Reward Management

There have been fundamental changes in remuneration practices in the UK over the last quarter century, with a substantial decline in collective bargaining as the major method of pay determination. In its place there has been a growth of more individualistic systems based on employee performance, skills and competency. While many of these changes have already been charted by writers in the human resource management field, the various texts available until now have been largely descriptive and prescriptive in their nature. This text is the first to adopt a critical and theoretical perspective. It covers the Institute of Personnel and Development's employee reward syllabus and tackles the conceptual issues missing from existing texts.

Each chapter:

- is written by a separate specialist author
- reviews and critiques the relevant academic literature. This enables both HR practitioners and those studying reward management to become acquainted with the range of literature and alternative viewpoints available
- contains examples and statistical material to illustrate key points and is completely up-to-date in terms of recent legislative changes, such as the minimum wage and minimum paid holiday entitlement.

The book includes the following chapters: Introduction – the context of reward management, Janet Druker and Geoff White; Determining pay, Geoff White; Trade unions and the management of reward, Edmund Heery; Grading systems and estimating value, Sue Hastings; Wages systems, Janet Druker; Salary progression systems, Marc Thompson; Benefits, Ian Smith; Financial participation schemes, Jeff Hyman; International reward management, Paul Sparrow; Coda – reward management into the twenty-first century, Janet Druker and Geoff White.

Geoff White is Reader in Reward Management at the University of Greenwich Business School. **Janet Druker** is Professor of Human Resource Management and Director of Research for the University of Greenwich Business School. Both are members of the Work and Employment Research Unit at the University of Greenwich and have written extensively in the fields of reward management and employee relations.

Routledge Studies in Employment Relations
Series editors: Rick Delbridge and Edmund Heery
Cardiff Business School

Aspects of employment relationship are central to numerous courses at both undergraduate and postgraduate level. Drawing on insights from industrial relations, human resource management and industrial sociology, this series provides an alternative source of research-based materials and texts, reviewing key developments in employment research.

Books published in this series are works of high academic merit, drawn from a wide range of academic studies in the social sciences.

Reward Management

A critical text

**Edited by Geoff White and
Janet Druker**

London and New York

First published 2000
by Routledge
11 New Fetter Lane, London EC4P 4EE

Simultaneously published in the USA and Canada
by Routledge
29 West 35th Street, New York, NY 10001

Routledge is an imprint of the Taylor & Francis Group

Typeset in Baskerville by
RefineCatch Limited, Bungay, Suffolk
Printed and bound in Great Britain by
Biddles Ltd, Guildford and King's Lynn

British Library Cataloguing in Publication Data
A catalogue record for this book is available from the British Library

Library of Congress Cataloging in Publication Data
Reward management: a critical text / edited by Geoff White and Janet
Druker.
    p.   cm. – (Routledge Studies in Employment Relations)
    Includes index.
    1. Compensation management.   2. Employee motivation.
I. White, Geoff.   II. Druker, Janet.   III. Series.
    HF5549.5.C67 R485   2000
    658.3′225 – dc21   00–020582

ISBN 0–415–19680–9 (hbk)
ISBN 0–415–19681–7 (pbk)

Contents

Figures and tables

Editors and contributors

Editors

Geoff White is Reader in Reward Management at the University of Greenwich Business School. Prior to becoming an academic, he worked for the major pay research organisation, Incomes Data Services, and was Managing Editor for Research for several years. Geoff became a university lecturer in 1991 and from January 1998 until December 1999 he was seconded on a part-time basis to the Low Pay Commission Secretariat as remuneration advisor. His previous books include *Managing People in Construction* (IPD 1996), also with Janet Druker, and *Employee Relations in the Public Services* (Routledge 1999), with Susan Corby. Geoff is currently involved in a three-year NHS-funded research project on pay and grading innovations in the NHS.

Janet Druker is Professor of Human Resource Management and Director of Research at the University of Greenwich Business School. Prior to working in higher education, Janet worked as a project officer at Warwick University where she also read for a PhD. She then worked for seven years with the Union of Construction Allied Trades and Technicians as head of research and organisation. Janet has researched and written widely on human resource management, especially on the construction industry and on self-employment. Her previous book, *Managing People in Construction* (IPD 1996) was also co-authored with Geoff White. Janet's current research is involved with employment bureaux. She also writes regularly for personnel practitioner journals.

Contributors

Sue Hastings is an independent consultant in pay systems, with a particular interest in gender aspects. She previously worked for the Trade Union Research Unit (TURU) at Ruskin College, Oxford and has written widely on the subject of Equal Pay and Equal Value. She has acted as advisor, primarily to unions and Applicants, on many Equal Value cases.

Edmund Heery has been Professor of Industrial Relations at Cardiff Business School since January 1996 and worked previously at Kingston University,

Imperial College, the City University and the London School of Economics. He has published widely on various aspects of industrial relations and human resource management and is engaged currently on an ESRC-funded research project examining the links between innovation and reward.

Jeff Hyman is Professor and Head of Research at the Napier University Business School in Edinburgh. Previously at Strathclyde University Business School, he has published widely in the field of employee financial participation schemes, including a major book, and general reward management issues. He is co-author with Bob Mason of *Managing Employee Involvement and Participation* (Sage 1995). He has also been a visiting fellow with the International Labour Organisation in Geneva.

Ian Smith is a Senior Lecturer in Management at the Cardiff Business School and worked in industry in both the UK and Canada before becoming an academic. Ian has a PhD from the University of Wales. He has published several books on remuneration practice, including *The Management of Remuneration: Paying for Effectiveness* (IPM 1983) and *Incentive Schemes: People and Profits* (Croner Publications 1989). He also acts as a consultant on reward management to a number of large businesses.

Paul Sparrow is Professor in International HRM at Sheffield University Management School. Prior to this appointment he was Lecturer in Organisational Behaviour at Manchester Business School and has also worked in consultancy. He has written widely on business psychology, HR strategy, management competencies and international HRM. He is joint author with Jean-Marie Hiltrop of *European Human Resource Management* (Prentice Hall 1994) and joint editor with Mick Marchington of *Human Resource Management: The New Agenda* (Financial Times/Pitman 1998).

Marc Thompson is currently a Research Fellow in Employee Relations at Templeton College, Oxford, which he joined after having been Principal Research Fellow at the Institute for Employment Studies. He has an established research track record in human resource and employment policy issues going back over ten years. Marc has published a number of studies on performance pay systems; age discrimination; gender discrimination in performance assessment systems; and recent developments in employee relations. His current research interests focus on strategic HRM and in particular the impact of HR strategies on firm performance. He recently published a literature review in this area (with Ray Richardson) for the IPD and is also working on an ESRC-funded research project on reward strategies in high technology companies.

Acknowledgements

The editors would like to convey their grateful thanks to the contributors to this volume. All of them are busy people with many and varied responsibilities yet they all managed to find time to provide us with the chapters published here. We also thank them for their continuing enthusiasm for this project through the lengthy editorial process.

We would also like to thank the staff of Routledge for their support, especially Stuart Hay and his successor Michelle Gallagher, and also the series editors Edmund Heery and Rick Delbridge at Cardiff Business School. As usual, we should add that any errors, misinterpretations or mistakes are our own! Finally, we would like to thank Doreen Foster, Research Secretary at the University of Greenwich Business School for her unfailing technical help with the manuscript.

This book is dedicated to Eddy and Frances, who have both provided us with reward in many ways, and to Doris and Fred, who have provided unstinting essential support through many years.

Geoff White and Janet Druker
University of Greenwich Business School
February 2000

Abbreviations

ACAS	Advisory, Conciliation and Arbitration Service
ADST	Approved Deferred Share Trust
APT&C	administrative, professional, technical and clerical
CBI	Confederation of British Industry
CBP	competence-based pay
DfEE	Department for Education and Employment
DSS	Department of Social Security
DTI	Department of Trade and Industry
ECJ	European Court of Justice
EDAP	Employee Development and Assistance Programme
EEF	Engineering Employers' Federation
EPA	Equal Pay Act
ESOP	Employee Share Ownership Plan
FDI	foreign direct investment
HERA	Higher Education Role Analysis
HRM	human resource management
ICR	Industrial Cases Report
ICT	information and communications technology
IDS	Incomes Data Services
IER	Institute for Employment Research
IES	Institute for Employment Studies
IHRM	international human resources management
IMS	Institute of Manpower Studies
IPD	Institute of Personnel and Development
IPM	Institute of Personnel Management
IPRP	individual performance-related pay
IRLR	Industrial Relations Law Reports
IRS	Industrial Relations Service
ISSP	International Social Survey Programme
IT	Industrial Tribunal
JE	job evaluation
JES	job evaluation scheme
LFS	*Labour Force Survey*

LPC	Low Pay Commission
LRD	Labour Research Department
MDW	measured day work
NAPF	National Association of Pension Funds
NBPI	National Board for Prices and Incomes
NEDO	National Economic Development Organisation
NES	*New Earnings Survey*
NHS	National Health Service
NMW	National Minimum Wage
NVQ	National Vocational Qualification
OECD	Organisation for Economic Co-operation and Development
OME	Office of Manpower Economics
OSP	Occupational Sick Pay
PBR	payment by results
PRP	performance-related pay
PSP	profit-sharing plans
RPI	Retail Price Index
SBP	skills-based pay
SERPS	State Earnings-Related Pension Scheme
SMP	Statutory Maternity Pay
SSP	Statutory Sick Pay
SVQ	Scottish Vocational Qualification
TUC	Trades Union Congress
ULC	unit labour cost
VET	vocational education and training
WERS	Workplace Employee Relations Survey
WIRS	Workplace Industrial Relations Survey

1 Introduction

The context of reward management

Janet Druker and Geoff White

This book is about the management of remuneration systems, today increasingly known as 'reward management' among personnel practitioners. This is a key element within human resource management and is a discrete area of study in its own right. Over the last twenty years there have been substantial changes in payment systems in Britain, most notably the decline in collective bargaining as the major method of pay determination and the growth of new pay practices which are more directly controlled by management. In the USA a new 'compensation and benefits' literature has emerged under the rubric of the 'New Pay' and, while historically conditions across the Atlantic have differed from British experience, this new paradigm has come to influence not just management practice but also government policy in Britain.

While subtly different in some respects to the 'New Pay' paradigm, thinking about 'reward management' in Britain (a term used by Armstrong and Murlis 1988), reflects many of the same management concerns. These revolve around two dimensions: (a) the need to take a holistic and integrated approach to all matters concerning the rewarding of employees for work done, and (b) the need for remuneration systems to be contingent upon business strategy.

The interest in reward management has been given added impetus by the rewriting of the UK Institute of Personnel and Development (IPD) professional education syllabus, which now contains a dedicated set of units under the generic title 'Employee Reward' and a specific textbook for the subject (Armstrong 1999). Prior to this, matters concerning payment systems fell under two separate headings – employee relations (which dealt with pay bargaining and legislation affecting pay) (Farnham 1993) and employee resourcing (which dealt with matters such as pay structures, job evaluation and benefits such as sick pay and pensions) (Torrington *et al.* 1991). The new IPD syllabus therefore gives a higher profile to the remuneration aspects of personnel management practice (although collective bargaining over pay is still located within the employee relations syllabus). This more holistic approach to pay and benefits matters has not, to date, been reflected in the academic literature, where there remains a strong dichotomy between the 'macro-economic' literature of the labour economists and the human resource management literature. The former is primarily concerned with the effect of pay determination upon the wider economy and, in particular, the impact upon employment, productivity and inflation. The latter, in contrast, draws both upon the industrial relations preoccupation with the regulation of the employment relationship and also on the organisational behaviour literature, with its emphasis upon motivation and equity theory. In recent years, the occupational psychology literature has been of increasing importance, but of course the determination of pay continues to be of interest to industrial sociologists too. Increasingly, however, there is a need for a more integrated approach to the study of remuneration and the reward management paradigm might provide a useful vehicle for this to develop.

The existing reward management textbooks, largely practitioner oriented, concentrate heavily on techniques rather than theory, and neglect the role which collective bargaining, and employee voice, continue to play in many UK organisations. Armstrong's key IPD text (1999) has only a one-page reference to collective bargaining and does not mention the fact that around a third of establishments (and indeed many of the larger employers) still negotiate about pay with trade unions and that over two-fifths of employees have their pay determined in this way (Cully *et al.* 1999). The parallel employee relations text by Gennard and Judge (1997) also has little to say about pay bargaining systems. Most importantly, the impact of power relations within the workplace and their influence upon reward management policies and practice are glossed over in the essentially managerialist IPD texts – the IPD *Core Personnel and Development* text by Marchington and Wilkinson (1996) being an honourable exception to this approach.

A critical approach

This book attempts to provide an integrated approach to reward management, drawing on the analytical traditions of industrial relations and the insights provided by specialist writers. It brings together the work of a number of contributors from a range of disciplines within the generic field of 'reward management'. Some are academics and some are consultants. The book is not intended to provide prescriptions for managers handling current problems; there are other texts that already do this job (Armstrong 1999; Armstrong and Murlis 1998; Hume 1995). Rather, it is intended as a guide through some of the themes and issues that are of current concern to employers, employees and government. The subtitle is a 'critical text', an important signal that this book seeks to provide a more theoretical and discursive approach to the subject than is normally found in practitioner texts. Each chapter not only summarises recent research on a particular aspect of reward management but also provides a critique of that research. This enables the student of reward management, be it at undergraduate or postgraduate level, IPD syllabus focused or not, a range of views about key aspects of managing payment systems.

The overall thrust of this book challenges the unitary or normative approaches taken in many other texts. It seeks to present a dispassionate analysis of trends and patterns and will hopefully provide students of both reward management and employee relations with some stimulating reading which will supplement the traditional material found on the human resources management (HRM) syllabus. It will also, hopefully, be of interest to the 'reflective practitioner' seeking new and independent thinking about reward systems.

The purpose of this introduction is to set the context for the chapters that follow. As indicated above, reward management has attracted increased attention in recent years (Stevens 1996). Pay structures and systems of pay determination are socially determined and are influenced by the context and culture in which they are implemented. Most importantly, they reflect power relations in the workplace between employers and employees. Inevitably this means that they have changed significantly over time and must be understood in historical context.

The renewal of interest in this field is part of a wider concern about changes in work and employment. For this reason we look first at the historical background, considering changes in work organisation and labour markets over the last twenty years. We consider the significance of innovation in work processes and technologies. Second, we look at the political framework for discussions and consider the ways in which it has affected the context for reward management. Third, we point to the associated changes in management theory and fashion – to the growth in human resource management and the ideological impetus towards 'individualisation' of the employment contract. We then relate the chapters of this book to the themes identified. In the Coda to this book we provide a conclusion and discuss the impact of 'New Labour' on reward systems.

Changing work organisation and processes

Although pay systems have been of recurrent interest during the twentieth century, there has been little agreement about their potential or actual role. Whilst the concept of a job is founded on a two-way commitment – the promise of pay in return for work performed, there are diverse views about the significance and composition of pay. The globalisation of business, moreover, raises questions about management across frontiers. To what extent does national culture affect the design of pay systems? How do multinational corporations tackle questions of international employment and reward (see, for example, Edwards *et al.* 1996).

Pay structures and the dispersion of pay reflect fundamental social values. Should there be a minimum level of reward for work below which no one should fall? If so, how should it be set and who should decide the level? Narrow pay differentials suggest a society with more egalitarian values, whilst a yawning gulf between the highest earners and the lowest paid points to wide social distinctions between these social groups. A widening of differentials may be taken as a proxy for increasing social inequality. Pay systems are an arena for conflict, wherein norms may be established and questions of equity are raised. There are questions about the responsibilities that business organisations may have to the wider community. To what extent should employers carry social costs for their employees – for example, for sickness, medical care, or old age (Standing 1997)? Will such arrangements disadvantage those who are outside of the labour market, or will they permit the state to provide more amply for this group? To what extent should the state ensure that social benefits are standardised at least at a minimum level and what impact will state benefits have on labour market participation?

There are questions too about the meaning that pay may have for the individual recipient and the extent to which it can be regarded as a means to improving performance. Questions of motivation have been explored (e.g. Maslow 1954; Herzberg *et al.* 1957; McGregor 1960; Vroom 1964; Porter and Lawler 1968) but not resolved, and such issues are best understood within their particular social and historical context since questions of culture, class and gender are relevant to our understanding. How important are pay and benefits as motivational tools when compared with the satisfaction of doing a particular job and doing it well? Money rewards are often perceived to be only a part of the real benefit derived from work. Theories of motivation point to the higher satisfaction that can derive from a job well done, but this seems to be a consideration that is applied more frequently to women's work in the caring professions than to the senior male executive in corporate life.

A discussion of reward management in practice must necessarily be located in the context of wider economic and social change. There is no easy or automatic correlation between forms of production and payment systems but some broad trends are evident. The legacy of (the overwhelmingly male) craft-based payment systems of the nineteenth century was challenged towards the end of the century by management theories and practices that sharpened the division of labour between the planning and organisation of tasks and their execution. The 'scientific management' theories of Frederick Winslow Taylor (1913) epitomised these developments. He asserted the principles of direct control through which management aggregates to itself the knowledge base that was previously the prerogative of the workforce (Braverman 1974). Through this process an organisational 'brain' is created, responsible for planning and work organisation. This was compounded by assembly-line production with management activities increasingly conducted separately from the shop-floor, where workers were to be spurred on to high performance by the use of incentive payments. The distinction between management and production processes that became more marked from the end of the nineteenth century was paralleled by a division within the workforce, with differential treatment in terms of pay and conditions for management, professional and administrative staff on the one hand and production workers on the other. Although time-based payment remained at the core of the employment relationship, payment was defined for employees associated with the management of the enterprise in terms of annual and monthly payments (salaries), whilst for production workers, calculations were often based on the notion of an hourly rate of pay, with associated incentive payments.

From the end of the First World War mass production came to be associated with standardised pay arrangements, often negotiated at industry level, through multi-employer bargaining. Pay was set on the basis of a 'rate for the job' and each job was a 'precisely defined aggregate of well-specified tasks and seniority' (Piore and Sabel 1984: 113). As Mahoney (1992: 338) comments, 'the concept of job was the unifying concept in the Scientific Management approach to organisation and management'. Moreover, the development of such systems led to 'the development and application of a concept of job ownership expressed in the labor movement and collective bargaining' (Mahoney 1992: 339). Trade union representation was based around particular skills or grades, and trade unions were engaged in a struggle to defend the interests and to improve the circumstances of those sections of workers – most often men – whose interests they represented. Time rates of pay, often determined through multi-employer collective bargaining, were often supplemented at establishment level with incentive payments which, together with shift and overtime pay, contributed significantly to total earnings for manual workers. Arrangements for administrative, professional and managerial staff were less standardised than those for craft or production workers in the private sector, but the principles of equity and public accountability that operated in the public sector encouraged a formalisation and standardisation on the basis of a recognised rate for the job.

Working women were at a significant disadvantage because social values emphasised women's domestic role and, outside of specific sectors of employment, such as the textile and garment industries, the social definition of 'skill' tended to exclude them from higher-paid work (Pollert 1981). Yet their growing labour market participation, coupled with changes in the law, encouraged women to challenge traditional patterns of discrimination. The notion of 'fair' employment standards that attached to the internal labour market provided a context for women to claim equality of treatment in terms of employment opportunity and pay – as Sue Hastings demonstrates in her chapter.

Over recent decades there have been fundamental changes in the nature of work and in the management of the employment relationship (Cappelli 1995). There has been a significant shift in the pattern of employment, a reduction in organisational size and a change in workforce composition, which have together redefined the context for reward practices. The reduction in manufacturing employment and the rise in unemployment during the 1980s were accompanied by a growth in the service sector that continued steadily during the 1990s. Employment in the heavily unionised areas of manufacturing and heavy industry in the UK – in engineering, mining, shipbuilding and steel – diminished whilst employment in the retail industry, in hospitality, the leisure industry, finance and business services increased. As full-time male employment dwindled, so part-time and predominantly female employment became more significant. The number of temporary workers and of temporary agency workers increased too. The decline in male, manufacturing activity called into question pay structures that had been associated with 'blue-collar' employment. The application of information and communication technologies (ICTs) blurred some of the distinctions between 'blue-collar' and 'white-collar' workers. Changes in work organisation through lean production (fewer workers) have been associated with changes in job content and in status-generating conflicting pressures – both for upskilling and for deskilling and creating the potential for new forms of control in the employment relationship within and across these groups (Crompton *et al.* 1996).

For many years it seemed that the concentration and centralisation of capital would inevitably be associated with a growth in organisational size as technology advanced and economies developed. Yet larger corporations now emphasise the benefits of decentralisation and business units have distinctive identities within complex corporate portfolios (Purcell and Ahlstrand 1994). Smaller, accountable units can more easily be bought and sold and work can be relocated from one country or region to another (Edwards *et al.* 1996). Larger firms have downsized whilst public sector organisations have been subject to compulsory competitive tendering and contracting out. Since the Bolton Committee's report in the early 1970s, small and medium sized enterprises have been seen as the engine of economic growth in the UK (Bolton 1971; Stanworth and Stanworth 1991). Establishment size is, in general, smaller than in the past and may be small even within global corporations.

Firm and establishment size is critical to reward management for a number of reasons. Larger establishments are more likely to employ personnel or compensation specialists and to be unionised. They are more likely to use job evaluation and to have recognised grading structures (Smith 1988; Cully *et al.* 1999). They are more likely to offer the benefits of continuous employment too, with a possibility of career progression within a salary structure of some kind. Smaller businesses with simpler, flatter structures – particularly those that are not subsidiaries of larger parent companies – are more likely to be associated with direct forms of management and communication and simpler payment structures (Cully *et al.* 1999). There is clear evidence that the lowest-paid workers, often associated with small businesses, have fairly simple payment systems with few additions to the basic rate of pay (White 1999).

Collective bargaining arrangements have been undermined and the scope of bargaining has diminished under the impact of these changes. Increased product market pressures and the drive for improved performance have encouraged employers to break with employers' associations and to seek to determine pay and conditions in relation to the needs and the performance of the individual business (Streeck 1987; Gospel 1992). Changes in work organisation and a growing employer interest in flexibility have encouraged the process of decentralisation (Katz 1993). Managerial discretion at enterprise and establishment level was enhanced where multi-employer collective agreements were dismantled – in the docks, engineering, banking and television (Jackson *et al.* 1993). Pay determination through industry-level bargaining was ended in at least sixteen industries covering more than one million employees in the late 1980s (Stevens 1996: 31). Even where unions continue to be recognised, they are now less likely to be involved in pay bargaining (Brown *et al.* 1998: 69). By 1998 only 41 per cent of the workforce was covered by collective bargaining and only 14 per cent by multi-employer collective bargaining (Cully *et al.* 1999: 106, 108).

At the individual level, the process of downsizing and the widespread experience of redundancy in the 1980s and 1990s undermined established notions of employment security and career progression – at least for the groups that had been previous beneficiaries, notably white-collar employees who had expectations of a 'career'. Leaner and flatter organisations have more limited scope for upward mobility, although those with key skills in the new technologies may have choices about movement within and between organisations (Warhurst and Thomson 1998; Stanworth 1998). Paradoxically, the diminished opportunities for progression within internal labour markets have been accompanied by increased emphasis on human resources as key assets and on growing concern to reward individual development and performance in ways that do not necessarily imply promotion (Lawler 1990: 139–150). Performance-related pay and competence-based payment systems have supported such developments. It is a process that challenges the traditions of job evaluation and the 'rate for the job' – including equal pay for work of equal value – which have been so important to notions of internal equity in the past.

Changing technologies and new forms of work organisation play an important part in defining the framework for employment too (Crompton *et al.* 1996). Information and communication technologies (ICTs) have eroded traditional skills and grading structures associated with apprenticeship training for (mostly) male entrants. Employers now seek new or enhanced skills that facilitate the rapid pace of ICT innovation (Gallie 1996). The reconfiguration of work processes and the demands of knowledge-based technologies mean that employees must adapt rapidly and use their skills and their discretion in the way that tasks are performed (Gallie 1996). Effective business performance relies on individual performance and seems to give further support to the notion of payment for the person, rather than payment for the job. It may be associated with forms of skill-based payments, with reward for the acquisition of skill or payment intended to mould behaviour and encourage greater responsiveness to change.

These changes in organisational structures and processes have not taken place in a vacuum. The political and economic context is also key to understanding the changes in pay which have taken place in Britain over the last twenty years.

The political and economic context

The election of Margaret Thatcher's Conservative government in 1979 heralded a period of major change in British politics. Elected on a radical right-wing manifesto, which sought to break the mould of existing consensus policies on employment and industrial relations matters, the years of Conservative governments between 1979 and 1997 saw a gradual erosion of existing labour market institutions. This was to be achieved through legislation designed to free business from government regulation on the one hand and to limit the freedom of trade unions to regulate employers' behaviour on the other. There was also some diminution in individual employment rights, although this was tempered by increasing European regulatory measures.

This is not the place to discuss in detail the ideological basis of the post-1979 Conservative government and its effects upon the employment relationship. This is covered elsewhere (e.g. Gospel 1992; Kessler and Bayliss 1998). Suffice to say that the Conservatives borrowed heavily, at least in their rhetoric, from the neo-classical economists of the New Right in both the USA and Britain. The government therefore rejected the post-war consensus belief in a planned econ-omy and a regulated labour market in favour of neo-classical theories of supply and demand and the 'unseen hand of the market'.

Attempts to control economic growth (and hence prices, wages and employ-ment) through statutory (or indeed voluntary) prices and incomes policies were rejected and unemployment rose to post-war record levels. Unemployment never fell below 1.5 million in the 1980s and 1990s whilst it never exceeded 1.5 million in the 1960s and 1970s. The growth in unemployment was seen by the Conserva-tives as a necessary discipline to curb trade union pay demands and high inflation, the latter seen as a direct result of trade union intervention in the labour market. In the private sector rising joblessness acted as a sharp brake upon earnings growth; consequently pay settlement levels fell rapidly in the early 1980s. At the same time new trade union legislation and the introduction of compulsory com-petitive tendering in the public sector weakened the power of trade unions in both the private and public sectors. The collapse of many traditional manufacturing industries in the early 1980s, coupled to the growth of new service sector com-panies, however, was to be a more important element in reducing the coverage of collective bargaining.

There was also a dramatic shift in the balance between the private and public sectors within the economy, with a considerable decline in the size of the public sector (see Shaoul 1999). Large parts of publicly owned industry and the public utilities were sold to the private sector and the remaining public services were opened up to private competition in the delivery of services to the public. Privatisation of the nationalised industries was to lead to major changes in pay arrangements for those employed in them, not least a substantial pay increase for senior managers. Compulsory competitive tendering for public services had sig-nificant effects upon the pay and conditions of staff working in these services, both those employed by the private contractors and those employed directly (Escott and Whitfield 1995; Colling 1999).

Government pay policy: the rhetoric and reality

If we seek to discover the views of the Conservative governments from 1979 to 1997 on pay matters, we must look in two places. First, we must consider their general rhetoric and stated objectives and specific legislative changes. Second, we must consider how they managed the pay and conditions of their own employees in the state sector.

In terms of the former, the government adopted a policy that encouraged employers to abandon various aspects of traditional pay determination. The polit-ical agenda on pay was set out by Kenneth Clarke, then Minister of State at the Department of Employment, in a speech to the City University Business School in February 1987. He stated that: 'We must move towards a system more clearly based on market forces, on demand and supply, on competition and on ability to pay' (quoted in Kessler and Bayliss 1998: 223). He went on to call for the ending of the national pay round, the going rate, comparability, job evaluation and national pay bargaining. He stated:

> If we can move to a system where pay increases are primarily based on performance, merit, company profitability and demand and supply in the local labour market, we will dethrone once and for all the annual pay round and the belief that pay increases do not have to be earned.
>
> (Quoted in Kessler and Bayliss 1998: 223)

Ten years later, in 1996, the President of the Board of Trade, Ian Lang, would argue that:

> Payment systems in Britain have been transformed over the last decade. The era when most workers were paid the same 'rate for the job' with little or no regard to their performance – or to business and local labour market conditions – is at an end.
>
> (DTI 1996)

So much for the rhetoric. In terms of the legislative programme, there was little in the way of new law specifically about pay, as opposed to the large amount of trade union legislation throughout the period. The major legislative changes were as follows:

- The repeal in 1980 of Schedule 11 of the Employment Protection Act, which had allowed claims to the Central Arbitration Committee that an employer was not observing industry-recognised terms and conditions, or was paying less than the 'general level' in industries without collective bargaining.
- The ending in 1983 of the Fair Wages Resolution, which had first been introduced in 1891 and which allowed the government to lay down minimum terms and conditions for those employed on government contracts.
- The Social Security Act 1983 which transferred the responsibility for state sickness benefit from the government to employers with the introduction of Statutory Sick Pay (SSP).
- The Wages Act 1986, which repealed the Truck Acts and introduced the right of employers to pay employees by credit transfer rather than in cash. This Act also reformed the existing Wages Councils by abolishing some and greatly simplifying the content of the wages orders of those remaining, including the exclusion of young people under the age of 21 from coverage.
- The various Finance Acts encouraging the growth of employee financial participation (see Chapter 8). The government established the legal framework for share ownership, profit-sharing and profit-related pay.
- The Social Security Act 1986 allowing employees to opt out of SERPS and out of their company occupational pension schemes in favour of private 'money purchase' schemes.
- The final abolition of the remaining twenty-six Wages Councils in Britain

under the 1993 Trade Union Reform and Employment Rights Act (although the three agricultural wages boards were to remain).

There were also, of course, changes caused by European employment and health and safety legislation, which tended to strengthen minimum rights in employment. They included the 1983 amendment to the Equal Pay Act, which introduced the concept of 'equal value' in grading systems, and the 1993 Working Time Directive, which set limits to working hours and provided for the first time a minimum statutory entitlement to paid holidays. The implementation of the latter was delayed until 1998 in the face of British government hostility.

The government's views on pay impacted directly on public sector workers. The earlier breakdown of the Labour government's approach to voluntary pay restraint – the 'Social Contract' – had led to the outbreak of strikes over pay restraint in the public services during the winter of 1978. The establishment of the Standing Commission on Pay Comparability under Professor Hugh Clegg to sort out these various public sector disputes came too late to avoid defeat for Labour. In contrast to the private sector, where the Conservatives saw no need for direct intervention on pay, in the public sector strict pay limits were continued (these had been initiated by the previous Labour government in 1976). The Conservatives, however, honoured the commitments of the Clegg Commission, leading to substantial 'catching up' awards in public sector pay. The 'pay provision figures' of the early 1980s were followed by less stringent controls during the Lawson boom years between 1986 and 1991 until strict limits were again imposed from 1992 (White 1996).

Within the remaining public services (civil service, NHS and local government), the government made major changes in pay determination arrangements. These included the ending of collective bargaining for nurses and professions allied to medicine in the NHS in 1983 and for school teachers in England and Wales in 1992. New pay review bodies were established for both of these groups. Moves to relate pay more closely to individual performance were begun in the civil service in the 1980s and spread quickly to other parts of the public sector, although with limited success in the NHS and local government. Individual performance-related pay became the norm for all civil servants but remained patchy in application in the NHS and local government, where it normally only applies to managers. There were also attempts to match pay more closely to market forces, through the use of pay supplements and extra benefits for those with skills in short supply. This was particularly the case in the mid- to late 1980s, when the Lawson boom and deregulation of financial services led to the 'vacuuming' of scarce skills from the public sector into the private sector. Lastly, the government pursued a long-term objective of introducing decentralised pay determination. This was achieved with the establishment of 'delegated' pay bargaining in the civil service from April 1996 and the introduction of two-tier bargaining arrangements into NHS Trusts from February 1995 (White 1999: 78). While decentralisation in the civil service remains, the NHS arrangements failed and led to a return to national bargaining. A new national pay system is currently under discussion with the NHS unions.

The outcomes of government policy

The economic outcomes of the Conservatives' policy on pay can be examined under three headings – income distribution, productivity and labour costs. In general, average earnings increased by a greater degree for women than for men between April 1979 and April 1997 (371 per cent for women compared to 303 per cent for men). This reflected some limited desegregation of women's work and the growth in employment in areas of better paid, female non-manual work. It also reflected the growing impact of equal pay laws, but women's weekly earnings remained at 73 per cent of men's in 1997 (Kessler and Bayliss 1998: 224). Taking into account inflation, however, both men and women saw a real increase in pay. Throughout the 1980s pay increases in the UK continued to outstrip inflation and indeed were greater than most of the UK's competitors. As Kessler and Bayliss (1998) comment, this fact is intriguing, given the very high unemployment throughout the period and the decline of trade union power. Earnings growth slowed in the early 1990s, following the major recession at the start of the decade, and has remained flat since, although earnings growth continues to outstrip inflation and is still high in comparison to competitor countries.

There were also changes in the distribution of earnings. Non-manual workers' pay increased much faster than that for manual workers and the earnings distribution widened considerably. While earnings continued to grow moderately for the lower paid, increases were much greater for the higher paid. The growing divide between the bottom decile of earners and the top (see Figure 1.1) was to be a major feature of the Conservative years. The relative wealth of the highest earners, moreover, was enhanced further by reductions in taxation which meant that they kept much more of their income. This widening of the earnings distribution was only exceeded by the USA (see Figure 1.2). The growing inequality in the UK has also been stronger than elsewhere. Looking at national sources, only New Zealand in the second half of the 1980s had inequality growing as rapidly as in

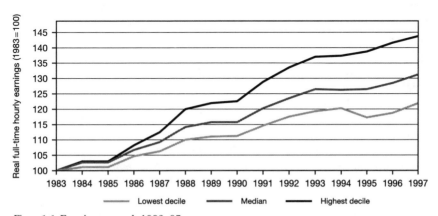

Figure 1.1 Earnings growth 1983–97

Source: Low Pay Commission (1999: 32) Crown copyright is reproduced with the permission of the Controller of Her Majesty's Stationery Office

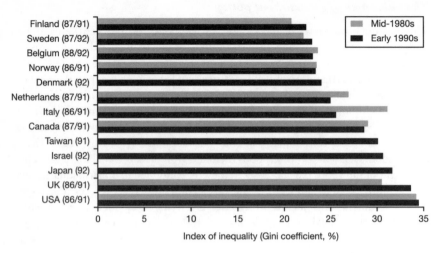

Figure 1.2 Income equality in the mid-1980s and early 1990s

Source: Hills (1998: 17)

the UK (Hills 1998: 17). In comparison, in many OECD countries the earnings distribution remained stable in the 1980s and in the case of Germany, France and Italy it actually narrowed. This contrary trend continued into the 1990s with the UK differing from the other countries in experiencing a widening earnings distribution (R. Dickens 1998: 192).

It was senior management pay that was driving wage inflation during the 1980s, rather than trade union pressures (McCarthy 1993). The growth of senior management and board members' pay was to become an increasingly difficult political issue for the Conservatives, especially when the newly appointed executives of the privatised public utilities were seen to have been given excessively large pay increases to bring them up to the level of other private sector managers. There was also a profusion of generous share option schemes which added to the total pay package. Given the government's rhetoric both about workers needing to demonstrate pay restraint and about the importance of linking pay to perform-ance, the fact that many senior managers were being granted extremely generous increases, even when their companies had experienced poor performance, pro-duced some hostile public and press reaction (Conyon 1995). Investors also began to show concern about how pay decisions were taken for such managers. As a result, three attempts at 'self-regulation' by employers were tried – the Cadbury Report in 1993, the Greenbury Report in 1995 and the Hampel Report in 1998. These recommended various degrees of voluntary regulation through intro-ducing more independent and transparent pay determination mechanisms but 'Top Pay' remains a political issue for the current government. There is still a threat that statutory regulation may be necessary.

According to R. Dickens (1998), in addition to these clear rises in wage differen-tials between the highest and lowest earners, there has also been an equally important rise in within-group pay dispersion. There are two possible reasons for this. The first is that it reflects a growing demand for skilled and educated workers and greater discrimination by employers in evaluating employee performance. The second reason is the changing role of labour market institutions. Gosling and Machin (1995 quoted in R. Dickens 1998) estimate that 20 per cent of the growing inequality can be attributed to the decline in unionisation. Similarly Bell and Pitt (1996 quoted in R. Dickens 1998) find that 20 per cent of the rise in variation in earnings is explained by declining union density.

In terms of productivity, there was a decline at the beginning of the 1980s but thereafter there were substantial improvements, especially in manufacturing. Between 1980 and 1996 output per person increased by 38.8 per cent within the whole economy and by 95 per cent within manufacturing. According to Metcalf (1989), the improvement in productivity was due to three factors: the shock effects of the recession in the early 1980s; more competitive product markets; and the reduction in union power. However, the view that Conservative policies were an unmitigated success has been challenged (see Nolan 1996 for example). Certainly the 'success' of the 1980s was not followed in the 1990s. If we compare labour productivity in various OECD countries in the period 1979 to 1995, UK growth was ahead of the USA and Germany but the same or less than many other OECD countries (OECD 1996). UK growth was exceeded by both France and Italy. Clearly, productivity was to some extent improved through increased pay flexibility but continued improvements relate more to such issues as capital investment and research and development, both of which remain low in the UK compared to competitor countries.

Labour costs per unit of output decreased from 1981 until 1986 but there was then a rapid increase until the recession of the early 1990s, when labour costs fell sharply. Over the period 1980–96 unit labour costs rose much less in manufacturing than in the whole economy. Increases in labour costs in the late 1990s have been low.

The political and economic agenda of successive Conservative governments had a profound effect on pay. Income distribution widened sharply, reflecting the declining role of trade unions in pay setting; inequality increased but productivity improved. Labour costs fell significantly. The question is whether this change reflects a transformation in reward management at the organisational level. In the next section we review the impact of human resource management upon pay practices.

Human resource management and the New Pay

The interest in human resource management (HRM) and in 'strategic pay' has accompanied the process of economic and social change. The ideas and the practices associated with HRM can be understood as part of a western, particularly American, response to the success of Japanese business from the 1980s (Legge 1995) as an attempt to challenge the legacy of traditional personnel management and industrial relations. Change was driven by the growing concern with product quality or service delivery and by attempts to streamline work processes. It is not our purpose to repeat here the discussions and debates about what does and does not constitute 'real' or leading-edge human resource management (see Guest 1990; Storey 1992; Sisson 1994; Legge 1995; Hope-Hailey *et al.* 1997). Debates about the meaning and evidence for human resource management have focused on the existence of a 'bundle' of HR initiatives. The composition of the bundle is a matter of debate. Critical factors include the strategic positioning of HR within the organisation; the relationship of the HR function to line management; the use of personnel 'levers', such as recruitment and selection and training and development; and the impact of HR on beliefs and assumption within the organisation (Storey 1992).

Reward management has a key position within HR theory for a number of reasons. Pay is a central organisational concern because questions of financial control and cost management are themselves fundamental to the organisation and to management decisions. Discussion and negotiation about those decisions and about the level and distribution of pay bring personnel or the HR function into a central organisational position. Reward management is one of the key levers to be deployed in pursuit of effective HRM. If pay is to 'deliver the goods' in terms of HR strategy, then it must be structured, it is argued, in order to meet HR objectives.

American 'New Pay' theorists have developed arguments along these lines, pointing to the pivotal link between business strategies and reward management. Edward Lawler III (1990) and Schuster and Zingheim (1992) have argued the case for this central relationship and the need for pay to be more explicitly linked to business performance. The 'New Pay' is intended to encourage an externally focused approach to reward, challenging traditional management approaches such as job evaluation, cost-of-living pay rises and external referencing (e.g. upper quartile position) for pay norms (Schuster and Zingheim 1992: 25). It follows, according to the logic of the 'New Pay', that as business performance can vary, so too should the levels of pay. In other words, the pay package should comprise pay which is 'at risk' as well as pay that is guaranteed. The 'New Pay' writers argue for the continuing need for adaptation in business practice in a dynamic business environment.

There are important qualifications that must be raised in relation to the work of the 'New Pay' theories. First it might be argued, the 'good for business' case should be questioned for the same reasons that a unitarist approach to HRM is challenged – namely that there are different interests at play within the business organisation and they cannot all be subsumed so easily in pursuit of business goals. The 'New Pay' treats employees as 'important partners' and it also assumes that 'when the organisation does well, employees should do well' (Schuster and Zingheim 1992: 38). Yet it is not clear that employees or their representatives are to be partners in determining the pay system itself or in deciding on the ways in which the benefits of organisational success should be shared. For trade union members this approach may suggest a silencing of employee voice – or at least it may seem to pre-empt negotiations. Trade unions have traditionally claimed representation rights around the issues that go to make up the pay package. There is within the collective bargaining process an implicit relationship between pay and benefits (such as sick or maternity pay or pension) or between pay and conditions (hours, holidays, rest breaks, etc). Whilst trade union membership has declined and collective bargaining has diminished in many industrial economies, trade unions retain the capacity to challenge the hegemony of business interest on behalf of employees.

Second, it is clear that 'strategic pay' may involve complex and sometimes contradictory objectives. A balance must be found between recognition and reward for the performance of the individual, for the group (and between different groups) and for the business as a whole. Payment 'for the person' which is emphasised by the 'New Pay' puts a premium on rewarding individual performance precisely because individual performance is seen as 'directly controllable' (Lawler 1990: 203). Yet individual performance-related pay may discourage employees from taking risks or from collaborating with others – even though these may be exactly what is required in terms of business development (Herriot 1995: 194). Interestingly, there are signs that a generalised interest in individual performance-related pay, and particularly in individualised performance management, has been challenged more recently by growing concern with team-working and with team-based payments (Pfeffer 1994, 1998; Mayo 1995).

Since the 'New Pay' is concerned with aligning pay structures with business objectives, attention must also be given to group and corporate performance and to the ways in which these different dimensions of performance may be rewarded. Schuster and Zingheim (1992) suggest that group variable pay may be appropriate to reward pre-determined team, business unit or organisational goals, but they have less to say on the ways in which the interests of the business, the team and the individual might be balanced. Lawler acknowledges that organisational or group performance is harder to influence than individual performance and so proposes that a larger amount of 'at risk' compensation should attach to group or corporate performance (Lawler 1990: 203). Finding the right compensation mix is clearly a complex process and one that may not easily be understood by those whom it is intended to motivate. It is not surprising that commentators point to the need for 'pay literacy' as a prerequisite for effective reward management (Stevens 1996: 25). Moreover these complex systems have still to relate to the underpinning terms of the individual employment contract. Here is a critical problem for the 'New Pay', since it is clear that the fundamentals of pay systems are not readily amenable to regular change or adjustment. In terms of the operation of 'New Pay' ideas, there is clearly a risk that they will become too sophisticated to be effective and too complex to be easily changed.

'Employee commitment' is one of the central tenets of HRM since it offers the possibility of something more in the employment relationship than the simple wage–effort bargain (Walton 1985). 'New Pay' approaches – concerned with pay for the person rather than pay for the job – seem to enhance managerial discretion to reward compliant behaviour patterns or the appearance of commitment. L. Dickens (1998) has identified the dangers inherent in HRM, with the potential for a 'gender model of commitment' and points to the risks of gender stereo-typing by managers. Collective pay determination and job evaluation were estab-lished according to principles of 'fair' treatment, yet they have not delivered equal pay for women. Yet it could be argued that pay for performance offers the poten-tial for more equitable treatment of women because their individual role and contribution will be rewarded. There is none the less a risk that the processes through which performance-based pay is determined – including individual objective setting and appraisal, will work to the disadvantage of women. The ways in which skills are perceived and valued underpin pay systems and no one pay system will deliver equal pay (Rubery 1995; L. Dickens 1998).

The meaning and significance of the psychological contract are relevant to the question of commitment too, since the unspoken assumptions of the worker and of the employer may have as much bearing on performance as the explicit terms of the employment contract. Schein (1988) drew on theories concerned with social contracts to identify the 'psychological contract' that exists between employer and employee. He was concerned with the unwritten rules and expect-ations of employees and managers and the way in which they shape human behaviour. The psychological contract includes expectations about pay and work-ing conditions, about the benefits and the security of the job in question. It is not so much a matter of legal rights – although these may help to shape expectations – as the expectation of fair and equitable treatment. It is important that these considerations were emerging at a time when 'lifetime employment' was said to be a thing of the past (Handy 1994). Cappelli (1995) has shown the lowering of morale brought about in the USA by growing workplace insecurities. Research in the UK in 1995 suggested that low trust by employees in the organisation was linked to the experience of redundancy (Kessler and Undy 1996). The growing contingent workforce may identify less with the organisation and its business objectives. Temporary workers, for example, may be denied some of the benefits of permanent employees and may have a lesser commitment to the organisation as a consequence (Gallie *et al.* 1998).

The psychological contract may be less robust in the context of the lean organ-isation where the 'career' has given way to 'portable skills' and training for a job has been replaced by transferable competencies (Herriot and Pemberton 1995). Research results in this area are conflicting. IPD research suggests more positive employee attitudes during 1996 and 1997 (Guest *et al.* 1996; Guest and Conway 1997). The Employment in Britain survey, by contrast, suggests that 'the striking fact remained the low level of commitment of employees to their organisations' (Gallie *et al.* 1998: 315). The 1998 Workplace Employee Relations Survey (WERS) points to more positive results with over half of the employees surveyed reporting high commitment, although with very different results for management and pro-fessional groups as compared with craft, production and process workers (Cully *et al.* 1999). Pay systems may well induce a 'calculative commitment' (Etzioni 1975, cited in Gallie 1998), but softer developmental approaches may be a more effect-ive inducement to commitment (Gallie 1998). It is clear though, even from the fairly positive picture painted by the WERS, that the unequivocal commitment to 'business objectives' is not one that will be uniformly or automatically endorsed by all of the workforce.

The contributions

The book is structured in ten chapters. Following this introduction, Chapters 2 and 3 consider the process of pay determination and the influence of trade union representation. Chapters 4, 5 and 6 look at grading structures, job evaluation and the effect of change on wage and salary systems. Chapters 7 and 8 discuss other dimensions of change within the overall package, including benefits and questions of financial participation. Chapter 9 discusses international issues in reward management. Finally in Chapter 10 we offer a brief conclusion in the Coda.

Chapter 2 sets the scene by considering the changing roles and patterns of pay determination. One fact remains clear – collective bargaining is no longer the major means of pay determination in Britain, with only 41 per cent of the workforce having pay fixed in this way (Cully *et al.* 1999: 242). There has been a clear growth since 1984 in the proportion of workplaces where pay is a matter solely for management discretion. While prescriptive personnel management writers suggest that pay determination should become more focused on the needs of the business organisation or unit, it is not clear whether there has been a shift in practice to more reliance on internal business criteria in setting pay. The influence of external factors, such as the cost of living and comparability with other organisations, appears to remain significant for many organisations, although the inability to raise prices in a low inflation environment is a major criterion (Ingram *et al.* 1999).

There has also been a clear shift towards more enterprise-based or establishment-level pay setting, even where collective bargaining remains, but research suggests that industry 'norms' continue to play a very important role (Arrowsmith and Sisson 1999). There is evidence of more contingent, variable and individualised payment systems, at least for non-manual workers. For manual workers, pay systems have become less complex and payment by results (PBR) systems continue to decline. The fact that pay determination is now effectively controlled solely by management in many workplaces, coupled to the growth of more variable pay, raises very important questions about the quality of pay information available to the personnel practitioner. Nevertheless, Arrowsmith and Sisson (1999) report that personnel practitioners feel very well informed about pay comparisons. There are certainly macro-economic ramifications of the increasing decentralisation of pay determination, as the number of 'pay control points' continues to increase. Pay setting at corporate level may well make sense to individual managers but the impact of these thousands of separate pay decisions can be quite contrary at the macro-economic level (see Philpott 1998). The decentralised nature of pay determination in Britain contrasts strongly with the more centralised systems in much of the European Union, where the discourse of 'social partnership' remains important in many countries.

The issue of employee voice in pay determination is covered in Chapter 3.

Edmund Heery explores the contribution that trade unions make within the pay determination process. His account is distinctive because it evaluates the union role after two decades of membership decline. Recognising the constraints and the limitations of union influence, it argues that, whilst the union contribution may be modest and variable, unions make a difference both to the substance and to the process of reward management. The chapter explores the union contribution across five critical decisions taken by the employer:

1   the level of reward
2   the distribution of reward through internal pay structures
3   the relationship between pay and performance
4   the range of rewards, including fringe benefits
5   the procedures concerned with the management of rewards, including the transparency of decision-taking.

Unions improve the position of union members as against non-members in terms of pay levels and the range of fringe benefits. They also tend to reduce income inequality, with particular benefits for women who still tend to be concentrated in low-paid jobs and to receive lower hourly pay than men. Unions have not always supported equality for men and women but their purpose now is concerned with equity of treatment as well as with extracting more pay for their members. Union campaigns and representation, for example, on the National Minimum Wage, have benefited women and lower-paid workers. Because unions seek to ensure the security and stability of earnings, they also support systems that are visibly equitable – so tend to resist merit pay and individual performance-related pay. However, where necessary, union representatives may negotiate about contingent pay if resistance to doing so may threaten their collective bargaining role.

The legacy of inequality, reinforced by prevailing social values, has served to shape the grading systems used within organisations, to the disadvantage of women, despite the importance of employment rules within internal labour markets. Sue Hastings, in Chapter 4, looks at the ways in which job evaluation has worked to the disadvantage of women, embodying discriminatory perceptions of women and women's skills. Paradoxically, the use of job evaluation has increased within the UK, even though 'new' pay systems might seem to work against the formulation of systems of internal relativities. This has been encouraged by changing technology and by new forms of work organisation which have required more flexible and sometimes more multi-skilled working. Job evaluation has also been encouraged by legislation on equal pay and equal value because it provides a line of defence in equal value claims. Equal value law has provided the terrain over which the challenge has been posed to the institutionalisation of gendered notions of skill and value. The chapter explores changing approaches to grading and the criteria on which it is based. The weightings given to particular types of skill and experience are shown to be important determinants of the outcomes in terms of grading and pay. Under-valuation of interpersonal skills, for example, might impact seriously on some female workers.

Women's labour force participation and career aspirations contrast with new pay systems – 'payment for the person' could work to women's disadvantage by removing provisions for 'equity' in favour of managerial discretion. However, for legal reasons alone, organisations are unlikely to abandon systems of internal relativities, Hastings argues. Competence-based systems offer some potential for ensuring equity of treatment but job evaluation still seems to be the majority choice.

Chapters 5 and 6 explore the breakdown in the distinction between wages and salary systems. Contextual change – both in labour markets and work processes – are key to understanding the erosion of the historic division between them. The difference between waged and salaried workers was bound up with the distinction between task management and execution. Different forms of management control applied to workers engaged on these processes. Harmonisation of conditions and single-status working have eroded the demarcations between different grades or occupations.

Chapter 5, by Janet Druker, points to the importance of hourly rates as a base for wage systems and for calculations for overtime and shift payment. Hourly rates are significant too as a reference point for other components in the wage package and as a benchmark for the National Minimum Wage. It is interesting to note that, whereas performance-related pay has become more important for white-collar employees, payment by results for manual workers is less common now than it was in the past. The role and value of incentive schemes have been intensely debated over many years. Advocates of individual incentive payments draw on Taylorist traditions – and their views continue to influence management thinking. Output-based reward systems enable employers – in theory anyway – to estimate and control more precisely the costs of production and to reduce supervision. PBR was the focus for workplace conflict during the 1960s and 1970s and its use has declined significantly since then. Detractors suggest that it is work method and organisation that are important in maximising productivity, rather than payment by results. This view seems to have had some effect, since there is evidence of innovation in terms of work organisation – growing interest in team-working that is strongly associated with moves to single status and harmonisation.

Harmonisation of terms and conditions and single-status working provide routes to facilitate change and to establish a framework that is more amenable to task flexibility. Although skills-based pay seems to provide a new framework to reward the acquisition of skill, there is an absence of hard evidence about the extent of its application in practice.

Chapter 6, by Marc Thompson, considers the changing nature of white-collar pay and pay progression systems. Non-manual workers have experienced major changes over the last twenty years. Seniority-based salary systems have been eroded by performance-based pay in many sectors, especially in the finance sector and public services where bureaucratic traditions had ensured the continuity of hierarchical and seniority-based career structures. In the 1980s many of these structures were abandoned in favour of much more contingent and variable pay systems although, as Thompson shows, the degree of change in white-collar pay systems is often overstated. Moreover, while performance-related pay continues to grow, there are already doubts arising as to its efficacy. Employers are now seeking to implement new forms of contingent pay progression based more on employee development, with so-called competency-based pay on the increase.

But pay systems do not simply consist of pay structures and progression systems. Benefits also represent a high cost to the employer and are of significant value to the employee. In Chapter 7 Ian Smith looks at why employers provide benefits and what purpose they serve within reward systems. The chapter provides an overview of the history of benefits provision and suggests that, surprisingly, given its cost and value, it has developed in a very ad hoc way. Employers have had a short-termist perspective even to benefits that require a major outlay, such as pensions or company cars. Some key changes are identified – through the extension of benefits because of harmonisation and through the modest growth in family-friendly benefits. Minimum levels of provision may be required by the state, but successive governments have been concerned to avoid the cost burdens associated with social benefits.

Benefits are valued by their recipients. They may serve to attract and retain staff or to encourage feelings of security and goodwill. In this way benefits may affect individual motivation and, it might be assumed, company performance. It is argued that benefits might be better managed to impact on performance. Flexible benefits are especially important in this context.

The 'New Pay' paradigm highlights the value of variable reward and recognition for the individual. Yet there is little evidence of this in the organisation and delivery of benefits. Flexible benefits have the potential both to reward the individual and to meet individual need. Yet take-up for cafeteria-style benefits within the UK is limited. Evidence of a strong link between benefits and performance is lacking. Where changes are initiated, they are very often based on pragmatic considerations and immediate pressures.

Chapter 8 considers the growth of financial participation schemes, one of the Conservative government's major contributions to reward policies and of enduring interest to New Labour. While concepts of profit-sharing and profit-based pay have been around for over a century, it was only with the passing of legislation in the 1980s which gave tax relief on such payments that profit-sharing and share ownership schemes really took off. Jeff Hyman looks at the development of such schemes and the ideological agenda behind them. As Hyman suggests, the key to the development of employee financial participation in the UK has been the association between political ideology and product market change. A substantial part of the political agenda was the lubrication of privatisation of public assets. The key message of this chapter is that unreserved claims that financial participation positively influences employee attitudes, behaviour or performance should be treated with caution.

International reward management for many years has been primarily concerned with the management of expatriate remuneration but, as multinational companies have sought increasingly to 'go local', interest has turned to the concept of national culture and its impact upon the design of payment systems. In Chapter 9 Paul Sparrow considers the impact of globalisation on reward systems and analyses the factors that international organisations should consider in managing their reward systems across national frontiers. The chapter considers whether convergence around flexible pay concepts is happening by comparing developments in three countries facing radical change – Germany, Japan and China. Sparrow goes on to examine the relationship of national cultures to management and employee preferences in reward systems. The chapter concludes that multinational firms attempting to harmonise reward systems across frontiers will face predictable patterns of resistance across different countries. These aspects of national culture can be changed but only for particular groups. While there may be convergence in pay philosophies across national systems, there remain important local factors that must be taken into account. Most importantly, it is how new pay ideas are 'sold' to the workforce which will play a key role in gaining acceptance.

One final point should be made about our contributors' chapters. Exponents of the 'New Pay' tend to encourage the notion that change in reward management must be radical and thorough-going. Many of the contributions in this book make the point that whilst there is significant evidence for change, it is often more modest and less coherent than the model requires. Not all of the trends that are identified conform to the prescriptions of the 'New Pay' and change is often partial and ad hoc.

Acknowledgement

Thanks are due to Ed Heery for comments on an earlier draft of this chapter.

References

Armstrong, M. [1996] (1999) *Employee Reward*. London, IPD.

Armstrong, M. and Murlis, H. (1988) *Reward Management. A Handbook of Remuneration Strategy and Practice*. London, Kogan Page.

Armstrong, M. and Murlis, H. (1998) *Reward Management. A Handbook of Remuneration Practice*. London, Kogan Page.

Arrowsmith, J. and Sisson, K. (1999) 'Pay and working time: towards organisation-based systems?'. *British Journal of Industrial Relations* 37 (1): 51–75.

Bell, B. and Pitt, M. (1996) *Trade Union Decline and the Distribution of Wages in the UK: Evidence from Kernel Density Estimation*. Oxford, Nuffield College, University of Oxford. Mimeo.

Bolton, J.E. (1971) *Report of the Committee of Enquiry on Small Firms*. London, HMSO.

Braverman, H. (1974) *Labor and Monopoly Capital: The Degradation of Work in the Twentieth Century*. New York and London, Monthly Review Press.

Brown, W., Deakin, S., Hudson, M., Pratten, C. and Ryan, P. (1998) 'The individualisation of employment contracts in Britain'. Research paper. London, DTI.

Cappelli, P. (1995) 'Rethinking employment'. *British Journal of Industrial Relations* 33 (4): 563–602.

Colling, T. (1999) 'Tendering and outsourcing: working in the contract state?'. In Corby, S.

and White, G. (eds) *Employee Relations in the Public Services. Themes and Issues.* London, Routledge.

Conyon, M.J. (1995) 'Directors' pay in the privatised utilities'. *British Journal of Industrial Relations* 33 (2): 159–71.

Crompton, R., Gallie, D. and Purcell, K. (1996) 'Work, economic restructuring and social regulation'. In Crompton, R., Gallie, D. and Purcell, K. *Changing Forms of Employment: Organisation, Skills and Gender.* London, Routledge, 1–20.

Cully, M., Woodland, S., O'Reilly, A. and Dix, G. (1999) *Britain at Work: as Depicted by the 1998 Workplace Employee Relations Survey.* London, Routledge.

Dickens, L. (1998) 'What HRM means for gender equality'. *Human Resource Management Journal* 8 (1): 23–40.

Dickens, R. (1998) 'Trends in wage inequality. Appendix 3'. *The National Minimum Wage. First Report of the Low Pay Commission.* Cm 3976. June. London, HMSO.

DTI (1996) *The Rewards of Success. Flexible Pay Systems in Britain.* London, Department of Trade and Industry.

Edwards, P., Armstrong, P., Marginson, P. and Purcell, J. (1996) 'Towards the transnational company? The global structure and organisation of multinational firms.' In Crompton, R., Gallie, D. and Purcell, K. *Changing Forms of Employment: Organisations, Skills and Gender.* London, Routledge.

Escott, K. and Whitfield, D. (1995) *The Gender Impact of CCT in Local Government.* London, HMSO.

Etzioni, A. (1975) *A Comparative Analysis of Complex Organizations.* New York, Free Press.

Farnham, D. (1993) *Employee Relations.* Management Studies. London, Institute of Personnel Management.

Gallie, D. (1996) 'Skill, gender and the quality of employment'. In Crompton, R., Gallie, D. and Purcell, K. *Changing Forms of Employment: Organisation, Skills and Gender.* London, Routledge, 133–59.

Gallie, D., White, M., Cheng, Y. and Tomlinson, M. (1998) *Restructuring the Employment Relationship.* Oxford, Clarendon Press.

Gennard, J. and Judge, G. (1997) *Employee Relations.* London, IPD.

Gosling, A. and Machin, A. (1995) 'Trade unions and the dispersion of earnings in British establishments 1980–1990'. *Oxford Bulletin of Economics and Statistics* 57: 167–84.

Gospel, H. (1992) *Markets, Firms, and the Management of Labour in Modern Britain.* Cambridge, Cambridge University Press.

Guest, D. (1990) 'Human resource management and the American dream'. *Journal of Management Studies* 27 (4): 378–97.

Guest, D. and Conway, N. (1997) 'Employee motivation and the psychological contract'. *Issues in People Management* 21. Third Annual IPD Survey of the State of the Employment Relationship. London, Institute of Personnel and Development.

Guest, D., Conway, N., Briner, M. and Dickman, M. (1996) 'The state of the psychological contract in employment'. *Issues in People Management* 16. London, Institute of Personnel and Development.

Handy, C. (1994) *The Empty Raincoat. Making Sense of the Future.* London, Hutchinson.

Herriot, P. (1995) 'The management of careers'. In Tyson, S. (ed.) *Strategic Prospects for HRM.* London, IPD, 184–205.

Herriot, P. and Pemberton, C. (1995) *New Deals: The Revolution in Managerial Careers.* Chichester, Wiley.

Herzberg, F., Mausner, B. and Snyderman, B. (1957) *The Motivation to Work.* New York, Wiley.

Hills, J. (1998) *Income and Wealth. The Latest Evidence*. Inquiry into Income and Wealth Distribution in the UK. ESRC Research Centre for Analysis of Social Exclusion. London School of Economics. York, Joseph Rowntree Foundation.

Hope-Hailey, V.V., Gratton, L., McGovern, P., Stiles, P. and Truss, C. (1997) 'A chameleon function? HRM in the 90s'. *Human Resource Management Journal* 7 (3): 5–18.

Hume, D.A. (1995) *Reward Management. Employee Performance, Motivation and Pay*. Oxford, Blackwell.

Ingram P., Wadsworth, J. and Brown, D. (1999) 'Free to choose? Dimensions of private sector wage determination. 1979–1994'. *British Journal of Industrial Relations* 37 (1): 33–49. March.

Jackson, M., Leopold, J. and Tuck, K. (1993). *The Decentralisation of Collective Bargaining*. London, Macmillan.

Katz, H. (1993). 'The decentralisation of collective bargaining: A literature review and comparative analysis'. *Industrial and Labor Relations Review* 47 (1): 3–22.

Kessler, I. (1995) 'Reward systems'. In Storey, J. *Human Resource Management. A Critical Text*. London, Routledge.

Kessler, I. and Undy, R. (1996) *The New Employment Relationship: Examining the Psychological Contract*. London, Institute of Personnel and Development.

Kessler, S. and Bayliss, F. (1988) *Contemporary British Industrial Relations*. 3rd edn. Basingstoke and London, Macmillan Business.

Lawler, E. (1990) *Strategic Pay: Aligning Organizational Strategies and Pay Systems*. San Francisco, Jossey Bass.

Legge, K. (1995) *Human Resource Management: Rhetorics and Realities*. Basingstoke, Macmillan Business.

Low Pay Commission (1999) *Pay Structures and the Minimum Wage*. Occasional Paper No. 3. London, Low Pay Commission.

McCarthy, W.E.J. (1993) 'From Donovan until now: Britain's twenty-five years of incomes policy'. *Employee Relations* 15 (6): 3–20.

McGregor, D. (1960) *The Human Side of Enterprise*. New York, McGraw-Hill.

Mahoney, T.A. (1992) 'Multiple pay contingencies: strategic design of compensation'. In Salaman, G. *Human Resource Strategies*. London, Sage.

Marchington, M. and Wilkinson, A. (1996). *Core Personnel and Development*. London, IPD.

Maslow, A. (1954) *Motivation and Personality*. New York, Harper & Row.

Mayo, A. (1995) 'Economic indicators of HRM.' In Tyson, S. (ed.) *Strategic Prospects for HRM*. London, IPD, 229–65.

Metcalf, D. (1989) 'Water notes dry up: The impact of the Donovan proposals and Thatcherism at work on labour productivity in British Manufacturing Industry'. *British Journal of Industrial Relations*, 27 (1): 1–31.

Murlis, H. (ed.) (1996) *Pay at the Crossroads*. London, IPD.

Nolan, P. (1996) 'Industrial relations and performance since 1945'. In Beardwell, I. (ed.) *Contemporary Industrial Relations. A Critical Analysis*. Oxford, Oxford University Press.

OECD (1996) 'Earnings inequality, low-paid employment and earnings mobility'. *Employment Outlook*, July. Paris, Organisation for Economic Co-operation and Development.

Pfeffer, J. (1994) *Competitive Advantage through People. Unleashing the Power of the Work Force*. Boston, Mass., Harvard Business School Press.

Pfeffer, J. (1998) 'Six dangerous myths about pay'. *Harvard Business Review* May/June: 109–19.

Philpott, J. (1998) 'Making pay work'. *Economic Report* 12 (1) February. London, Employment Policy Institute.

Piore, M. and Sabel, C. (1984) *The Second Industrial Divide: Possibilities for Prosperity*. New York, Basic Books.

Pollert, A. (1981) *Girls, Wives, Factory Lives*. London, Macmillan.

Porter, L. and Lawler, E.E. (1968) *Management Attitudes and Behaviour*. Homewood, IL, Irwin Dorsey.

Purcell, J. and Ahlstrand, B. (1994). *Human Resource Management in the Multi-divisional Company*. Oxford, Oxford University Press.

Rubery, J. (1995) 'Performance-related pay and the prospects for gender pay equity'. *Journal of Management Studies* 32 (5): 637–54.

Schein, E.H. [1965] (1988) *Organisational Psychology*. Engelwood Cliffs, NJ, Prentice Hall.

Schuster, J.R. and Zingheim, P. (1992) *The New Pay: Linking Employee and Organisational Performance*. New York, Lexington Books.

Shaoul, J. (1999) 'The economic and financial context: The shrinking state?' In Corby, S. and White, G. (eds) *Employee Relations in the Public Services. Themes and Issues*. London, Routledge.

Sisson, K. (1994) 'Personnel management: paradigms, practice and prospects'. In Sisson, K. *Personnel Management: A Comprehensive Guide to Theory and Practice in Britain*. Oxford, Blackwell, 3–50.

Smith, R.S. (1988) 'Comparable worth: limited coverage and the exacerbation of inequality'. *Industrial and Labor Relations Review* 41: 227–39.

Standing, G. (1997) 'Globalisation, labour flexibility and insecurity: the era of market regulation'. *European Journal of Industrial Relations* 3 (1): 7–37.

Stanworth, C. (1998) 'Telework and the information age'. *New Technology, Work and Employment* 13 (1): 51–62.

Stanworth, J. and Stanworth, C. (1991) *Work 2000. The Future for Industry, Employment and Society*. London, Paul Chapman Publishing.

Stevens, J. (1996) 'Pay at the crossroads'. In Murliss, H. (ed.) *Pay at the Crossroads*. London, IPD, 24–38.

Storey, J. (1992) *Developments in the Management of Human Resources*. Oxford, Blackwell.

Streeck, W. (1987) 'The uncertainties of management in the management of uncertainty: employers, labor relations and industrial adjustment in the 1980s'. *Work, Employment and Society* 1 (3): 281–308.

Taylor, F. (1913) *The Principles of Scientific Management*. New York and London, Harper & Bros.

Torrington, D., Hall, L., Haylor, I. and Myers, J. (1991) *Employee Resourcing*. Management Studies. London, Institute of Personnel Management.

Vroom, V. (1964) *Work and Motivation*. New York, Wiley.

Walton, R. (1985) 'From control to commitment in the workplace'. *Harvard Business Review* 63 (2): 76–84.

Warhurst, C. and Thompson, P. (1998) 'Hands, hearts and minds: changing work and workers at the end of the century'. In Thompson, P. and Warhurst, C. (eds) *Workplaces of the Future*. Basingstoke, Macmillan.

White, G. (1996) 'Public sector pay bargaining: comparability, decentralization and control'. *Public Administration* 74 (1): 89–111.

White, G. (1999) 'The remuneration of public servants. Fair pay or New Pay?' In Corby, S. and White, G. *Employee Relations in the Public Services*. London, Routledge, 73–91.

2 Determining pay

Geoff White

Determining pay has never been an exact science. Fixing the appropriate level of pay and benefits is at the core of reward management systems and there is a substantial literature on the techniques and data available to do this. Various criteria may be used in fixing the pay of an individual, both within the organisation and in relation to the external labour market. While establishing relationships between different jobs and occupations which meet the needs of internal equity is a primary concern in the design of pay systems, linking these pay and grading structures to the external labour market and keeping pay levels competitive is also a vital concern. As Robinson (1973: 7) has argued:

> The concept of fairness when applied to wages is inevitably a concept which requires comparisons. It is not possible to decide whether someone is fairly paid until one knows what other people are paid. . . . Differentials and relativities lie at the very heart of the concept of equity as applied to wage determination.

The tension between concerns for internal equity and external markets for jobs remains one of the key problems for organisations in the design of effective reward systems.

In recent years there have been major changes in the manner in which pay is determined, with a substantial decline in the use of collective bargaining and its replacement by systems that depend far more on management discretion (Millward *et al.* 1992; Milner 1995; Brown *et al.* 1998; Bland 1999). Even in the sectors where pay remains subject to joint regulation, there have been significant moves away from industry-wide pay determination and towards organisation-based structures (Brown *et al.* 1995; Brown and Walsh 1991; Millward *et al.* 1992). This might indicate a growing preoccupation with enterprise performance, with 'ability to pay' paramount but, on the other hand, there has been a growing emphasis on the external market as the key factor in fixing pay levels. These changes pose important questions for both organisations' pay information systems and for providers of pay data.

This chapter considers the changing nature of pay determination and its impact upon the management of pay. It covers three main areas – the method and locus of pay determination (where and how decisions about pay levels are taken); the criteria used to determine the level of pay increases; and finally the changing role of pay information sources. We begin by looking briefly at the relationship between internal pay structures and the external labour market, especially the concepts of hierarchy and market. We then consider the major forms of pay determination and the levels at which pay is fixed. The criteria affecting pay increases are then considered. Finally we consider the implications of these changes for the management of pay and for pay information systems.

Introduction

The concept of exchange is at the heart of the employment relationship. Every employment is made up of two elements – the wage-rate bargain (how much the employee is paid) and the effort-bargain (how much work is produced in return for the pay). Employees expect that their remuneration will reflect their contribution to the work and the employer expects to pay what is considered to be a fair price for the work done.

In reaching an agreed value for the work done, a number of work contingencies are considered. These, argues Mahoney (1989), consist of performance contingencies, job contingencies and person contingencies. The first of these, performance contingency, is the simplest in that payment primarily relates to the output or outcome of the work – the more the employee produces, the more he or she is paid. The second, job contingency, relates primarily to the job held and the time worked. The third, person contingency, relates to the personal qualities of the individual employee, including the value of those tacit skills which they bring to the organisation. There are also non-work contingencies which come into play, such as certain employee benefits which provide various forms of income security for the employee in cases of ill health or in retirement. These reflect more social need than work-based contingencies, argues Mahoney. Pay will relate to a combination of these contingencies and provide the base upon which differentials are created between different jobs or individuals.

The relative worth of each job or individual employee is subject to various influences. These include both market value and the social value that is placed upon particular skills and duties – both of which can change over time. Achieving internal equity, or the fair distribution of remuneration within an organisation, is a major task for employers (see Chapter 4). The creation of a grading or pay structure provides the basis for differentials and also identifies what is expected in the way of job content for employees for different levels of pay. It does not, however, create the basis for pricing individual jobs. The pricing of jobs – as opposed to their internal evaluation or ranking – is usually done by some reference to the external labour market. This often involves some form of pay comparability with other organisations or occupational norms, or at least some reference to external economic indicators such as the cost of living or average earnings movements. External comparability has been central to pay theory and practice for two reasons. First, jobs have no demonstrable inherent value and hence employers gauge the value of a particular post by reference to external comparators. Second, the pay package is the only part of a job offer which applicants can readily compare with other offers (Fay 1989). Fay identifies three main approaches to external equity:

1   Setting recruitment rates at market level for entry-level jobs but then basing pay progression on internal career ladders (the internal labour market approach)
2   Setting across-the-board positioning to place an organisation's complete salary structure at some percentage of the market rate (e.g. many companies claim to be 'upper quartile' companies)
3   Where collective bargaining is present there may be industry-wide agreed minimum rates that apply to the organisation or there may be enterprise- or establishment-level bargaining over pay levels. In these cases negotiations will take place against comparator data on pay levels and pay increases in other industries and organisations, as well as other factors such as company profitability (ability to pay) and employee productivity. But the degree of bargaining power exerted by the union will also clearly affect ultimate levels of pay.

Pay levels are therefore determined through both internal and external factors. But there is a dynamic tension between the needs of the internal market for equity and fairness and the differential price at which labour can be purchased in the external labour market. The balance that organisations create between these two factors plays an important role in reward strategy. In the next section we look in more detail at the importance of internal and external comparisons, in particular the concept of markets versus hierarchies.

Internal versus external labour markets?

The design of pay systems relates primarily to the construction of a social order in which employees' remuneration is linked in some way or another to the perceived value of particular individuals, occupations or skill levels both within the organisation and in the external labour market. The issue of internal equity and the design of fair grading systems is covered separately in Chapter 4 but it is briefly worth considering here the choice of emphasis which employers make in determining pay – whether to stress the importance of internal equity or external relativities.

Two differing approaches to managing the employment relationship have been identified – one based on hierarchical relationships (so-called internal labour markets) and one based on concepts of commercial contracts within a market (external labour markets) (Doeringer and Piore 1970). In the classical model of the labour market, buyers and sellers of labour meet to transact their business on a completely open basis and pay rates are fixed for every job through the laws of demand and supply. But in reality, the labour market operates in much more complex ways. According to Kerr (1954, cited in Doeringer 1967), there are numerous distinct labour markets determined by geographical, occupational and institutional factors. However, all labour markets are of two broad types: (a) the structureless and (b) the structured. In the former there is no attachment except the wage agreed between the worker and the employer, while in the latter there are clear internal and external labour markets for particular jobs and occupations. As Doeringer (1967: 207) comments:

> The theoretical construct of the internal labour market, as introduced by Kerr, may be more precisely defined as an administrative unit within which the market functions of pricing, allocating and often training labor are performed. It is governed by a set of institutional rules which delineate the boundaries of the internal market and determine its internal structure. These institutional or administrative hiring and work rules define the 'ports of entry' into the internal market, the relationships between jobs for purposes of internal mobility and the privileges which accrue to workers within the internal market.

The structure of such internal markets is typified by three factors:

1   the degree of openness to the external labour market, as determined by the number and location of the ports of entry
2   the dimensions, both horizontal and vertical, of the methods of internal movement (e.g. promotion or downgrading)
3   the rules which determine the priority in which workers will be distributed among jobs within the internal market (Doeringer 1967).

Williamson (1975) draws on the work of Doeringer and Piore and the work on human capital by Becker to highlight the value of internal systems. Like Doeringer and Piore, Becker argued that 'incumbent employees who have received specific training become valuable resources to the firm' and hence are offered a premium to discourage turnover (Becker 1964, cited in Williamson 1975: 59). Williamson indicates that internal, long-term, flexible employment relationships avoid the transaction costs associated with the external 'contract' model, such as continuous recruitment costs, a continual renegotiation of the effort-bargain with workers and constant measurement and evaluation of performance in order to enforce the contract. While contracts may be long-lasting and subject to an authority relationship, all employees are doing essentially is 'continuously meeting bids for their jobs in the spot market', akin to a system of subcontracting (Williamson 1975: 67). The internal labour market, in contrast, 'achieves a fundamental transformation by shifting to a system where wage rates are attached mainly to jobs rather than workers. The incentives to behave opportunistically, which infect individual bargaining schemes, are correspondingly attenuated' (Williamson 1975: 74). The major method for rewarding performance in an internal market is not through incentive schemes, which would reimpose individual bargaining – 'a series of haggling encounters over the nature of the *quid pro quo*' (Williamson 1975: 77) – but through promotion via the grading hierarchy.

According to Williamson (1975: 78):

> Reliance on internal promotion has affirmative incentive properties because workers can anticipate that differential talent and degrees of cooperativeness will be rewarded. Consequently, although the attachment of wages to jobs rather than to individuals may result in an imperfect correspondence between wages and marginal productivity at ports of entry, productivity differentials will be recognised over a time and a more perfect correspondence can be expected for higher-level assignments in the internal labour market job hierarchy.

In the USA the development of this internalised system of employee management, in which seniority became the most important criterion governing employment, dates from after the First World War (Cappelli 1995). It was a product of both trade union demands for equity and the development of modern personnel management systems that sought to rationalise policies and improve the ability for long-term planning. It is interesting to note that in Britain, 'most British employers did not build strong internal labour systems, but relied more on market mechanisms for obtaining labour, fixing its price, and disposing of workers as supply and demand dictated' (Gospel 1992: 179). Historically, only a few large British manufacturing firms (and the finance and the public sector) developed more extensive internal systems, but from the 1930s there was a growing shift towards more internalised, bureaucratic labour management systems. Overall, though, internalised systems are still much less common in Britain than in the USA, Germany or Japan.

The development of internalised employment systems was characterised by a shift away from individualised incentives such as piecework and towards payment systems that were based less on individual output, such as measured day work. In internalised systems, each job had a narrowly specified description and jobs were allocated to grades via elaborate job evaluation schemes. Union pressure also helped tie pay rates to job titles and seniority rather than individual attributes (Cappelli 1995).

So what has happened in recent years? According to Arrowsmith and Sisson (1999), while the shift towards more enterprise-based employment systems is clear, the implications are not. One view is that the arrival of HRM is leading to greater internalisation. But there is also evidence of a shift towards more marketisation of the employment relationship in both the USA (Cappelli 1995) and the UK (Rubery 1994, 1996). This implies decreasing collective regulation of the employment relationship and increased scope for managerial discretion in framing the individual worker's terms and conditions (rather than necessarily a return to market forces as the major method of determining pay). In pay determination terms, this has meant increasing individualisation of pay, especially the growth of individual performance-related pay, widening pay dispersion, increased variability of income for employees, and more insecurity of income (Cappelli 1995; Rubery 1997).

There is also evidence that some organisations have increasingly sought to insulate themselves from external decision-taking. In pay determination terms, in the UK there has clearly been a shift away from multi-employer arrangements towards more specifically enterprise- or establishment-based systems, which by their very nature are more internalised (Brown *et al.* 1995; Brown and Walsh 1991; Millward *et al.* 1992; Walsh 1992). This would infer a greater degree of internal control over pay. As Walsh (1993: 409) comments: 'It is now commonplace within the human resource management literature that decentralised bargaining, performance-related pay and individualised remuneration schemes consolidate and extend earlier moves by companies towards internal labour markets.'

But this pattern can be interpreted differently. Bargaining fragmentation and the shift towards individualism, argues Walsh (1993), have weakened many of the organisational principles underpinning internal labour markets and the consequences for employers may be negative and costly. Reflecting back upon Williamson's (1975) observations about the nature of employment relations, and particularly pay, in internal labour markets, Walsh (1993) argues that recent developments in pay systems may have weakened the non-individualistic wage bargaining attributes of internal labour markets. By making pay more contingent and more 'person' based, the problems associated with 'contract' relations are re-introduced. As Arrowsmith and Sisson (1999) comment, many of the implications of marketisation are the antithesis of the internalisation model.

There is therefore a conundrum in this picture of greater organisational control and independence of approach to remuneration on the one hand and greater emphasis on individualisation of the employment relationship on the other. This conundrum is illustrated in the US 'New Pay' literature (Lawler 1990; Schuster and Zingheim 1992; Gomez-Mejia and Balkin 1992; Mahoney 1992). The New Pay literature emphasises the need to shift from 'internal', job-related pay struc-tures to 'external', person-related pay. It also argues that pay levels should be determined according to business circumstances ('ability to pay', 'affordability'), and on an individual rather than a collective basis. The market is seen as the ultimate arbiter in fixing pay levels for individual employees. For example, Lawler (1995: 14) says that: 'The new pay argues in favour of a pay-design process that starts with business strategy and organisational design. It argues against an assumption that certain best practices must be incorporated into a company's approach to pay.' He also argues that organisations must abandon concepts of 'rate for the job' in favour of rewards based on the individual employee's value in the external market. Lawler states that: 'Paying people according to their value in the market pays. After all, it is people who move from job to job and from company to company' (1990: 153). Furthermore, internal comparisons for setting wages 'run the great risk of producing pay rates that are not competitive and they focus the attention of individuals away from where it should be: on their competitors' (Lawler 1990: 192).

In the UK a shift towards more strategic and contingent systems of employment management, especially in relation to pay, has been encouraged by government (Department of Employment 1988), the CBI (CBI 1995) and by various (often US-based) management consultancies operating in the UK (see for example, Hewitt Associates 1991; Flannery, Hofrichter and Platten (the Hay Group) 1996).

There is a major question regarding the extent to which these exhortations to create more strategic and contingent pay systems have actually been heeded in practice. The evidence from the USA might indicate a change, although American pay and grading structures have traditionally been more rigid than in the UK, with the extensive use of job evaluation. The picture in the UK is less clear. Here there has been little systematic empirical analysis of the impact of the shift to organisation-based arrangements (Arrowsmith and Sisson 1999: 52). In the following sections we look at the declining coverage of collective bargaining and at the criteria that determine employers' approach to pay determination in both unionised and non-unionised environments.

The changing nature and locus of pay determination

Two major points can be made about the changes in pay determination over the last twenty years. The coverage of collective bargaining has diminished and pay fixing has become more decentralised, in both unionised and non-unionised sectors. The main source for information on the changing nature and locus of pay determination in the UK is the series of Workplace Industrial Relations Surveys (WIRS) that were conducted in 1980, 1984, 1990 and 1998. The overall figure for collective bargaining coverage for non-managerial employees in the latest 1998 Workplace Employee Relations Survey (WERS) is 31 per cent of workplaces (Cully *et al.* 1999: 109).[1] In terms of employees covered, WERS 1998 indicates that 41 per cent of employees are covered by collective bargaining (Cully *et al.* 1999: 242). This compares with aggregate coverage of 54 per cent in 1990 and 70 per cent in 1984 (Millward *et al.* 1992: 93). The WIRS series indicates a clear reduction in the numbers of both employees and establishments covered by collective bargaining between 1980 and 1990 (see Table 2.1). This reduction does not necessarily mean, however, a shift to greater management discretion over pay. One reason for the reduction in collective bargaining coverage in the public sector is the substantial growth in the number of public sector employees covered by independent pay review bodies since 1980 (the nurses and professions allied to medicine from 1983 and school teachers in England and Wales from 1992) (White 1999). None the less, the major reduction in coverage has been in the private sector and here the shift has most definitely been to more management discretion over pay determination. As Table 2.2 demonstrates, public sector establishments are much more likely to be covered by collective bargaining than those in private manufacturing and private services, and manual workers generally have higher coverage than non-manual. The rise in coverage between 1980 and 1984 was primarily the result of greater coverage in the private services sector. Closer analysis by sector (see Table 2.2) shows a steady decline in coverage in private

Table 2.1 Basis for most recent pay increase, all sectors, WIRS 1980, 1984 and 1990. Percentage of workplaces

	Manual			Non-manual		
	1980	1984	1990	1980	1984	1990
Direct result of collective bargaining	55	62	48	47	54	43
Most important level:						
Multi-employer	32	40	26	29	36	24
Single employer/multi-plant	12	13	13	11	13	15
Plant/establishment	9	7	6	4	4	3
Other answer	1	1	2	2	1	1
Not result of collective bargaining	44	38	52	53	46	57
Locus of decision about increase:						
Management at establishment	–	20	31	–	30	37
Management at higher level	–	11	15	–	15	17
National joint body	–	5	4	–	2	5
Wages Council	–	3	2	–	1	*
Not stated	–	1	*	–	*	*

Key:
– Data not available
* Fewer than 0.5%

Source: Millward *et al*. (1992) Table 7.1, p. 219

manufacturing and some decline in the public sector, although from a very high baseline. WERS 1998 shows that collective bargaining coverage in the public sector has fallen from 80 per cent of employees in 1990 to 63 per cent in 1998. In private manufacturing the fall was slight – from 51 per cent to 46 per cent, while in private services it fell from 33 per cent to 22 per cent (Cully *et al*. 1999: 242).

   This pattern of decline is reinforced by figures from the *Labour Force Survey*, which surveys employees rather than establishments (see Table 2.3 below). In 1993 the LFS began collecting data on the extent to which an employee's workplace recognises trade unions for the purposes of negotiating the pay and conditions of employees, although this question did not allow employees to report on whether their own pay and conditions were the subject of collective bargaining. From 1996 a new question was added which established whether an employee was actually covered or not. Table 2.3 shows the results from 1996 to 1998. In 1998, around 35 per cent of employees had their pay determined by collective agreement.

   A small-scale survey of 676 private sector establishments carried out by the Institute for Employment Studies (IES) in 1997 for the DfEE found pay was determined by collective bargaining in only 27 per cent of production establishments and 17 per cent of service sector establishments (Giles and Atkinson 1997).

   The LFS data also allow some analysis of industrial variations in collective

Table 2.2 Basis for most recent pay increase by major sector, 1980, 1984 and 1990. Percentage of workplaces

	1980	*1984*	*1990*
Result of collective bargaining			
Private manufacturing:			
Manual	65	55	45
Non-manual	27	26	24
Private services:			
Manual	34	38	31
Non-manual	28	30	26
Public sector:			
Manual	–	91	78
Non-manual	–	98	84
Not result of collective bargaining			
Private manufacturing:			
Manual	35	45	55
Non-manual	73	74	76
Private services:			
Manual	66	62	69
Non-manual	72	70	73
Public sector:			
Manual	–	9	22
Non-manual	–	2	16

Key: – Data not available

Source: Millward *et al.* (1992). Tables 7.2, 7.5 and 7.8

Table 2.3 Collective bargaining in Great Britain

Year	*No. of employees whose pay is determined by collective agreement (000s)*	*Percentage of employees whose pay is determined by collective agreement*
1996	8,091	36.5
1997	8,058	35.5
1998	7,984	34.5

Source: *Labour Force Survey*, 1996, 1997 and 1998

bargaining coverage (see Table 2.4). The highest coverage is found in public administration, followed by the public utilities (water, gas and electricity) and education. While private sector health has fairly low coverage, in the public sector health establishments employing twenty-five or more employees the figure is much higher at 77 per cent. The lowest coverage is found in hotels and restaurants; agriculture, forestry and fishing; and in real estate and business services.

As Milner (1995) indicates, there are both definitional and data problems in estimating the coverage of collective pay setting. The tightest possible definition is the proportion of employees in employment whose pay is directly determined by

Table 2.4 Percentage of employees covered by collective bargaining by workplace characteristics and union membership; Great Britain; Autumn 1998

	All	Private		Public	
		Less than 25 employees	25 or more employees	Less than 25 employees	25 or more employees
All employees	34	7	31	61	78
Industry:					
Agriculture, forestry and fishing	9	*	*	*	*
Mining and quarrying	31	*	*	*	*
Manufacturing	33	5	39	*	77
Electricity, gas and water supply	69	62	70	*	*
Construction	22	6	19	91	91
Wholesale and retail trade	14	3	25	*	*
Hotels and restaurants	7	2	8	*	64
Transport and communication	46	14	47	67	92
Financial intermediation	44	46	43	*	57
Real estate and business services	12	3	11	62	82
Public administration	79	*	33	68	84
Education	64	*	32	64	72
Health	50	6	14	59	77
Other services	26	4	20	48	76
Union membership					
Member	81	59	80	81	87
Not a member	14	2	12	37	62

Key: * Sample size too small for reliable estimate

Source: *Labour Force Survey*, Autumn 1998

collective agreement. Bargaining can be at plant, organisation or multi-employer level, but the key issue is whether or not pay is directly determined – i.e. the agreement sets out exactly what each category of employee will be paid. For example, in the civil service there are still negotiations with trade unions about the overall pay budget but virtually all civil servants now have their pay increase determined through individual performance appraisal. A less stringent definition is the proportion of workers affected by collective bargaining through a collective agreement. For example, an employer party to an industry-level agreement may decide to top up the nationally agreed award at local level. The difficulty with this second definition is that it is difficult to ascertain whether an employee's pay is actually affected by a collective agreement. This can also lead to double counting of coverage where an employee is covered by both a national agreement and a local 'domestic' agreement. The third and loosest definition of coverage includes workers whose employer follows a collective agreement without actually being party to it. For example, some employers in the construction and printing industries follow the relevant industry pay agreements without actually having any members of the signatory unions present in their workplace. The WIRS data are based on a question asking the management respondent 'What proportion of workers are represented by unions recognised for negotiating pay and conditions either at this workplace or higher in the organisation, if applicable?' The WIRS data therefore use a fairly tight definition of coverage.

It is also important to place this decline in collective bargaining coverage within a historical context. Using various official sources of changes-in-rates of pay data, Milner (1995) has compiled a chronological series of data on collective bargaining coverage from 1895 to 1990. These time series include both estimates of all those covered by voluntary collective agreements and statutory machinery (the trade boards established in 1909) together and those covered just by voluntary national agreements. The main series shows a rise in overall coverage from around 7 per cent in 1895 to around 50 per cent in 1990 but this overall rise masks a number of fluctuations. Overall coverage expanded dramatically during the First World War and its immediate aftermath (partly because of the huge growth in numbers covered by statutory trade boards in the period), reaching 50 per cent by 1918. The data indicate that at least one-third of British employees were covered by collective bargaining in the form of national agreements at this time.

Numbers covered continued to increase in the early 1920s, reaching 60 per cent in overall coverage and at least 35 per cent coverage by collective bargaining. There was then a very large drop in coverage in the late 1920s and early 1930s. Overall coverage dropped to less than 30 per cent and voluntary collective bargaining to less than 20 per cent. There was then a gradual rise again from the late 1930s through the Second World War to reach 50 per cent again for overall coverage and nearly 40 per cent for voluntary collective bargaining in 1945.

After the war, overall coverage increased again to reach 70 per cent in 1950 and around 50 per cent covered by collective agreements alone. Coverage began to increase again in the late 1960s to reach 80 per cent at the beginning of the 1970s and around 85 per cent by the mid- to late 1970s. Most of this increase was through the spread of voluntary collective bargaining, as statutory wage-fixing machinery (the Wages Councils) was in decline during this period. By the end of the 1970s, collective bargaining coverage had reached around 80 per cent. Both overall coverage and coverage by collective bargaining began a precipitous drop in the second half of the 1980s to around 50 per cent (statutory pay-fixing machinery, except in agriculture, was ended with the abolition of the Wages Councils in 1993).

Three main findings emerge from Milner's analysis:

1 Collective bargaining coverage is now lower than at any point since the Second World War.
2 The gap between collective bargaining coverage and union density has narrowed to an unprecedented degree.
3 The proportion of employees who are not members of a union but are covered by collective bargaining is lower now than any time since the 1920s.

Milner's study also indicates the importance of multi-employer or industry-wide collective bargaining in the development of UK industrial relations up to the early 1980s. The collapse of industry-wide collective agreements in the late 1980s and 1990s has had important ramifications for the overall coverage of collective bargaining as a pay determination system. The shift away from multi-employer pay determination began as early as the 1950s (Brown and Walsh 1991), and by the time of the Donovan Report (1968) the effects of such decentralisation were being remarked upon. Donovan commented on the increasing tendency to wage drift (the increasing divergence between the centrally negotiated rates and the actual earnings at company level) resulting from decentralisation. This led some employers to weaken their agreements so that the national agreements simply provided a minimum wage floor upon which company pay structures were erected.

In the 1970s employers increasingly opted out of multi-employer agreements altogether to establish their own company agreements (Brown and Terry 1978). According to Brown and Walsh (1991: 48), 'By 1978 the dominance of single-employer over multi-employer agreements in manufacturing had already become clear' and this process accelerated in the 1980s (Brown 1981; Daniel and Milward 1983; Millward and Stevens 1986; CBI 1988). The 1986 CBI survey of collective bargaining structures found that 87 per cent of employees in plants with collective bargaining had their basic rates of pay determined at the level of the establishment or company (CBI 1988: 67). So 'by 1986 single employer bargaining was dominant across the whole remuneration package' (Purcell and Ahlstrand 1994: 121).

Decentralisation of pay determination

The second major observable trend in pay determination is the decentralisation of decision-making about pay. Even where collective bargaining continues as the major method of pay determination, there has been a clear shift away from multi-employer (industry-wide) bargaining and, to a lesser degree, establishment-level bargaining, towards enterprise-level agreements. By 1998 only 14 per cent of establishments were covered by multi-employer bargaining and most of these agreements were in the public sector, where 35 per cent of establishments were still covered by multi-employer agreements (Cully *et al.* 1999: 108). As shown in Table 2.1, from 1984 the proportion of workplaces covered by multi-employer bargaining for manual workers declined from 40 per cent to 26 per cent in 1990 and from 54 per cent to 43 per cent for non-manual workers. Plant/establishment-level bargaining also declined slightly from 9 per cent in 1980 to 6 per cent in 1990 for manual workers and from 4 per cent to 3 per cent for non-manual workers. WIRS indicates that the growth has been at single-employer/multi-plant level.

The 1997 survey by the Institute for Employment Studies (IES) for the DfEE (Giles and Atkinson 1997: 37) found that only 17 per cent of private services establishments and 12 per cent of private production establishments determined pay at national/multi-employer level. Some 67 per cent of private production establishments and 59 per cent of private services establishments determined pay at establishment level.

Table 2.5 Basis for most recent pay increase 1990. Percentages by sector

	Manual employees			Non-manual employees		
	Private manufac- turing	Private services	Public sector	Private manufac- turing	Private services	Public sector
Result of collective bargaining	45	31	78	24	26	84
Multi-employer	16	11	58	7	5	67
Single employer, multi-plant	8	16	13	5	19	13
Plant/establishment	19	4	1	9	1	*
Other answer	2	*	5	2	*	3
Not result of collective bargaining	55	69	22	76	73	16
Management at establishment	44	44	1	59	50	*
Management at higher level	9	21	11	17	24	5
National joint body	3	3	7	2	1	11
Wages Council	2	3	*	–	1	–
Not stated	1	–	1	*	*	*

Key:
– Data not available
*Fewer than 0.5%

Source: Millward *et al.* (1992), Tables 7.2, 7.5 and 7.8

This acceleration in the shift away from industry-level pay determination was partly driven by government exhortation. The Conservative government made clear its opposition to industry-wide bargaining which it criticised as 'cosy' arrangements between employers' bodies and trade unions. It saw these as establishing inflexible pay structures which could not respond to economic changes and which discouraged regional variations to reflect local labour markets (Department of Employment 1988). In the public sector, where it had direct powers, it introduced more flexibility based on 'merit, skill and geography' into the national agreements, although its attempts to introduce geographical decentralisation never really materialised. When decentralised bargaining finally emerged in the civil service in 1996, it was based on organisational restructuring into departments and agencies, rather than geographical decentralisation.

Another pressure leading to decentralisation has been the shift to multidivisional organisational structures in the private sector. As firms increase in size and diversify their activities, they tend to break away from multi-employer bargaining and develop more enterprise-specific pay determination systems (Aoki 1984, cited in Brown and Walsh 1991). Single-employer bargaining is more likely to be found in larger multi-plant organisations, foreign-owned companies and high-concentration industries (Booth 1989). Multi-employer bargaining tends to be more associated with large numbers of small employers and relatively low capital requirements (Deaton and Beaumont 1980; Booth 1989; Gospel and

Druker 1998). A survey of multi-establishment enterprises in 1985 (Marginson *et al.* 1988) found that the degree of decentralisation within an enterprise is related to such factors as the extent of product diversification and the intensity of competition. Organisations that produce a heterogeneous range of goods and services are more likely to have individual establishment bargaining, whereas organisations that produce fairly standardised products or services are more likely to have enterprise-wide bargaining. Decentralisation of pay determination therefore appears to be dictated more by changes in corporate structure and product markets than by labour market considerations.

There is also some evidence that the approach to bargaining may differ by ownership and multinationality. Marginson *et al.* (1993: 59) found that UK domestic companies were most likely to bargain on a multi-employer basis, and in a single set of negotiations covering all sites within the enterprise. Conversely, they were least likely to bargain at individual establishment level. Establishment-level bargaining predominated among both UK and overseas-owned multinationals. The same survey also found that establishment-level negotiations predominated in the manufacturing sector. In the service sector, centralised bargaining was more common, with company-level bargaining being as important as establishment-level. Conglomerate companies were least likely to bargain at the level of the individual establishment. Territorially based divisional organisation was strongly associated with company-level bargaining, as was the presence of divisions covering one single business. Sites designated as profit centres were less likely to be part of company-level bargaining systems, and more likely to negotiate at site level, than were those designated as cost centres (Marginson *et al.* 1993: 60).

Three main reasons for decentralisation have been identified (Walsh 1992). First, the withdrawal from multi-employer arrangements was aimed at bringing pay determination under the direct control of the employer. Second, the organisational restructuring of companies into different geographical and product markets has led local managers to seek to extend their control over pay by reshaping bargaining arrangements around the contours of smaller, profit-related business units. Third, employers believed that devolving pay negotiations allowed them to secure changes in work practices more easily. Research by Purcell and Ahlstrand (1994), which specifically considered pay determination in multi-divisional companies, found that for employers the major aim of decentralisation was to link pay more closely to organisational performance. This reflected a shift away from concern with pay rates and levels of pay increases to more fundamental issues of control over labour costs.

There is, nevertheless, some tension between centralised and decentralised decision-taking in most organisations. While decisions about pay levels and allocation may be taken by local managers, there is often central control over general pay policy and establishment/divisional budgets.

The advantages and disadvantages of the various levels of pay bargaining have been discussed fully elsewhere (see for example, Palmer 1990; Towers 1992; Purcell and Ahlstrand 1994) and the factors affecting greater decentralisation/ centralisation analysed using a strategic choice model (Purcell and Ahlstrand

1994). However, as Walsh (1993: 428) argues, by 'glossing over the distinction between "internalisation" and "decentralisation", the human resource management literature underplays the potential tensions and contradictions of any strategy designed to fragment and individualise the employment relationship'. There is also economic evidence that decentralised bargaining might be inherently inflationary compared to more centralised or at least co-ordinated pay determination systems (see Calmfors and Driffill 1988; Layard 1990). In this way decentralisation of bargaining may lead to economic problems (Philpott 1998). The trend towards more decentralised systems may make wage restraint harder to achieve because, without any mechanism for co-ordination, local pay bargainers are unable or unlikely to take account of the macro-economic results of their actions. Whether this still applies in a very low inflation environment, such as in the UK in 2000, remains a moot point but this has not deterred the Chancellor of the Exchequer, Gordon Brown, from stressing the importance of 'responsible' wage bargaining and the need for a 'sense of national purpose' in forthcoming wage negotiations (annual Mais Lecture at City University, London, 19 October 1999).

The criteria for determining pay changes

A corollary of a move to more internalised pay systems might also imply less concern with external criteria when deciding increases to pay. There is much management rhetoric about the decline of 'going rates' and the rise of 'ability to pay' as the major criterion for pay increases, especially in the light of low inflation. Certainly this is the view expounded in much of the practitioner press and was a major feature of the policy agenda of successive Conservative governments in the 1980s and 1990s. But have the criteria for pay increases changed? Have employers shifted away from comparability with other employers (the 'going rate') and economic factors (such as inflation) and moved towards more business-focused concerns (i.e. profitability and productivity)? If they have, this might have important implications for pay information services and for labour market intelligence (which we deal with in the next section).

According to classical labour market theory, under competitive conditions the wage an employer pays is neither under his control nor under that of the workers. As Blanchflower and Oswald (1988: 364) describe this approach: 'The going rate of pay is fixed by conditions in the whole economy, and most especially by the total demand for and supply of labour. Each firm must pay that going rate.' Nevertheless, this deterministic view of the labour market has been challenged by those who argue for an 'insider–outsider' theory of wages. This approach stresses the importance of the organisation's internal activities and financial performance. Under this framework, wages are determined at least in part by how well the employer is doing. If sales are high, insiders will demand higher pay from their employers, while outsiders (e.g. the availability of replacement labour from the unemployed pool) have little or no influence on this internal market. In reality there is no such thing as a 'going rate' for a particular job but rather an array of rates. For example, an American study of twenty-one aerospace firms fifteen years ago found that the top-paying firm paid more than 21 per cent above the average pay and the bottom one paid more than 13 per cent below the overall average (Foster 1985 cited in Milkovitch and Newman 1996).

In examining how the labour market operates, it is important to look at the relative importance of external and internal pressures upon pay levels. In this section we review the criteria used by employers (and unions where present) in determining pay decisions. Three main factors affecting the level of pay have been identified (Milkovitch and Newman 1996): viz. labour market pressures (supply and demand); product markets (level of competition and product demand); and organisational factors (such as the industry, technology, size and business strategies).

US studies of the relative importance of factors in setting pay levels indicate some shift in priorities between 1978 and 1983 (Freedman 1985). While industry comparisons were in first place in 1978, by 1983 this factor had fallen to fourth place. The top three factors in 1983 were, in rank order: company productivity or labour trends; expected company profits; and local labour market conditions and wage rates. The consumer price index was ranked fifth.

So what is the picture in Britain? There are two main British sources of information about the criteria used in reaching pay decisions – the infrequent WIRS surveys and the much more regular CBI Pay Databank surveys. The most recently available WIRS data show that in 1990 the cost of living remained the most important influence upon pay decisions but, of course, inflation was much higher then. In the private sector three other factors were important: labour market conditions; ability to pay; and comparisons with another pay settlement. For those not covered by collective bargaining, individual employee performance was also a factor.

The second and more up-to-date source is the CBI Pay Databank, established in 1979, and now covering both private sector manufacturing and service sectors. Around 1,300 pay awards are logged each year and average levels of increase calculated. The CBI survey also asks what influences are strongest in reaching the decision about pay increases. We show the results over time since 1979 in Table 2.6.

Ingram *et al.* (1999) argue that, despite claims that pay determination has become more subject to internal factors, the CBI data indicate that external influences are still very important, particularly the rate of inflation and comparability with other pay awards. The RPI was found to be a modal influence in any year of the sample. This was important as both a downward and upward influence on pay decisions. Around 40 per cent of manufacturing firms and 35 per cent of service sector firms consider the cost of living very important. On the other hand, the inability to raise prices (a proxy for external product market conditions) has also become more important since 1984. Almost 50 per cent of manufacturing firms and 25 per cent of service sector firms see this factor as a major impediment to pay increases. Around half of all firms invoke some form of comparability as a contributing factor in pay determination. Only within-

Table 2.6 Pressures on private sector wage increases: percentage where influence very important. CBI Pay Databank Survey Data

Influence	Pressure	Manufacturing			Services
		1979–84	*1984–89*	*1989–94*	*1989–94*
Upward pressures					
Cost of living	E	44	37	39	31
Ability to increase prices	E	4	4	2	3
Need to recruit and retain labour	I	9	18	14	22
High or increasing profits	I	16	21	11	15
High or improving orders	I	N/a	11	8	5
High or improving productivity	I	N/a	16	15	16
Industrial action threatened	I	1	1	1	0.3
Industrial action taken	I	1	1	1	0.2
Any external		46	39	41	33
Any internal		25	44	33	38
Downward pressures					
Falling cost of living	E	N/a	13	19	20
Inability to raise prices	E	51	40	49	26
Low or falling profits	I	54	27	41	27
Risk of redundancy	I	30	14	22	17
Employee involvement policies	I	3	4	5	3
Low or falling orders	I	N/a	9	29	15
Low or falling productivity	I	N/a	3	4	3
Any extenal		49	45	57	40
Any internal		61	38	54	40
Comparability					
Company level	I	23	21	14	16
Industry level	E	15	19	17	29
Local comparisons	E	17	24	21	16
National comparisons	E	18	20	19	20
Any form of comparability		52	53	43	51

Key: I = internal pressure, E = external pressure. Figures are five-year averages

Source: Ingram *et al.* (1999), Table 2

company comparisons appear to be in decline. The research also shows that concepts of a 'going rate' for settlements have weakened since 1984/5. Variation in settlement levels has increased since 1984/5, indicating a greater dispersion in pay award levels and the disappearance of a single 'going rate'. Nevertheless, Ingram *et al.* conclude that: 'While internal settlement pressures appear to be important features of pay determination, there is little evidence from our sample that internal factors have replaced the role of external factors' (Ingram *et al.* 1999: 42).

A survey of pay in the private sector by the IES in 1997, already cited, looked at factors raising and constraining pay costs too (Giles and Atkinson 1997). It also found that the cost of living was considered to be by far the most important influence over higher pay costs in both production and service establishments. There were, however, some sectoral differences. The emphasis on rewarding individual performance was the second most important factor among service sector employers whilst it was less important in the production sector. In contrast, economic performance and staff promotions seemed to have more impact in production establishments than in services.

A survey of pay and benefits trends by the CBI and Hay in 1995 (CBI 1995) also found that, despite low inflation and a concurrent slow-down in market movement, market comparisons remained an important element in salary management. Three-quarters of the sample made external market comparisons. However, as expected, the comparisons varied from group to group, although – with the exception of manual workers – the most important was the specific business sector in which the organisation operated.

Evidence in support of both the internalisation and market referencing of pay determination can be found in work by Arrowsmith and Sisson (1999) (see Table 2.7). In their establishment survey of four sectors (printing, engineering, retail and health), they found that business results (or revenue in the case of NHS Trusts) were reported as the single most relevant factor in pay decisions, while employee productivity was important in engineering and printing. The RPI and comparisons with national competitors were also cited by many respondents. The pay award 'seems to be the outcome of a complex process which simultaneously involves issues of 'ability to pay' and assessments of the external 'going rate', mediated by labour market pressures' (Arrowsmith and Sisson 1999: 60). Interestingly, there were few instances of pay being linked to changes in technology or work organisation and few employers linked pay to changes in working time. Most importantly, this work showed that there are strong sectoral patterns in both pay practices and pay movements and that these appear to occur regardless of whether workplaces have collective bargaining or not.

The implications for pay information systems

The changes in payment systems since the 1980s raise some important questions about the pay information systems upon which decisions are based. The literature on the development of pay information systems is not great and certainly there is little data on the use made by employers and unions of such sources (one exception is recent work by Arrowsmith and Sisson 1999). In this section we review the historical development of the range of pay data sources which are available before considering some of the implications for such sources of the changes discussed in the previous section.

In a pamphlet entitled 'Wages – Fog or Facts', published over thirty years ago, David Layton (the founder of Incomes Data Services, the major commercial

Table 2.7 Factors relating to the most recent pay award. Percentage of respondents

Factor	Degree of importance											
	Engineering			Printing			Health			Retail		
	High	Med.	Low	High	Med.	Low	High	Med.	Low	High	Med.	Low
Business results (1)	72	25	3	57	32	12	83	10	8	71	29	0
Employee productivity (2)	48	46	7	40	44	16	19	36	45	47	11	42
RPI	37	44	18	13	41	47	11	60	29	33	56	11
Recruitment retention	25	45	30	13	51	37	33	45	22	45	40	15
Pay compared with UK competition (3)	13	53	35	17	36	47	35	47	18	30	60	10
Cost compared with UK competition (4)	16	49	35	18	36	46	80	11	9	10	50	40
Employee expectations	–	–	–	16	71	13	18	63	18	15	75	10
Trade union pressure	9	38	53	20	29	51	11	57	33	5	25	70
TU pressure: where pay negotiated	11	57	32	24	20	56	14	64	21	20	80	0
Pay comparisons: international comparisons (5)	4	12	84	3	8	90	4	22	74	0	5	95
Cost comparisons: international comparisons	19	28	53	8	13	79	–	–	–	0	5	95
Base	All respondents											

Key:
Health sector questions: (1) Revenue; (2) Employee performance (also retail); (3) Pay comparisons with other Trusts; (4) Costs; (5) Pay comparisons with non-NHS employers.

Source: Adapted from Arrowsmith and Sisson (1999)

British pay research organisation), argued that there was a strong case for examining the adequacy of published information used for pay determination (Layton 1965). This pamphlet, written against the backdrop of centralised incomes policy and disputes at shop-floor level over incentive schemes, suggested that there was a dearth of data on the collective agreements on pay and conditions negotiated at company level, especially at workplace level. In response, Layton called for changes in the collection of pay information under the following main headings – pay claims; rates of pay; an informed and regular appraisal of pay and hours statistics; and the systematic study of terms and conditions. Most importantly, Layton argued for the regular publication of such information so that it might be made available in the public domain. Such data were seen as a basis for economic modelling but they would also provide essential information for those who made the political and industrial decisions on pay and benefits.

According to Brown and Walsh:

> In the mid-1950s there were probably only a few hundred distinct bargaining units with separate agreements in Britain. Twenty-five years later in 1980 the first Workplace Industrial Relations Survey, covering services as well as manufacturing, permitted a rough estimate that there were 'probably well over 30,000 bargaining units covering twenty-five or more employees'. From the 1980 survey it was estimated that there were 'something of the order of 10,000 pay control points covering twenty-five or more employees . . . 1,000 pay control points covering 1,000 or more employees . . . 100 such points covering 10,000 or more employees'.
>
> (Brown and Walsh 1991: 48–49)

As the number of bargaining units proliferated, the range of sources of pay data also grew. Until the 1960s the sources available to government, employers and unions were limited in the main to government sources. Much of this data was broad macro-economic information but data on industry agreement wage rates were collected by the Board of Trade from 1910 (and latterly published in the Ministry of Labour's own *Time Rates and Hours of Work*) (Milner 1995). From 1970 the government's *New Earnings Survey* (NES), a 1 per cent sample of all full-time workers' pay in Great Britain, made available detailed analysis of earnings. And from 1973 the *Labour Force Survey* (LFS) collected pay data from private households, albeit on a two-yearly basis until 1984 when it became annual (and quarterly from 1992). Trade unions also monitored pay agreements in their own sectors but employers had little access to published pay information. This absence of published pay information partly reflected the overwhelming predominance of industry-wide agreements and the assumption that such rates were actually paid at company and establishment level. Other pay information was considered to be confidential to the parties concerned. It is interesting to note that pay information about actual organisations is much less common in Europe, where multi-industry agreements still predominate, but is common in the USA, reflecting the prevalence there of pay determination at the enterprise and establishment level.

The recognition of the growth of workplace pay bargaining, following the Donovan Commission Report (1968), and the growing interest in industrial relations at company and establishment level, led to a burgeoning of sources of pay and benefits information. The two major British commercial pay information services – Incomes Data Services (IDS) and Industrial Relations Services (IRS) – date from 1966 and 1972 respectively (IDS introduced its monthly Pay Chart in 1980 and IRS its monthly Databank Chart in 1983). These two organisations began to publish wage rates and salary scales from named organisations so that such data came into the public arena for the first time. In 1979 this development was followed by the establishment of the CBI Pay Databank, which collected data from member firms through a regular survey of pay increases. Unlike IDS and

IRS, the CBI data were anonymous and presented as survey results. While initially the CBI survey only covered manufacturing, from 1983 the survey included private services. In 1980 the Engineering Employers' Federation established its own survey of engineering firms. Then in 1983 the trade union-funded Labour Research Department (LRD) began publishing settlement data. Also in 1983 the Office of Manpower Economics (OME), set up in 1971 to service the independent public sector pay review bodies, began surveying pay settlements to inform the civil service pay negotiations from 1984 (and latterly the Police Negotiating Board). The (unpublished) OME survey is conducted on a quarterly basis across a representative sample of non-manual private sector staff pay awards (Charles *et al.* 1998). The main features of these six sources are shown in Table 2.8. It should be noted that the CBI, EEF and OME surveys only cover the private sector.

Other sources of pay and benefits information which have been developed since the 1970s include: published surveys from consultants, professional bodies or other sources; consultants' databases (using data collected from clients); surveys carried out by or for 'pay clubs' of employers, who regularly exchange information; and bespoke surveys carried out for a particular organisation or purpose. A *Directory of Salary Surveys* published by IDS lists over 270 such sources (IDS 1998) and this excludes international surveys. Two major points about such salary surveys should be made. The first is that the quality and cost of such information can vary greatly. The second is that, while providing statistical evidence about the level of salaries and benefits for particular occupational groups or industries, the information usually tells us little about changes in pay practices or the composition of pay.

By the late 1980s a large number of pay settlements were reported annually by IDS and IRS. This is not to say that there were many more settlements that were not reported, but that the range of those that were reported was such that they gave a fairly accurate picture of pay changes in the economy as a whole, especially among larger employers. This success was in part achieved through the fact that,

Table 2.8 Comparisons of settlement data sources

Organisation	Structured sample (*Y/N*)	No. of settlements	Settlement source	Earnings (E) or Basic (B)	Includes public sector (*Y/N*)	Median/ average/ range
CBI	Y	2,700	Employer	E	N	All
EEF	N	2,700	Employer	B	N	All
IDS	N	1,100	Employer	B	Y	Range
IRS	N	1,500	Employer	B	Y	All
LRD	N	1,000	Trade unions	B	Y	All
OME	Y	500+	Employer	B & E	N	All

Abbreviations: CBI = Confederation of British Industry; EEF = Engineering Employers' Federation; IDS = Incomes Data Services; IRS = Industrial Relations Services; LRD = Labour Research Dept; OME = Office of Manpower Economics

Source: Charles *et al.* (1998)

under collective bargaining, there are two parties (and hence two views) of the outcomes of a settlement – the employer and the union. Interpretations of agreements could therefore be compared. Moreover, there were always two sources for the information. Collective agreements were much more likely to be placed in the public domain and thus open to scrutiny than where pay changes were dictated by management alone. In that sense, Layton's original objective was largely achieved by the end of the 1970s. But it was at this point that several changes in the labour market began to occur which have created increasing difficulty for those providing impartial reporting of pay awards.

The implications of these changes in pay systems have already been highlighted in the USA. The growth of more 'at risk' pay, either based on individual performance or on organisational profitability, presents increasing difficulties for those monitoring pay. So too does the ending of clear job descriptions (often used to benchmark salaries against the market) and the development of broad-banded pay progression systems, which allow greater flexibility in individual pay. As one US writer puts it;

> How do you use salary surveys when there are no jobs? How do you match jobs when there are no jobs to match? And when jobs end and there is just work to be done, how do you address external equity?
>
> (Davis 1997: 18)

Another American, Fay, states:

> Base pay is becoming a smaller part of the total compensation package for an increasingly broader range of employees, making it unclear what incumbents in a job actually make. It is certainly more difficult to make comparisons across very different pay systems. When 'at risk' pay may take the form of lump sum bonuses, payments into employee stock ownership or savings plans, or additional time off with pay, comparison of salary figures which may include only base pay or direct cash payouts becomes misleading.
>
> (Fay 1989: 88)

As indicated elsewhere, in the UK the shrinkage in the coverage of collective bargaining and the shift away from multi-employer collective agreements have been accompanied by a growth in discretionary and variable pay systems, particularly the growth of individual performance-related pay. While it has always been the case that a gulf may exist between basic rates of pay and total earnings, the growth of variable pay systems – in which earnings are composed of several separate components – has made the measurement and evaluation of earnings growth increasingly difficult. Many important elements in the total pay and benefits package may be missed if we only concentrate on increases to base rates, such as annual profit-sharing bonuses, profit-related pay, share option schemes, etc. The importance of some of these additions to basic pay is shown by the effect that the annual profit-sharing bonuses have on the government's Average Earnings Index (IDS 1998: 8).

There is therefore increasing imprecision in the composition of what is termed a pay increase. For example, of the six main providers of pay data discussed above, the CBI and OME surveys provide estimates of total earnings increases arising from the award whilst the others generally report only increases in basic pay. It is in the treatment of merit pay that the problems become most apparent. The CBI and OME data will include bonuses, merit pay, etc. in their earnings definition. In the past IDS usually reported the 'new money' increase on the lowest basic rate but this has now been modified to include 'all merit' increases. Where all pay increases are based on individual performance ratings, IDS reports the average merit award or the merit percentage of the paybill, which relies on accurate estimates from employers. In contrast, IRS specifically excludes bonus or merit payments from its analysis unless there is a single identifiable increase to basic pay. In the case of the NES, the growth of merit pay for non-manual workers over the last twenty years is almost invisible because 'all merit' salaries are included as basic pay and not defined as PBR (which includes bonuses, incentives, commission payments, etc. only when separately identified).

The number of 'pay control points', moreover, has probably increased further since the WIRS 1980 data referred to by Brown and Walsh (1991). This is because of the continuing decline of industry-wide collective bargaining, the increasing number of non-union workplaces where pay tends to be determined at establishment level, and the increasing individualisation of pay and benefits. The NES reflected the substantial decline in industry-wide collective agreements in 1997 by abandoning its reporting of individual private sector agreements and providing only aggregate information by size of organisation. Figures for individual agreements are still, however, provided for the public sector and private not-for-profit sector (e.g. universities).

For many workers in non-union workplaces, pay is now nominally determined through individual negotiation between the manager and employee or simply at management discretion (WERS 1998 indicates that only 2 per cent of employees negotiated their own pay – 50 per cent had their pay determined by management alone). In reality there may be a high degree of uniformity in the contracts of employment and terms and conditions offered to employees supposedly on individual contracts. The most recent evidence, from a large-scale study by Cambridge University's Centre for Business Research, suggests that as far as non-pay terms and conditions are concerned, there is increasing standardisation across employee groups (Brown *et al.* 1998), although clearly where cafeteria benefits systems exist, there will be individualisation of choice within the remuneration package. This research shows, however, that pay is likely to be more differentiated and more open to employer interpretation of the employee's job requirements than in the past. Where such individualisation is present in the reward system, there is much less scope for 'rate for the job' and 'going rate' arguments. The number of grades has often been reduced and this has been linked to the broadening of job responsibilities in so-called 'broad-banded' pay structures. In some cases, instead of a series of pay points or incremental points, there is now only a minimum, a maximum and possibly a mid-point, leaving the employer wide discretion as to where to appoint new starters and how to progress individual employees through merit ratings or competencies. Even in quite low-paid occupations, such as fast-food counter staff and retail assistants, local managers may now have a considerable degree of freedom to vary individual wage rates according to both local labour market pressures and individual performance. In many cases, therefore, pay awards only lay down minimum rates. The scope for 'pay drift' – the gap between basic pay increases and actual increases in earnings – within such arrangements remains wide.

These changes mean that, increasingly, commercial pay information sources provide only a partial picture. Instead of reporting actual rates of pay, organisations are increasingly quoting scale minima and maxima or average merit increases or indeed total paybill increases. As indicated earlier, without the ability to check such estimates with a second party, there is scope for a high degree of mystification by employers. This is problematic for both employees, for government and for academic research. In particular, as highlighted by Rubery (1995) in a study of the effects of performance-related pay on gender pay equity, opportunities to monitor pay trends will decrease as the spread of such payment systems reduces the transparency of the labour market.

Nevertheless, despite this observation, research by Arrowsmith and Sisson (1999) indicates that managers may be very knowledgeable about the pay climate surrounding their own organisation. In a range of questions about sources of pay and working time information, many were confident of their ability to locate themselves in the wider context. Their answers revealed that they used a wide range of information (see Table 2.9). The authors conclude that 'this extensive availability of information means that there is little or no need for a more formal co-ordination of approach to pay and working time' (Arrowsmith and Sisson 1999: 68).

Conclusions

This chapter has discussed the ways in which employers make decisions about pay comparisons. We began by contrasting two main approaches to pay determination – internalisation (in which the emphasis is primarily upon internal equity) and external referencing (in which the emphasis is primarily upon comparisons with external competitors for labour). It was argued that there is a fundamental conundrum in the New Pay literature between these two approaches, with greater emphasis upon individual business circumstances being coupled to a strong attachment to market rates. Of course, as Arrowsmith and Sisson (1999) argue, in reality most organisations use a combination of these two approaches in determining pay.

The chapter has also identified two major changes in pay determination over the last thirty years – a substantial decline in collective bargaining as the major method of pay determination in the British labour market and its replacement by

Table 2.9 Information sources on pay and working time (total numbers with number of 'most important' source in parentheses)*

Information source	Engineering		Printing		Health		Retail	
	Pay	Time	Pay	Time	Pay	Time	Pay	Time
British Retail Consortium							9 (0)	6 (0)
NHS Executive					47 (22)	40 (16)		
Trust Federation					21 (4)	17 (2)		
NAHAT					26 (2)	18 (0)		
AHHRM					18 (3)	32 (16)		
Pay Review Bodies					52 (30)	32 (16)		
EEF	128 (82)	120 (78)						
BPIF			78 (54)	74 (51)				
CBI	23 (10)	50 (5)	8 (1)	6 (0)	1 (0)	0 (0)	7 (2)	6 (0)
Management networks	38 (15)	36 (11)	20 (7)	17 (8)	39 (14)	33 (12)	13 (8)	13 (7)
Consultants (e.g. Hay)	10 (2)	4 (0)	1 (0)	1 (0)	15 (4)	7 (0)	11 (3)	7 (1)
Independent surveys	44 (8)	36 (5)	4 (3)	5 (2)	24 (4)	16 (4)	13 (3)	9 (1)
Benchmarking exercises	11 (3)	10 (5)	11 (9)	9 (8)	14 (3)	12 (1)	8 (3)	6 (2)
Specialist media (e.g. IDS, IRS)	16 (7)	18 (7)	2 (1)	3 (1)	39 (14)	30 (11)	13 (5)	11 (3)
Higher organisational level	33 (7)	29 (13)	14 (5)	13 (4)	–	–	–	–
Other	4 (3)	2 (1)	6 (4)	4 (2)	9 (5)	7 (4)	2 (1)	1 (1)
No external sources used	6	14	3	4	0	0	1	2

Base: All respondents
Abbreviations: NHS = National Health Service; NAHAT = National Association of Head Teachers; AHHRM = Association of Healthcare Human Resource Management; EEF = Engineering Employers' Federation; BPIF = British Printing Industries Federation; CBI = Confederation of British Industry; IDS = Incomes Data Services; IRS = Industrial Relations Service

Source: Arrowsmith and Sisson (1999)

an increasingly large segment of non-negotiated pay, where employer discretion rules. There has also been an associated decentralisation of pay determination (in both unionised and non-unionised workplaces) away from industry level and towards enterprise level. The growth of establishment-level pay determination has primarily taken place in the non-union sector. Most of the 'High Street' service sector employers – retail, fast-food and finance sector firms – maintain company-wide pay determination methods, and decentralisation in the public services has been limited largely to the civil service. There is, however, increasing variability in the individual grade rates within the organisation, with a growth of contingent 'at risk' pay components and substantial management control over pay progression.

Despite the growing decentralisation of pay determination, the criteria used by employers in fixing pay levels remain largely unchanged. Inflation and pay comparisons with competitor firms remain very important. There is little evidence that internal factors such as 'ability to pay' and 'performance/productivity' have become more important, although price competition with rivals has become a more significant factor. Most important is the observation that sectoral patterns in pay determination remain strong, despite the decline of industry-wide arrangements.

Finally, it is concluded that 'pay intelligence' has become increasingly problematic as collective bargaining has declined and payment systems have become more individualised. The issue of 'pay drift' was a major concern in the 1970s as collective bargaining became more decentralised and the growth of incentive pay was often disguised. The fragmentation of pay and grading systems, the growing absence of co-ordination of pay changes, and the degradation of pay monitoring mean that the threat of 'pay drift' could return to haunt both governments and employers again. More importantly, to return to the quote from Robinson (1973) cited earlier, the concept of fairness when applied to wages is inevitably tied up with comparisons. If employees cannot know what others are paid, there can be no assurance that they are fairly paid. The changes to pay determination over the last decade may have given employers increasing power over employees' remuneration, but the outcomes may have important ramifications at the macro-economic level, in terms of pay drift, and for employees in terms of transparency.

Note

1 There are two figures available for the coverage of collective bargaining in 1998. The original WERS 1998 First Findings (Cully *et al.* 1998) stated that 45 per cent of establishments had union recognition for the purposes of collective bargaining but this includes workplaces where there are no union members. The recently published *Britain at Work* (Cully *et al.* 1999: 106) shows that 31 per cent of workplaces had collective bargaining for non-managerial employees. Unfortunately, no overall figure including managerial employees is given. In terms of coverage of employees, WERS 1998 indicates that 36 per cent of non-managerial employees are covered by collective bargaining.

References

Aoki, M. (1984) *The Co-operative Game Theory of the Firm*. Oxford, Oxford University Press.

Arrowsmith, J. and Sisson, K. (1999) 'Pay and working time: towards organisation-based systems?' *British Journal of Industrial Relations* 37 (1): 51–75. March.

Becker, G. (1964) *Human Capital*. Chicago, University of Chicago Press.

Blanchflower, D.G. and Oswald, A.J. (1988) 'Internal and external influences upon pay settlements'. *British Journal of Industrial Relations* 26 (3): 363–70. November.

Bland, P. (1999) 'Trade union membership and recognition 1997–98: an analysis of data from the Certification Officer and the *Labour Force Survey*'. *Labour Market Trends*, 107 (7): 343–53.

Booth, A. (1989) 'The bargaining structure of British establishments'. *British Journal of Industrial Relations* 26 (3): 226–34. November.

Brown, W. (1981) *The Changing Contours of British Industrial Relations: A Survey of Manufacturing Industry*. Oxford, Blackwell.

Brown, W. and Sisson, K. (1975) 'The use of comparisons in workplace wage determination'. *British Journal of Industrial Relations* 13 (1): 25–53. March.

Brown, W. and Terry, M. (1978) 'The changing nature of national wage agreements'. *Scottish Journal of Political Economy* 25 (2): 119–33.

Brown, W. and Walsh, J. (1991) 'Pay determination in Britain in the 1980s: the anatomy of decentralisation'. *Oxford Review of Economic Policy* 7 (1): 44–59.

Brown, W. and Walsh, J. (1994) 'Managing pay in Britain'. In Sisson, K. (ed.) *Personnel Management: A Comprehensive Guide to Theory and Practice in Britain*. Oxford, Blackwell.

Brown, W., Marginson, P. and Walsh, J. (1995) 'Management: pay determination and collective bargaining'. In Edwards, P. (ed.) *Industrial Relations: Theory and Practice in Britain*. Oxford, Blackwell.

Brown, W., Deakin, S., Hudson, M., Pratten, C. and Ryan, P. (1998) *The Individualisation of Employment Contracts in Britain*. Research paper for the Department of Trade and Industry. Centre for Business Research, Department of Applied Economics, University of Cambridge. June.

Calmfors, L. and Driffill, K. (1988) 'Centralisation of wage bargaining and macroeconomic performance'. *Economic Policy* 6: 13–61.

Cappelli, P. (1995) 'Rethinking employment'. *British Journal of Industrial Relations* 33 (4): 563–602. December.

CBI (1988) *The Structure and Processes of Pay Determination in the Private Sector: 1979–1986*. London, Confederation of British Industry.

CBI (1995) *Trends in Pay and Benefits Systems*. 1995 CBI/Hay Survey results. London, CBI.

Charles, G., Bailey, D. and Palmer, S. (1998) 'Pay and earnings data. An analysis of the sources'. Office of Manpower Economics. February. (Unpublished)

Cully, M., O'Reilly, A., Millward, N., Forth, J., Woodland, S., Dix, G. and Bryson, A. (1999) *The 1998 Workplace Employee Relations Survey. First findings. ESRC, ACAS, PSI*. October. London, Department of Trade and Industry.

Daniel, W.W. and Millward, N. (1983) *Workplace Industrial Relations in Britain*. London, Heinemann Educational Books.

Davis, J.H. (1997) 'The future of salary surveys when jobs disappear'. *Compensation and Benefits Review* 29 (1): 18–26.

Deaton, D. and Beaumont, P. (1980) 'The determinants of bargaining structure: some large scale evidence for Britain'. *British Journal of Industrial Relations* 18 (2): 202–16. July.

Department of Employment (1988). *Employment for the 1990s*. London, HMSO.

Doeringer, P.B. (1967) 'Determinants of the structure of industrial type internal labour markets'. *Industrial and Labour Relations Review* 20: 206–20.

Doeringer, P.B. and Piore, M.J. (1970) *Internal Labour Markets and Manpower Analysis*. (Mimeo). Office of Manpower Research. US Department of Labour. May.

Donovan Commission (1968) *Royal Commission on Trade Unions and Employers' Associations*. Cmnd 3623. London, HMSO.

Fay, C.H. (1989) 'External pay relationships'. In Gomez-Mejia, L.R. (ed.) *Compensation and Benefits*. ASPA/BNA Series. Vol. 3. Washington DC, Bureau of National Affairs Inc.

Flannery, T.P., Hofrichter, D.A. and Platten, P.E. (The Hay Group) (1996) *People, Performance and Pay. Dynamic Compensation for Changing Organisations*. New York, Free Press.

Foster, K.E. (1985) 'An anatomy of company pay practices'. *Personnel* September: 69–70.

Freedman, A. (1985) 'The new look in wage policy and employee relations'. *The Conference Board*. New York.

Giles, L. and Atkinson, J. (1997) *Multi-purpose Survey of Employers: Sweep 2. Pay in Private Services Module. Commentary.* Falmer: Institute for Employment Studies (IES).

Gomes-Mejia, L. and Balkin, D. (1992) *Compensation, Organizational Strategy and Firm Performance.* Cincinnati, South Western.

Gospel, H. (1992) *Markets, Firms, and the Management of Labour in Modern Britain.* Cambridge, Cambridge University Press.

Gospel, H. and Druker, J. (1998) 'The survival of national bargaining in the electrical contracting industry: a deviant case?' *British Journal of Industrial Relations* 36 (2): 249–67. June.

Hewitt Associates (1991) *Total Compensation Management. Reward Management Strategies for the 1990s.* Oxford, Blackwell.

IDS (1997/8) *Directory of Salary Surveys 1997/98.* IDS Management Pay Review Research File 43, August. London, Incomes Data Services.

IDS (1998) 'What is happening to bonuses and variable pay?' *IDS Report 770.* October. London, Incomes Data Services.

Ingram, P., Wadsworth, J. and Brown, D. (1999) 'Free to choose? Dimensions of private-sector wage determination, 1979–1994'. *British Journal of Industrial Relations* 37 (1): 33–49. March.

Kerr, C. (1954) 'The balkanisation of labour markets'. In Bakke, E.W. and Hause, P.M. (eds) *Labour Mobility and Economic Opportunity.* Cambridge, Mass., MIT Press.

Layard, R. (1990) 'How to end pay leapfrogging'. *Employment Institute Economic Report* 5 (5): 1–8.

Layton, D. (1965) *Wages – Fog or Facts?* Eaton Paper 7. London, Institute for Economic Affairs.

Lawler, E.E. (1990) *Strategic Pay. Aligning Organisational Strategies and Pay Systems.* San Francisco, Jossey Bass.

Lawler, E.E. (1995) 'The New Pay: a strategic approach'. *Compensation and Benefits Review.* July–August: 46–54.

Mahoney, T.A. (1989) 'Employment compensation and strategy'. In Gomez-Mejia, L.R. (ed.) *Compensation and Benefits.* ASPA-BNA Series (3). Washington DC, The Bureau of National Affairs, Inc.

Mahoney, T.A. (1992) 'Multiple pay contingencies: strategic design of compensation'. In Salaman, G. (ed.) *Human Resource Strategies.* London, Sage.

Marginson, P., Edwards, P.K., Martin, R., Purcell, J. and Sission, K. (1988) *Beyond the Workplace: Managing Industrial Relations in the Multi-establishment Enterprise.* Oxford, Blackwell.

Marginson, P., Armstrong, P., Edwards, P., Purcell, J. and Hubbard, N. (1993) *The Control of Industrial Relations in Large Companies: An Initial Analysis of the Second Company Level Industrial Relations Survey.* Warwick Papers in Industrial Relations, No. 45, December. Industrial Relations Research Unit. University of Warwick. Coventry.

Millward, N. and Stevens, M. (1986) *British Workplace Industrial Relations* 1980–1984. London, Gower.

Millward, N., Stevens, M., Smart, D. and Hawes, W.R. (1992) *Workplace Industrial Relations in Transition. The ED/ESRC/PSI/ACAS Surveys.* Aldershot, Dartmouth Publishing Company.

Milkovitch, G.T. and Newman, J.M. (1996) *Compensation.* 5th edition. Burr Ridge, IL, Irwin.

Milner, S. (1995) 'The coverage of collective pay-setting institutions in Britain, 1895–1990'. *British Journal of Industrial Relations* 33 (1): 69–91. March.

Palmer, S. (ed.) (1990) *Determining Pay. A Guide to the Issues*. Wimbledon, Institute of Personnel Management.

Philpott, J. (1998) *Making Pay Work*. Economic Report. Vol 12 (1). February. London, Employment Policy Institute.

Purcell, J. and Ahlstrand, B. (1994) *Human Resource Management in the Multi-divisional Company*. Oxford, Oxford University Press.

Robinson, D. (1973) 'Differentials and incomes policy'. *Industrial Relations Journal* 4 (1): 4–20. Spring.

Rubery, J. (1994) 'Internal and external labour markets: towards an integrated analysis'. In Rubery, J. and Wilkinson, F. (eds) *Employer Strategy and the Labour Market*. Oxford, Oxford University Press.

Rubery, J. (1995) 'Performance-related pay and the prospects for gender pay equity'. *Journal of Management Studies* 32 (5): 637–54. September.

Rubery, J. (1996) 'The labour market outlook and the outlook for labour market analysis'. In Crompton, R., Gallie, D. and Purcell, K. (eds) *Changing Forms of Employment*. London, Routledge.

Rubery, J. (1997) 'Wages and the labour market'. *British Journal of Industrial Relations* 35 (3): 337–66. September.

Schuster, J.R. and Zingheim, P.K. (1992). *The New Pay. Linking Employee and Organisational Performance*. New York, Lexington Books.

Towers, B. (1992) *Choosing Bargaining Levels: UK Experience and Implications*. Issues in People Management No. 2. Wimbledon, Institute of Personnel and Development.

Walsh, J. (1992) 'Managing fragmented pay bargaining: some UK evidence'. *Personnel Review* 21 (7): 3–13.

Walsh, J. (1993) 'Internalisation and decentralisation. An analysis of recent developments in pay bargaining'. *British Journal of Industrial Relations* 31 (3): 409–32. September.

White, G. (1999) 'The remuneration of public servants. Fair pay or New Pay?' In Corby, S. and White, G. (eds) *Employee Relations in the Public Services. Themes and Issues*. London, Routledge.

Williamson, O.E. (1975) *Markets and Hierarchies: Analysis and Antitrust Implications*. London, Free Press.

3 Trade unions and the management of reward

Edmund Heery

Introduction

The proportion of the British workforce who are members of trade unions has fallen continuously since 1979. By 1998 it was estimated that only 30 per cent of the total workforce was unionised and that in the private sector union membership was confined to a mere fifth of employees (Bland 1999). In parallel with this decline in union membership there has been a long-term, and even sharper, decline in the proportion of the workforce who have their pay determined by collective bargaining. According to Milner (1995), collective pay-setting institutions covered approximately 80 per cent of British workers in the mid-1970s. The most recent estimate of bargaining coverage from the annual *Labour Force Survey*, however, suggests that now only 35 per cent of employees have their pay set through institutions of this kind (Bland 1999). Given these trends, what is the justification for writing today about the influence of trade unions on reward management? I believe three reasons make this a worthwhile exercise. First, while unions have declined, they maintain a significant presence in the economy and continue to function as mass organisations of employees: the percentage figures for union density and bargaining coverage for 1998 refer to 7.1 and 8 million workers respectively. Second, the introduction of a statutory recognition procedure by the Labour government has presented unions with an opportunity to reverse their decline and raised the prospect for managers of having to deal with unions and negotiate pay in companies where they previously have been absent or marginal. Third, the decline of unions and collective bargaining has been described as 'the counter-revolution of our time' (Phelps Brown 1990) and a systematic review of the union impact on reward provides a means of assessing this enormous social and economic change. By examining what unions do, we can reach a conclusion about whether their decline adds to or subtracts from our national economic life (Freeman and Medoff 1984).

The process of reward management within employing organisations can be conceived as a series of strategic decisions, each of which might potentially be influenced by union pressure. Five of these decisions are particularly important and provide the framework for the following review of trade union effects. These critical decisions embrace:

- setting the *level* of reward through processes of pay determination
- deciding the *distribution* of rewards through an internal pay structure
- selecting reward *systems* which relate earnings to work performed
- determining the *range* of rewards which, in addition to pay, can include fringe benefits, career progression, opportunities for development and psychological rewards, such as job satisfaction and recognition
- establishing *procedures* for the management of rewards.

Thus, the review is concerned with the extent to which unions raise the pay of their members relative to non-union workers; compress pay differentials (including those between male and female workers); inhibit the use of payment systems which link rewards to performance and thereby place earnings at risk; extend or restrict the range of rewards which organisations offer to their employees; and promote due process and transparency in the management of reward. The majority of evidence presented is taken from Britain but, where appropriate, data from the United States and continental Europe are also used and there is an emphasis throughout on tracking recent trends in union policy and effects. The objective, moreover, is not simply to describe trade union influence on reward management but to offer an explanation in two senses: first by uncovering the rationale and motives that guide union behaviour and, second, by identifying the structural features of organisations and unions themselves which serve to facilitate or constrain union influence.

Reward level

Trade unions classically are bargaining agents which seek to enhance their members' pay and conditions of employment. In Samuel Gompers' concise summary of union purpose, unions want 'More!' and exist to 'achieve a continually larger share for labour' within the existing system of capitalist production (quoted in Hecksher 1988: 20). Available research on the union 'wage effect' suggests that they have been reasonably successful in fulfilling this basic purpose and that the wages of union workers, on average, are higher than those of equivalent workers who are not covered by collective bargaining. The purpose of this section is to review this evidence and summarise what is known about the size and trend over time of the union effect on wages. It also deals with three important additional questions:

1 Under what conditions are unions effective in raising pay?
2 Is the union objective simply to maximise pay or do other concerns also influence pay bargaining behaviour?
3 What are the wider consequences of union wage bargaining for employers and employees, including those who are not members of trade unions?

Opponents of trade unionism have argued that they distort the operation of the labour market, inhibit company performance and raise the earnings of their members largely at the expense of non-union workers (Minford 1985). Supporters, in contrast, claim that union wage bargaining has a relatively benign effect on the economy (Freeman 1992). The aim here is to consider which of these competing interpretations is closest to the truth.

According to Metcalf (1994: 140), there 'is now general agreement that, on average, unionised workplaces pay higher wages than otherwise comparable non-union ones'. Such agreement amongst labour economists is based on a series of cross-sectional estimates of the union wage-gap which compare the hourly, weekly or annual earnings of individual union members or unionised workplaces with those of their non-union equivalents, while seeking to control for other possible influences on earnings, such as employees' level of human capital. A review of these studies by Booth (1995: 164–70; see also Mishel *et al.* 1999: 183–5) concludes that they consistently produce estimates of higher earnings for union members, which in Britain vary between 3 and 19 per cent and which in the USA vary between 12 and 20 per cent. The average estimate of the mean union wage-gap from cross-section models, according to Booth, is around 15 per cent for the USA and 8 per cent for Britain. Averages, however, can conceal as much as they reveal and it is apparent that union membership is worth more in relative terms to some groups of employees than it is to others. In Britain the general pattern is for the union wage-gap to be higher for manual workers than it is for non-manuals and for women than it is for men (Booth 1995: 164–7). According to Main (1996: 229), the union/non-union wage-gap in the mid-1980s was 'of the order of 9.0 per cent for manual males, 0.1 per cent for non-manual males, 15.7 per cent for female full-time employees, and 8.0 per cent for female part-time employees'.

While there is broad agreement that union wages, on average, are higher, there is less consensus over whether this effect is declining over time, with studies in both Britain and the USA yielding seemingly contradictory findings (Freeman 1992: 152; Metcalf 1994: 142–3). In Britain, research using the CBI Pay Databank and the Workplace Industrial Relations Survey (WIRS) points to an erosion of the union mark-up in the 1980s with higher pay increases being recorded for non-union firms and establishments. Individual data, in contrast, drawn from the British Social Attitudes and Family Expenditure Surveys, suggest that the union wage differential remained broadly stable over the same period. Metcalf's conclusion is that the bulk of evidence points to a decline and this is perhaps the safest conclusion to draw, given the tougher environment unions have faced since the 1970s, the exposure of mature, unionised industries to more intense competition and other evidence of both a qualitative and quantitative kind which points to a decline in union power (see also Brown *et al.* 1998). In recent years union strike activity has reached an historic low. There is evidence that the scope of bargaining has narrowed and that managers have been able to secure bargaining concessions from unions; moreover research points to the marginalisation and even derecognition of unions in a sizeable portion of the economy (Claydon 1996; Cully *et al.* 1999; Davies 1998; Dunn and Wright 1994; Edwards and Heery 1989b; Marchington and Parker 1990; Smith and Morton 1993). Given these findings, it seems sensible to take at face value evidence which points to a similar erosion of union bargaining power over pay.

Disaggregated data indicate that not all union workers receive a wage premium and suggest that particular conditions are required if unions are to raise the pay of their members. Analysis of WIRS indicates that two types of condition are important (Booth 1995: 169). First, the size of the wage-gap is influenced by union organisation, with higher relative earnings where membership is high, where there is a pre-entry closed shop and where there is multi-unionism with separate collective agreements. Second, the product market conditions faced by the establishment are also important and in 'the vast majority of establishments facing competitive product market conditions, unions are unable to achieve wage levels above those paid elsewhere to comparable non-union workers' (Metcalf 1994: 142). Operating in international markets appears to have a similar effect, suggesting that foreign competition constrains union influence. The union effect on reward levels, therefore, is conditional on union organisational power but also on the capacity of employers to yield concessions to unionised workers. In the language of labour economics, where unions possess monopoly power they are in a position to extract a share of economic rents for their members from employers who, themselves, operate in relatively sheltered product markets.

Differences in union organisation and product market conditions appear to determine the size of the union wage-gap *within* national economies. However, if one examines differences between countries, then the structure of collective bargaining appears to be the key explanatory variable. Table 3.1 contains estimates of the union/non-union wage-gap in a series of developed economies provided by Blanchflower and Freeman (1992). It indicates that where bargaining is centralised at national or industry level, as in Germany, Austria and Switzerland, or where there are mechanisms for extending pay settlements, as in Australia, then the union wage premium tends to be lower. Blanchflower and Freeman also report that there is a low wage-gap in Japan, where the Spring

Table 3.1 Estimates of the union wage-gap in OECD economies

Structure of collective bargaining	Estimate of union wage-gap (%)
Decentralised bargaining	
USA	22
Canada	10–20
UK	10
Co-ordinated bargaining	
West Germany	8
Australia	8
Austria	7
Switzerland	4

Source: Blanchflower and Freeman (1992)

Labour Offensive operates as an equivalent co-ordinating mechanism. Where pay determination is mainly at company or workplace level, however, as is the case in North America and Britain, then unionised workers are in a position to maximise relative gains through the exertion of bargaining power.

While co-ordinated bargaining may limit the size of the union wage-gap, it can enable unions to pursue other goals. Within co-ordinated systems, unions operate as 'encompassing' organisations which must have regard to the effects of their bargaining behaviour on the national economy and level of employment and which are in a position to act as a social partner and exchange pay restraint for a macro-economic policy and tax and welfare regime beneficial to the broad mass of working people (Visser 1988a, 1998c). The motives underpinning union wage bargaining in this kind of system, therefore, extend well beyond Gompers' insistence on 'more', and may be influenced by a complex set of trade-offs between earnings growth, employment and social welfare. Even within decentralised systems, however, Gompers' demand is tempered by other concerns and there is evidence for both Britain and the USA of unions acting as 'efficient' bargainers which seek to balance wage and employment objectives. For example, Freeman (1992: 152–3) reports research which shows that wages in the unionised sector are more responsive to changes in competition and the economic climate. He argues that union preparedness to surrender their members' share of economic rents in hard times stems from a desire to bargain over employment as well as wages. 'Ordinarily, unions seek to preserve the jobs of existing members', he notes, '[and] very rarely raise wages to extract the maximum rent when a firm begins to fail.'

Conservative critics of unions disregard arguments of this kind and tend to claim that union wage bargaining not only has adverse effects on business and the wider economy, but also that it rebounds against employees themselves. In using monopoly power to raise pay, it is argued, unions disrupt the operation of the labour market, reduce demand for labour in the unionised sector of the economy, and generate an oversupply of labour in the non-union sector which leads to low wages alongside high unemployment (Minford 1985). Perversity arguments form part of the stock-in-trade of conservative intellectuals (Hirschman 1991) and have tended to elicit two responses from economists favourable to trade unionism. The first is to dispute the scale and significance of the union contribution to unemployment by pointing both to the modesty of the union wage-gap and to the fact that the decline in union bargaining power has failed to solve the problem of mass unemployment (Main 1996; Metcalf 1994). Dunn and Metcalf (1996: 92), for example, make the crude but effective point that, whereas in the post-war heyday of union power unemployment never went above one million, since the early 1980s it has been consistently well above this figure.

The second, more ambitious response, has been to argue that union wage bargaining contributes positively to national economic performance and so may not only help generate employment but lead to the production of relatively good jobs which are secure, well-paid and require high levels of skill. Union wage bargaining is claimed to have this effect through two separate mechanisms. First, by raising wages it can 'shock' employers into attempts to seek compensating improvements in productivity and second, by promoting the interests of employees, it can reduce workplace grievances and labour turnover (Freeman and Medoff 1984; Nolan and Marginson 1990). Some of these claims find clear support in the research record. Unionised workers are less likely to report dissatisfaction with their pay (though they tend to be more critical of management), have lower quit rates and turnover and on average receive more training and development (Arulampalam and Booth 1998: 529–30; Bryson and McKay 1997; Freeman 1992: 148–9). The evidence of the union effect on productivity, however, is ambiguous and is best regarded as inconclusive. Some research does point to an enhancing effect and in the 1980s the rate of productivity growth in unionised workplaces appeared to be higher, but this evidence can also be interpreted in terms of unionised firms restoring productivity as union power declined (Metcalf 1994: 145). The first defence of union wage bargaining, therefore, that its negative effects have been exaggerated by critics, appears sustainable but the second defence, that collective bargaining generates a series of positive consequences within the economy, is supported by some but not all empirical indicators.

Reward structure

A second dimension of reward which unions potentially can influence is the structure or distribution of pay, both within the individual firm and the wider economy. That structure may be relatively extended, with large differentials in pay between the higher and lower paid, or it may be relatively compressed, with a pay floor raising the earnings of the less-skilled relative to the pay of those in better jobs. The purpose of this section is to establish what impact unions have on the distribution of earnings and to review the extent to which they compress pay structures and eliminate low pay. The gendered nature of the pay structure and the extent to which women continue to be paid less on average per hour than men and to be disproportionately clustered in low-paying jobs (Cully *et al.* 1999: 159–63), highlights the need for an examination of the effectiveness of unions in representing women workers. Accordingly, the section also considers the issue of 'equality bargaining' (Colling and Dickens 1989) and the extent to which unions have acted to counter the relative disadvantage of women in the labour market.

Potentially, unions can have two effects on the dispersion of pay. First, they can widen pay inequality by raising the earnings of their members relative to those of non-members. Second, they can narrow pay inequality by bargaining for a compressed pay structure in companies where they are recognised. Evidence from Britain, the USA and other countries points strongly to the latter effect (Freeman 1992: 149–50). In the UK, the dispersion of pay is lower both across establishments and within establishments where there is coverage by collective bargaining. Moreover in the UK, there is also evidence that unionised workers are more concerned about pay inequality, which suggests that unions sensitise their members to this issue (Bryson and McKay 1997: 36). Analysis suggests, moreover, that the narrowing of pay dispersion within the unionised sector outweighs the widening of pay dispersion which stems from the union wage-gap, so that the net effect of union wage bargaining is to reduce income inequality (Blanchflower and Freeman 1992: 65). As a consequence, national economies with relatively high union density and coverage by collective bargaining have a more compressed, less unequal wage structure (Freeman 1992: 150; see also Dex *et al.* 1999).

Most commentators argue that the union effect on pay structure arises from two separate concerns. The first is a desire to establish standard rates of pay that reduce management's scope to award differential payments to workers in the same occupational category or grade: unions 'attach wage rates to jobs rather than to individuals' (Booth 1995: 179). The second is a desire to lift the pay floor and eliminate low pay through bottom-loaded wage agreements; indeed, it is union success in raising the earnings of manual workers relative to non-manual workers which accounts for much of the narrowing of the pay structure in union-ised firms (Freeman 1992: 149). A consistent finding from the WIRS series is that there are relatively few low-paid workers in establishments covered by collective bargaining (Cully *et al.* 1998: 25; Millward *et al.* 1992: 364) and for this reason the vast majority of employees affected directly by the National Minimum Wage (NMW) (83 per cent) do not work in unionised companies (Low Pay Commission 1998: 35). Despite the latter fact, the unions have campaigned consistently for a statutory pay floor since the mid-1980s and their support has probably been decisive in translating the policy into legislation (Thornley and Coffey 1999). Legal regulation has been used to complement joint regulation through collective bargaining, therefore, as a way of raising the pay floor.

Although unions continue to compress the pay structure, there is evidence that their ability to do so is declining. During the 1980s pay inequality expanded in unionised establishments, though at a lower rate than in non-union workplaces (Metcalf 1994: 144), in part because unions lost bargaining power and were forced to concede systems of pay determination which give greater scope for rewarding individual employees (see below). The decline in trade unionism and coverage by collective bargaining, moreover, has contributed to the rapid widen-ing of income inequality across the economy since the 1970s. According to Machin (1996: 60), about a fifth of the rise in wage inequality in Britain and the United States over the past two decades is directly attributable to trade union decline (see also Freeman and Katz 1994; Goodman *et al.* 1997: 280; Mishel *et al.* 1999: 185–9).

While union density and bargaining coverage are important determinants of union capacity to shape pay dispersion, comparative research also points to the effect of bargaining structure. Estimates of the variation of earnings amongst *unionised workers* in six countries, produced by Blanchflower and Freeman (1992: 66), indicate that countries with a co-ordinated system of collective bargaining (Germany, Austria, Switzerland and Australia) have less inequality than countries where bargaining is fragmented (UK, USA). Where the system of pay determin-ation allows unions to pool their bargaining power and limit bargaining by nar-rowly defined occupational groups, therefore, they are more able to pursue a 'solidaristic' wages policy which reduces differentials. Where the system does not permit this, or where power in the trade union movement is dispersed and concentrated at workplace level, then the union impact on pay dispersion is less pronounced. In Britain, the narrowing of the pay dispersion in the 1970s (which was associated with a decline in real earnings for many of the better paid) came to an end as local bargainers and union activists rebelled against incomes policy and pushed their unions into the Winter of Discontent strike wave of 1979–80.

Union success in raising the pay floor is the primary reason why union wage bargaining generates a bigger wage-gap for unionised women workers: women are more likely to be found in the lower reaches of the pay structure and therefore benefit more from the upward compression of earnings. It is also open for unions to engage in deliberate 'equality bargaining', that is to make the issues of equal pay and equal treatment a bargaining priority and seek a reform of pay structures and systems that operate to the detriment of women workers and effectively consign them to the base of the pay structure. It is still common for women workers to be concentrated in separate pay grades at the base of company pay structures, to be covered by separate pay agreements to their male co-workers, for grading procedures not to take account of the competencies possessed by women workers, and for opportunities to earn supplements, bonuses and overtime payments to be restricted largely to male, full-time employees. Where unions are recognised, they can seek to challenge arrangements of this kind, though available research suggests that they frequently do not. Colling and Dickens's (1989) review of equality bargaining in the 1980s suggested that most union negotiators were unaware of or unconcerned about possible sex discrimination within collective agreements and few attached priority to equality issues when negotiating pay and conditions of employment (see also IRS 1991). The trend, however, is for more unions to take this issue seriously and in a range of industries (including local government, gas, electricity supply, banking and supermarket retail) unions have negotiated changes to pay and grading structures to combat indirect discrimination against women workers (Arthurs 1992; Colling and Dickens 1998; Gilbert and Secker 1995; Hastings 1992; Jackson *et al.* 1993: 94). A feature common to several of these cases has been union sponsorship of women pursuing equal pay cases against their employers through the employment tribunal system, as a means of putting pressure on managers to negotiate the introduction of new job evaluation and grading procedures. In local government and supermarket retail this combination of union tactics has been used successfully and has resulted in regrading and substantial pay increases for members of two numerous and largely female occupations: home helps and check-out operatives. Indeed, virtually all equal pay cases arise in unionised environments and it seems that unions have an important 'mediating' role in facilitating the enforcement of the legal right to equal pay (Dickens 1989; Millward 1995).

The reasons for growing union commitment to equality bargaining are complex. Partly, it arises from the new opportunities which have been afforded by developments in employment law and particularly the 1983 equal value amendment to the Equal Pay Act, which gave women the right to equal pay for work of equal value. In the wake of this amendment a series of judgments by the European Court of Justice has clarified and further strengthened the entitlement to equal pay and has given the unions the chance to use the law as a lever to open up equality bargaining. Increased commitment, however, is also a function of union decline and, in some cases crisis, and the fact that union fortunes are increasingly dependent on their capacity to recruit women members. As a consequence, the Trades Union Congress (TUC) and many of its affiliates have developed policies that promote the cause of sex equality with the intention of re-positioning unions as the representatives of working women (Heery 1998a, 1998b). Policy change has not occurred solely under duress, however; but is also a function of change within unions. There are increasing numbers of women activists and the associated shift in union ideology and definitions of purpose have led a proportion of male representatives to attach priority to equality bargaining (Colgan and Ledwith 1996; Heery and Kelly 1988). British unions, it can be argued, are undergoing a process of 'frame extension' in which their core constituency is re-defined to include women workers and gendered categories in the labour market, such as part-timers. This shift is a function partly of externally induced crisis but also of internally generated change (see Cornfield and Fletcher 1999).

Although the union bargaining agenda has been extended to embrace equality issues, it is apparent that there are powerful constraints on this development. Several of these are internal and, notwithstanding change, it remains the case that the majority of union negotiators and representatives are male and many remain attached to a traditional and narrow bargaining agenda (Cully *et al.* 1999: 195–7; Kelly and Heery 1994: 57). There are also potent external constraints, and a number of studies of equality bargaining have pointed to the limited impact of equality bargains on the relative rewards of women workers. Colling and Dickens's (1998) study of British Gas, for instance, describes how an ambitious equality agreement was nullified as the company was exposed to new competitive pressures by the gas regulator. The business was restructured into a series of semi-autonomous units, and responsibility for negotiations devolved on the management side from central personnel to divisional line managers and on the union side from national officers to predominately male shop stewards (see also Gilbert and Secker 1995). The effect of these changes was to remove the impetus from equality bargaining as the need to cut labour costs became management's main priority and as the architects of the agreement, in the central personnel function and amongst union full-time officers, lost influence.

The British Gas case points once again to the importance of the structure of collective bargaining as a determinant of union effects on reward, and this is equally apparent if one examines international differences in gender equality. Research on the gender pay-gap has consistently shown that women tend to earn more relative to men in countries with a centralised or co-ordinated system of collective bargaining (Blau and Kahn 1995; Rubery and Fagan 1994; Whitehouse 1992). The gap is particularly narrow in the Nordic countries, where central wage agreements have traditionally narrowed the wage dispersion within and between industries and raised the pay floor to the benefit of relatively low-paid women workers (Almond and Rubery 1998). In countries like Britain, Ireland and the USA, in contrast, which have more fragmented systems of pay determination, the gender pay-gap is wider, notwithstanding developments in equal pay law and labour movements which have become more receptive to an equality agenda. The union impact on gender pay divisions, therefore, cannot be reduced solely to a matter of motive and the preparedness of unions to embrace equality bargaining, but is also a function of the inherited structure of industrial relations which constrains trade union action. Within a decentralised bargaining structure, the adoption of equality bargaining has the potential to narrow the gender pay-gap *within* employing organisations which recognise trade unions but has very little capacity to influence differences in male and female earnings across firms and industries. Women earn less when they work only with women (Millward 1995); consequently if unions are to address the combined effects of pay discrimination and occupational segregation in economies like Britain, then they must rediscover ways of regulating the labour market at industry or national levels. Perhaps the greatest service the British trade union movement has done for women workers in recent years has been to campaign for a National Minimum Wage, 72 per cent of the recipients of which are women (Almond and Rubery 1998; Low Pay Commission 1998: 142).

Reward systems

A third strategic issue which unions potentially can influence is the selection of reward or payment systems. The latter can be defined as procedures for relating pay (and possibly other rewards) to work. They fall into two broad categories: *input-based reward systems* link pay to the skills, competence or time which employees invest in their work while *output-based systems* link pay to measures of worker performance, such as output, productivity, achievement of objectives, sales and profit (Kessler 1995). The measures of worker performance used in the latter category may relate to an individual employee, a work group or team or to all members of a particular enterprise, as occurs with profit-sharing and profit-related pay. The bulk of research on unions and payment systems is concerned with their relationship to output-based systems and these are the focus of the following section. It considers:

- union influence on the incidence of output-based payment systems
- the nature of the union policy response to their spread
- the methods which unions use to ensure payment systems operate without detriment to their members' interests
- the factors that allow unions to exercise control over contingent pay.

The incidence of a number of payment systems is related to the presence of trade unions. In some cases, unions seem to encourage the use of particular forms of contingent reward and in the USA gain-sharing plans are associated with a union presence (Eaton and Voos 1992), while in Britain large unionised firms are more likely to use profit-sharing (Millward *et al.* 1992: 263; see also Pendleton 1997; Poole 1989: 94). Other systems are less common where unions are present and, outside the large-firm sector in Britain, profit-sharing is found mainly in non-union firms and the same is true for the United States (Eaton and Voos 1992). Another system which is less common in the unionised sector is individual performance-related pay (IPRP) or merit pay. Schemes of this kind relate salary increases or bonuses to the results of an individual performance appraisal and have increased in frequency in recent years. In Britain, Ireland and the USA the presence of IPRP is inversely correlated with union recognition (Blanchflower and Oswald 1990; Freeman 1992: 150; Gunnigle *et al.* 1993: 75). This has led some to suggest that this payment system expresses a new 'individualism' within the employment relationship and represents a sharp break with earlier forms of payment-by-results, which were integral to the 'pluralist industrial relations tradition' (Gunnigle *et al.* 1998: 574). Partly for this reason, the union response to IPRP is considered centrally in what follows.

Table 3.2 shows results from a national survey of union policy on IPRP in Britain and indicates that the majority of unions are opposed and, indeed, the introduction or extension of IPRP schemes has been a cause of industrial disputes in a number of sectors, including the civil service, education, banking and television. Many unions clearly regard IPRP as undesirable. However, rather than representing a break with the past in response to the peculiarly threatening nature of this system of payment, such opposition represents continuity, as other forms of output-based payment system have also attracted widespread resistance. Baddon *et al.* (1989: 44) characterise the dominant union response to the recent spread of profit-sharing, a seemingly more collectivist payment system, as one of 'bored hostility' (see also Poole 1989: 96–9), and accounts of union responses to the use of manual worker incentives tell a similar story. The spread of shop-floor incentive schemes was resisted by American unions in the 1950s and in the major automobile companies the United Auto Workers' Union was successful in blocking their use (Slichter *et al.* 1960: 4930–6; see also Brown and Philips 1986). Research from British manufacturing in the 1960s reveals an identical pattern of majority opposition to incentive schemes amongst shop stewards and occasional successful attempts to secure their removal (Brown 1973: 13–15), while beyond

Table 3.2 Union policy on IPRP (trade unions and staff associations in Britain, 1994)

Policy	Nos	%
Opposed and committed to resistance	16	26.2
Opposed but prepared to accept IPRP	26	42.6
Pragmatic, neither opposed nor in favour	10	16.4
Supportive, ready to accept IPRP	4	6.6
Supportive, the organisation advocates IPRP	1	1.6
There is no policy on IPRP	4	6.6
Total	61	100

Source: Heery and Warhust (1994)

manufacturing the National Union of Mineworkers (NUM) conducted a long campaign against piecework within the coal industry (Gidwell 1977; see also Heywood *et al.* 1997).

The reasons for this recurrent pattern of trade union opposition to contingent payment systems appear to be fivefold.

1 This kind of payment system can pose a threat to union members and particularly to the security and stability of their earnings. This is a factor in union hostility to profit-sharing and profit-related pay and some of the sharpest union resistance to IPRP has arisen where schemes have involved the replacement of cost-of-living with 'merit-only' pay increases.

2 Unions have claimed incentives generate perverse effects and can frustrate, rather than promote effective labour management. In coal mining, a major reason for opposition to piecework was its association with mining accidents (Edwards and Heery 1989a). Moreover unions have used academic research to argue that IPRP is counter-productive because of its tendency to demotivate employees and erode teamwork (Heery and Warhurst 1994). Unions of professional workers, such as teachers, lecturers, nurses, doctors and probation officers, have particularly argued that IPRP is perverse in its effects and likely to erode the commitment that is required for the effective delivery of professional services (e.g. NUT 1999).

3 Unions have opposed contingent pay because of its impact on pay structure and its tendency to widen the dispersion of pay by generating differences in earnings between individuals, work groups, work-sites and men and women. These differences, moreover, are viewed as 'unfair' because in many cases they reflect not genuine differences in performance but the accidents of job content, job context and management style, and the pernicious effects of gender and race discrimination.

4 Unions have regarded incentives as divisive and threatening to their own capacity to develop collective organisation and purpose amongst employees. In coal mining, the reintroduction of incentives in the late 1970s was opposed by many in the NUM because it threatened to divide the industry into low- and high-paid areas and make it difficult to mount effective national strike action in support of pay claims or against pit closures. Similarly, IPRP has been opposed because of its potential to detach individuals from union membership and so 'disorganise' the union from within.

5 Unions have opposed contingent pay because it may pose a threat to their procedural role as the collective representatives of employees and be linked to attempts by employers to exclude unions from the process of pay determination. The primary reason for union opposition to profit-sharing has been 'the non-negotiable nature of schemes' (Baddon *et al.* 1989: 45) and opposition to IPRP has been particularly intense because of its association with explicit or tacit moves to derecognise unions (Heery 1997a).

While there is a history of union opposition to contingent pay, this is not the only response and in many cases union policy towards payment systems of this kind is marked by ambivalence. This is demonstrated in Table 3.2, which indicates that unions vary in their depth of opposition to IPRP, with many acknowledging the need for pragmatism, and a minority even declaring in favour. Regardless of what academic commentators might claim about the essential 'individualism' of this kind of payment system, many unions regard its use as compatible with a continued role for themselves. The reason for union acceptance of IPRP, and other contingent pay systems, is in many cases simple acknowledgement of *force majeure*, that the union is incapable of preventing the introduction of incentives. In other cases, however, contingent pay may be recognised as beneficial for employees and a source of union strength. In the USA in the 1950s, opposition to payment-by-results softened as it became apparent that it provided a 'rich source of indirect wage increases' (Slichter *et al.* 1960: 497) and in British coal mining the reintroduction of incentives in the 1970s was supported by the NUM's moderate leadership on the grounds that it would raise pay, allow members to escape the constraints of government incomes policy, and revive pit-level bargaining (Edwards and Heery 1989a). Similar examples are available for more recent payment systems, with unions acceding to IPRP because it provides a means to raise public service salaries or permits members in management jobs to escape from the constraints of a compressed pay structure (Heery and Warhurst 1994). For a range of different contingent pay systems, moreover, there is evidence of union policy moderating over time as the new method of reward is institutionalised within a particular enterprise, sector or occupation. It is notable that the preparedness of unions to accept IPRP is associated statistically with the proportion of members exposed to this system of payment (Heery and Warhurst 1994: 14; see also Baddon *et al.* 1989: 49; Slichter *et al.* 1960: 496).

The primary condition for union acceptance of contingent pay systems appears to be the opportunity to regulate schemes jointly with management through collective bargaining (Kessler 1994). Unions are 'irredeemable bargainers' (Crouch 1982: 117) and their main purpose when faced with contingent pay is to shape its form and operation through collective agreement, essentially to minimise the disadvantages listed above. With regard to IPRP, for instance, unions have sought to reduce the at-risk element in total remuneration and ensure stability of earnings is maintained through parallel cost-of-living awards. Furthermore they have instituted monitoring and appeal procedures to reduce the risk of unfair treatment and have sought to limit management discretion through formal rules governing performance appraisal and procedures which allow for the joint review of IPRP schemes (Brown *et al.* 1998; Heery and Warhurst 1994). These kinds of measure, moreover, echo the response to earlier forms of contingent pay and underline the continuity in union policy. The re-introduction of group incentives in the coal industry, for example, took the form of a supplementary bonus paid on top of a negotiated day rate. It also included provisions for the protection of earnings in the event of machine breakdown or geological problems, allowed for the payment of lieu bonuses to surface workers to ensure the dispersion of pay did not widen excessively, and embraced a number of regulations governing management's setting of effort standards, including the entitlement to negotiate over work study estimates of standard performance (Edwards and Heery 1989a).

Three-quarters of UK unions with members covered by IPRP report they have negotiated collective agreements regulating IPRP schemes (Heery and Warhurst 1994: 12). Despite the apparent 'individualism' of merit pay, therefore, unions have been reasonably successful in drawing it within the compass of joint regulation. It remains the case, though, that this kind of payment system is associated with non-unionism and de-recognition and that many unions have members covered by IPRP schemes which have not been bargained collectively (Bacon 1999; Brown *et al.* 1998; Heery 1997a). Necessarily, therefore, unions have had to develop ways of representing members where joint regulation has come to an end. Three main responses are apparent, though it should be noted that two of them have as their ultimate purpose the restoration of collective bargaining.

1   The first response has been to develop an advisory and representation service for union members on personal contracts with IPRP: this has been a particular feature of managerial unions in the privatised utilities. The union role in this case has become one of supporting members who negotiate their own salary, for example, through the provision of pay data, and acting as an advocate on behalf of individuals who believe they have been unfairly assessed. According to some commentators (Bassett and Cave 1993), this form of representation is most appropriate to the new 'individualism' in employment relations. However, as we have seen, there is nothing to prevent collective bargaining over IPRP, and even where this does not apply, alternative or additional methods of representation are available.

2   The second response, for instance, has been to campaign against IPRP, in order to discredit it in members' and managers' eyes and secure either its withdrawal or its reform. Some unions have displayed considerable imagination in campaigning and have commissioned academic research on the effects of IPRP, generated publicity, involved the media, and commissioned surveys of members' opinion in order to reveal the extent of opposition or discontent (Heery and Warhurst 1994).

3   The third response might form part of a campaign and involves the use of employment law to challenge management's operation of IPRP. Two bodies of law have been used. First, in organisations where unions remain recognised for issues other than IPRP, they have used the law on disclosure of information to obtain data on the level and distribution of performance payments. Second, they have used discrimination law, and particularly the law on equal pay, to question the fairness of IPRP and to secure greater transparency and formality in its operation (Heery and Warhurst 1994). In both cases, the law has been used as a lever to open up IPRP schemes to union influence.

In addition to the law, research on the determinants of union influence over payment systems has identified a range of factors which can allow unions to shape contingent pay. Classic studies of piecework bargaining (Brown 1973), for instance, have pointed to the combined influence of buoyant product markets and slack systems of management control in allowing workers to influence the operation of incentive schemes (see also Heery 1984). Other studies have pointed to worker control of key stages of the labour process as a basis for influence (Edwards and Heery 1989a) and it is clear that union bargaining power with regard to contingent pay is largely a function of aspects of the economic and organisational context which endow unions with leverage over management.

Research on the determinants of union success in bargaining over IPRP points to additional influences, including management strategy and the structure of collective bargaining. With regard to the former, it is notable that unions of professional and managerial employees have been less successful in securing collective agreements on IPRP, reflecting the fact that many employers regard joint regulation as illegitimate at higher organisational levels (Brown *et al.* 1998; Heery 1997a). With regard to bargaining structure, it is notable within the public sector that the civil service unions have had most success in securing collective bargaining over IPRP and that this has been secured through the medium of industry-wide collective agreements. In local government and the National Health Service, in contrast, IPRP has been introduced largely at the initiative of local managers, who have used the effective decentralisation of pay determination to escape from union influence (Heery 1997a). In the past, locally introduced incentive schemes have been viewed as a stimulus to workplace trade union activity, but in a period of union decline and weakness, local experiments with contingent pay may take place on management's terms and decentralisation lead effectively to de-recognition (Beaumont 1995: 28).

While influence over pay systems is largely a function of structural context and the 'positional power' which unions possess, it may also be a function of the union's 'organisational power': its ability to shape members' response to contingent pay. Case studies of the introduction of incentives in strongly unionised sectors, for instance, have revealed how workplace union leaders may seek a 'disciplined' reaction to the new payment system and enforce norms on effort levels and the distribution of earnings opportunities. In coal mining the reintroduction of incentive schemes in some pits was accompanied by the adoption of pooling arrangements for bonus earnings, the discouragement of 'excessive' earnings by individual work teams, and controls on the allocation of workers to 'high' and 'low' paying jobs (Edwards and Heery 1989a; see also Batstone *et al.* 1977: 143–5). In these cases, therefore, the union was using its collective strength and control over its members to influence the operation of an incentive scheme and minimise perceived unfairness and consequent division. Where the local union lacks 'organisational power', however, this kind of disciplined, collective response to contingent pay will be absent. Research on IPRP schemes in local government, for example, has revealed quite extensive employee dissatisfaction with schemes and a latent demand for union involvement, but also a failure on the part of unions to satisfy that demand through the articulation of grievances (Heery 1997b). Scope for union influence over IPRP and other payment systems may not be realised, therefore, because of the absence of an authoritative workplace leadership. Given the substantial weakening of shop steward organisation in recent years (Terry 1995), it is likely that the passive, ineffectual response to IPRP seen in local government characterises many other workplaces as well.

Reward range

A fourth decision which unions potentially can influence concerns the range or form of reward. While payment in cash remains the primary reward for work for most employees, remuneration for many also embraces benefits, such as pensions, healthcare and company cars. Moreover, beyond remuneration, other aspects of the employment relationship may function as rewards, including the opportunity for personal development, job satisfaction and recognition of achievement. Reward can therefore comprise both extrinsic elements, which are consumed away from the workplace and often function as 'compensation' for work, and intrinsic elements, which are integral to work activity and enable employees to enjoy a more satisfying working life. The role of unions in influencing the range of rewards has not been a major concern of academic researchers. However, a persistent theme in discussion has been that unions narrow the span of reward and focus on short-term and cash returns to their members at the expense of deferred and non-pay rewards (Brown *et al.* 1998: 27; Hill 1981: 131; Strauss 1998: 103). Accordingly, this section tests these beliefs and considers the role of unions in either narrowing or broadening the range of rewards with regard to two areas: the provision of fringe benefits and opportunities for training and development. Throughout, the emphasis is on the union role at enterprise level. In Britain and Europe unions have often contributed to the development and even administration of systems of social insurance and vocational training but this societal role, typically pursued through political action, is not considered here. Instead, the focus is on the unions' function in restricting or broadening the range of employment rewards in their direct dealings with employers, principally through the medium of collective bargaining.

With regard to benefit provision, there is clear evidence from the United States that unions extend the range of rewards and that unionised workers receive both more and more valuable fringe benefits than their non-union counterparts (Freeman 1992: 149). US unions have been particularly successful in improving pension and health insurance provision for their members and if the cash value of these and other benefits are accounted for, the wage-gap for unionised workers rises by another two to three percentage points (Booth 1995: 171; Mishel *et al.* 1999: 184–5). There is supporting, though less extensive evidence for Britain, and analysis of individual data from the mid-1980s by Green *et al.* (1985) indicates that unionised workers are more likely to receive company sick pay, a company pension, subsidised meals and paid holidays. More recent research on the last of these benefits has found that, there is a difference of about 11 percentage points between the chances of unionised and non-unionised workers getting any paid holidays, and a further difference of some 5.5 days on average between the holiday entitlements of those receiving paid holidays in recognised and in non-recognised workplaces.

(Green 1997: 252)

At an aggregate level, therefore, unions both broaden their members' remuneration by adding fringe benefits and generate a benefit differential which reinforces the differential in earnings between unionised and non-unionised workers. Evidence for unions narrowing the reward range is not apparent and in both countries it seems that unions have played an important role in securing 'deferred' rewards for their members which contribute to lifetime security. Not all fringe benefits are found more frequently in unionised workplaces, however, and in Britain benefits in kind, company cars and private healthcare are less common in the union sector (Green *et al.* 1985). The probable reasons for this are twofold: that certain benefits may be associated with a paternalist management style which leaves little room for joint regulation or, like private healthcare in the UK, may conflict with union support for a high level of state provision.

While unions may improve benefit provision for their members, their impact on the distribution of benefits is less certain. Historically, the latter has been very uneven and has reflected an underlying status division between salaried and hourly paid employees (Price and Price 1994). There has been and continues to be a tendency for non-pay benefits to increase with job status and for manual workers, women, part-timers and those in jobs of short tenure to be relatively disadvantaged when it comes to benefit provision (Brown and Walsh 1994). Over the past two decades, however, there has been a broad movement towards the harmonisation of employment terms within enterprises. The achievement of single status, with common benefit provision for the entire workforce, has become an aspiration if not a reality across much of the economy. To what extent have unions promoted this development and contributed to the narrowing of benefit dispersion in the way that they have compressed the dispersion of pay? In the past in Britain, occupational unionism, with separate unions for manual, craft and white-collar workers, undoubtedly reinforced status divisions, though increasingly unions have pursued single status within collective bargaining. The 'new style' agreements of the 1980s and the 'partnership' deals of the 1990s have typically provided for integrated benefit provision (Bassett 1986; Thomas and Wallis 1998), and in public services unions have pressed for the harmonisation of conditions of employment, most notably in local government where a collective agreement on single status was signed in 1997. Despite these developments, there is no economy-wide tendency for single status to be associated with a trade union presence (Millward 1995: 112). There is a tendency, however, for single status to reflect both union structure and the structure of collective bargaining; where there is a common union covering both manual and non-manual employees and where there is single-table bargaining at enterprise level, then single-status benefit provision is more likely both within the union sector and across the economy at large

(Millward 1994: 111; see also Brown *et al.* 1998). Unions promote harmonisation, therefore, where the structures of representation and bargaining facilitate their doing so.

Another recent development in benefit provision has been the introduction of cafeteria or flexible benefits, which allow employees an element of choice over the form in which they receive rewards. This change is sometimes used as an indicator of the 'individualisation' of the employment relationship, like the spread of IPRP, and in some cases has been associated with union derecognition (Brown *et al.* 1998: 27). While there is no evidence of unions advocating cafeteria benefits, at least in the UK, there is evidence of unions pushing for a more flexible system of benefit provision in two senses. First, unions have advocated the extension of benefits (and wider equal treatment) to atypical workers so that employees who choose to work on a non-standard pattern are not penalised for doing so. Second, union policy has engaged increasingly with the issue of 'family-friendly' working arrangements and has sought to establish a flexible pattern of working time with supportive benefits for those workers who have to integrate paid employment with childcare or care of elderly relatives. At European level, concrete expression of these dual concerns can be seen in the negotiation of collective agreements on parental leave and part-time employment which subsequently have been adopted as European directives (Falkner 1998). The latter, in turn, have stimulated bargaining activity at company level, like earlier and related legislation in the fields of equal pay and maternity leave (Price and Price 1994). How extensive and successful have been attempts to negotiate benefits that support flexible working by employees remains uncertain. However, in Britain, the United States and other countries it is possible to identify cases of successful innovation and a shift in formal union policy (TUC 1996; Visser 1998b: 296; Wever 1998). In the United States, according to York (1993), unions have been most successful in recent years in bargaining for parental leave and in extending the circumstances in which leave for family care can be taken. They have been less successful, but nevertheless have made advances, in negotiating various forms of subsidised childcare (York 1993). What these and associated developments suggest is that unions are seeking to extend the agenda of collective bargaining in order to embrace greater diversity of employee interests, partly in order to reposition unions as the representatives of an expanding female and contingent labour force (Heery 1998a).

Union voice also seems to be associated with greater provision of training and, for the UK, a series of studies have demonstrated a link between union presence and worker access to training. Thus, Arulampalam and Booth's (1998) analysis of the British Household Panel Survey of 1991 indicates that the receipt of continuing training is associated with the presence of a recognised trade union; Knight and Latreille (1996) use survey data from engineering firms in the 1980s to demonstrate a link between union presence and the provision of apprenticeships; and Green *et al.* (1999) use a combination of data from the *Employers' Manpower and Skills Practices Survey* 1991 and the *Labour Force Survey* 1993 to show that employees working in establishments with a recognised trade union are more likely to receive training than their non-union counterparts (see also Cully *et al.* 1999: 149).

Similar findings are available for Australia and the United States (Booth 1995: 210; Kennedy *et al.* 1994). Another UK study by Heyes and Stuart (1998) has measured the depth of involvement in company training policy of union representatives in manufacturing and found a correlation with both the level and form of training received by members. In companies where the union influenced policy, access to training was broader and employees were more likely to obtain qualifications and receive a pay increase. This suggests that the effect of union involvement is to ensure a more even division of the benefits of training between employer and employee.

The current trend in Britain and in other countries is for unions to try and extend their influence over training and, where possible, add it to the bargaining agenda. An interest in the regulation of training has long been characteristic of craft unions, but today general and white-collar unions are equally likely to attach priority to this issue. In Britain, the TUC has lobbied for a statutory duty for employers to bargain over training and through its 'Bargaining for Skills' campaign has sought to promote the negotiation of training agreements by its affiliates. Several of the latter, moreover, have placed training at the heart of a 'new bargaining agenda' and have adopted as a core objective the entitlement of all employees to five days continuing training per year (Dundon and Eva 1997; Heyes and Stuart 1998; Rainbird and Vincent 1996). The unions have also embraced the objective of 'lifelong learning' and in some cases have negotiated programmes that allow for personal development and access to continuing education beyond the requirements of the immediate job or occupation. The best-known examples are the Ford UK EDAP agreement (Employee Development and Assistance Programme), which echoes a similar initiative in the United States, and the 'Return to Learn' programme developed by Unison, which aims to negotiate access to education for relatively low-paid and largely unqualified public service workers (Hougham *et al.* 1991).

The reasons for this shift in union policy towards education and training appear to be twofold. First, it is another attempt to re-position unions as the representatives of a changing workforce. The GMB's embrace of the target of five-days' training, for instance, derived from market research it commissioned which indicated that there is a strong demand for training and development amongst workers which is not being met through existing union agreements (Storey *et al.* 1993). Unison's 'Return to Learn' programme also represents an attempt to make policy more responsive and extend opportunities for development to the unskilled and to part-timers who have been excluded from this kind of benefit in the past. Second, it represents an attempt to engage employers and develop 'partnership' around an issue which is seemingly positive-sum in nature. The TUC has placed the joint regulation of training at the heart of its attempts to secure a new social partnership with business. It believes the advocacy of training by trade unions can promote not only the employability of workers, but also the long-term competitiveness of British industry (TUC 1997). According to Streeck (1992: 254), union involvement in skill formation could become the defining feature of their role in 'the post-Keynesian political economy' and form the centrepiece of a new supply-side industrial relations in which the primary economic function of unions is to promote a plentiful supply of skilled and flexible labour.

Although unions have registered successes in attempting to bargain over training and development, commentators have pointed to the continuing limits to their influence (Claydon 1998; Green *et al.* 1999). The primary constraint which unions face is their lack of bargaining power and the fact that many employers are simply not disposed to extend joint regulation beyond a limited customary agenda. Thus, the 1998 Workplace Employee Relations Survey found that union representatives negotiated over training in less than 5 per cent of workplaces and that in 43 per cent of establishments where unions were present, there was no involvement in training whatsoever (Cully *et al.* 1999: 104–5). The lack of union bargaining power at workplace level is doubly significant in Britain because the national system of vocational education and training (VET) provides very little support for union involvement. Previous arrangements for the tripartite regulation of training at national and sectoral levels were largely done away with in the Conservative reform of VET in the 1980s and the resulting system is primarily responsive to the interests of employers (Gospel 1998; Rainbird and Vincent 1996). This is in stark contrast to arrangements in other European countries, where unions can influence training policy either directly or indirectly through works councils. The Employment Relations Act 1999 contains a provision for employers to consult with recognised unions on training at six-monthly intervals, but this falls short of a duty to bargain and it remains to be seen whether it is effective in allowing unions to extend the range of rewards they negotiate for their members.

Reward processes

The previous four sections have dealt with union influence over substantive issues in reward management, but unions also can shape *procedure* and determine the processes through which rewards are managed. It is union influence over reward procedure which is the concern of this final section and it considers the role of unions in providing for employee participation in determining rewards, in formalising reward procedures, in establishing due process mechanisms for the resolution of disputes, and in providing for the transparency of reward practice through monitoring, audit and review. This procedural role of unions can be extremely important and according to some commentators, it increasingly defines the contribution of unions within business. Brown *et al.* (1998: 73) claim that, as unions' capacity to 'earn rents' and directly determine the substance of reward policy has declined, so their role in representing individuals and functioning as a vehicle for 'representative consultation' has increased. While unions may be less able to raise pay rates in a more competitive economy, therefore, they may still be able to shape the way in which reward is managed and the purpose of what follows is to describe the typical and changing concerns of unions with regard to reward procedure.

The main concern of unions with regard to participation has been to secure the right to bargain over reward on behalf of members. Unions, as has been pointed out, are irredeemable bargainers and seek to draw all aspects of reward management within the compass of collective negotiation and agreement. As a consequence, they can alter fundamentally the process of decision-making within the field of reward and can displace unilateral regulation by employers with a system of union-mediated worker participation or collective joint regulation. This raises the question, however, of the representativeness of unions and the extent to which collective bargaining genuinely allows for employee participation in the determination of rewards. Clearly, goal displacement can occur within unions, as in any bureaucracy, and the institutional interests of the union come to dominate those of its members. In the majority of cases, however, it is likely that this tendency is kept in check, partly because of the salience of reward for union members, which gives them an incentive to hold representatives to account, and partly because most unions have internal systems of participation which allow members to influence decision-making. WIRS 1990 recorded that union negotiators consulted members over pay settlements in 77 per cent of bargaining units for manual workers and 70 per cent for non-manual workers. The survey also identified a trend towards more formal and privatised consultation of members through workplace and postal ballots, which arguably provide a more accurate measure of worker opinion and are less susceptible to manipulation (Millward *et al.* 1992: 235; see also Kelly and Heery 1994).

Another way of assessing the efficacy of collective bargaining as a form of participation is to see if there are functional alternatives which operate in non-union workplaces. Writers on reward frequently advise managers to involve employees directly in the design and operation of reward systems (Lawler 1990). In the absence of a union, employers may develop systems of participation which are focused on the individual employee or provide for negotiation through non-union channels. In the majority of non-union companies, this does not appear to be the case and while there may be particular examples of good practice, in the absence of unions the collective negotiation of pay is a rarity (Cully *et al.* 1999: 104). Other evidence concerns the operation of 'personal contracts', which seemingly provide for individual bargaining over reward. In most cases these contracts are 'standardised packages, individually wrapped' and there is little scope for employees to vary their contracts in a meaningful way (Evans and Hudson 1994; see also Brown *et al.* 1998). For all but senior managers and those with highly marketable skills, it is likely that transaction costs preclude individual negotiation of the reward package (Cully *et al.* 1999: 109).

If the first effect of unions on reward procedure is to encourage joint decision-making, then the second is to formalise reward practice. Evidence for this can be seen in Table 3.3, which presents further data from the survey of union responses to IPRP and which indicates that a priority of unions with members covered by schemes has been to formalise the method of appraisal and the link between appraisal and reward. A similar process can be seen in the field of reward structure, where union presence is associated with the use of formal job evaluation procedures for establishing pay grades and differentials (Millward *et al.* 1992: 269). Indeed, the growing interest of some unions in securing equal pay for work of

Table 3.3 Union attempts to influence the form of IPRP schemes (unions with members covered by IPRP schemes, N = 38–41)

Change in IPRP scheme	Attempted	Not attempted
Introduction of more 'objective' system of performance review	73.7 (55.3)*	26.3
Insisting managers follow explicit rules when awarding IPRP	68.4 (52.6)	39.0
Introduction of an appeals procedure	73.2 (63.4)	26.8
Union access to information on the distribution of performance payments	75.0 (65.0)	25.0
Gender monitoring	60.0 (57.5)	40.0
Ethnic monitoring	45.0 (42.5)	55.0
Commitment from management to joint review of IPRP	60.0 (50.0)	40.0

Note: * Percentage reporting success in their attempt shown in brackets

Source: Heery and Warhurst (1994)

equal value for women workers has led to the further extension and refinement of job evaluation in a search for procedures that fully capture the relative demands of jobs and eliminate scope for discrimination. This effect of unions, in formalising or bureaucratising the employment relationship, has been widely noted; indeed, forty years ago it was identified by Slichter and colleagues (1960) as one of the primary effects of unions on management. It originates in a number of abiding union concerns. Formal rules effectively constrain management decision-making and reduce the scope for arbitrary treatment or favouritism, a concern that has been particularly acute for unions whose members are covered by individualised systems of contingent pay. In limiting management discretion, formal rules also serve to standardise the employment relationship and provide for the consistent treatment of employees who, for example, are paid a standard rate for the job rather than a 'personal' salary fixed by the employer. For this reason, employees are likely to develop a common interest. Moreover, in requiring fair and consistent treatment of its members, the union can also develop its own institutional strength, based upon the shared interests and collective identification of employees who experience reward management in common (Edwards and Heery 1989b).

Table 3.3 also indicates that most unions faced with IPRP have sought to establish an appeals procedure through which individuals can question management's assessment of their performance and seek redress. The table shows that unions have generally been successful in this regard and other research on IPRP has demonstrated that schemes are more likely to include a right of appeal when they have been negotiated with a union (Heery 1997a: 219). Another effect of unions on reward management, therefore, is likely to be the institution of formal procedures for questioning management decisions and resolving disputes over the setting of work standards, the assessment of performance, the grading of individuals, the award of training and fringe benefits, deductions from wages, under-payment of wages and so on. General research on industrial relations has demonstrated that procedures of this kind are more common where a union is recognised and also that they are more likely to be used, essentially because individual employees can draw upon representative skills and have more confidence that they will not be penalised for questioning a management decision (Eaton and Voos 1992).

Within the specific field of reward, WIRS 1990 has demonstrated that procedures are found with much greater frequency in unionised establishments: a formal channel for resolving disputes over pay and conditions was reported in 81 per cent of workplaces with a recognised union but only 48 per cent of those without (Millward *et al.* 1992: 190). The purpose of these procedures, once again, is to set formal boundaries around management decision-making and import greater fairness or equity into the management of reward, such that individual employees are not penalised for actions beyond their control or through mismanagement. Their effect is to qualify the management prerogative by establishing a system of organisational justice through which managers can be held to account for the decisions they take and conflicts resolved in an equitable way.

The scrutiny of management decision-making is one of the central functions of unions within the enterprise and while this function can be discharged through formal appeal mechanisms, it can also be achieved by measures which make the process of management transparent. Unions can pressure managers to provide information about the functioning and outcomes of reward systems and so make it possible to check for inconsistency, unfairness or other problems that are emerging. Table 3.3 demonstrates that making reward management transparent in this way has been a primary concern of unions with members covered by IPRP schemes. Thus, a majority of unions report attempts to gain access to the distribution of performance payments, to establish a system of gender monitoring, and secure management agreement to the joint review of IPRP schemes. A substantial minority also report attempts to institute ethnic monitoring of schemes. In the vast majority of cases these attempts to secure greater transparency in the operation of IPRP were successful. What this suggests is that an important activity of unions is the generation of management information as managers are encouraged to review reward systems and share information with representatives. In performing this role, moreover, unions can draw upon supportive legislation, such as that requiring the disclosure of information for the purpose of collective bargaining and the laws and associated statutory codes of practice on sex and race discrimination, equal pay and the equal treatment of part-time workers. The effect, once again, is to qualify the management prerogative by making the process and outcomes of management transparent and available for scrutiny.

Conclusion

The primary message that can be drawn from this review of trade unions and reward management is that unions 'make a difference' (Pendleton 1997). Their impact on reward may be variable and often modest in scope but in aggregate, and with regard to each of the five strategic decisions which have been examined, there is evidence of unions affecting the substance and process of reward management. Thus, unions continue to raise the pay of their members relative to non-union workers; they compress the pay structure and increase the relative pay of women; they restrict the use of contingent pay systems that place earnings risk; they extend the range of rewards; and they affect the process of reward management by instituting worker participation through collective bargaining and limiting management discretion through formal rules, due process and transparency.

These effects derive from the main function of unions in industrial relations systems characterised by collective bargaining, namely to engage in distributive bargaining and secure a larger share of the economic surplus for their members. They also derive from other purposes, however, and it is clear from the review that unions pursue a range of objectives within the field of reward. Two deserve particular emphasis. First, unions do not simply want more reward for their members they also want *fair* rewards and much of their activity is concerned with shaping a moral economy informed by notions of just process and just outcomes. With regard to process, the themes of consistent treatment and the right to protection from arbitrary management loom large. With regard to outcomes, unions tend to stress equality (the rate for the job), equivalence (a fair day's work for a fair day's pay) and redistribution (a compressed pay structure and single-status benefits). The second objective is reflected in the attempts by unions to 'reposition' themselves as the representatives of women and atypical workers, which were referred to above. It would be wrong to exaggerate the extent or depth of this change, but in recent years there has been a shift towards equality bargaining and a greater concern with representing the specific interests of women workers and part-timers in union policy. Arguably, what is happening in at least sections of the labour movement is a process of redefining the interests which unions exist to represent and this, in turn, is shaping the kinds of effect they generate within reward management. In concrete terms, as unions have become more dependent on recruiting women workers and as women have become more active in unions, so unions have tried to negotiate equal value pay structures, have opposed IPRP because of the risk of sex discrimination, have pressed for the inclusion of part-timers in benefit programmes, and have tried to institute the gender monitoring of rewards.

While the theme of multiple and evolving purposes runs through the review, so does the theme of multiple and evolving constraints. Again, two deserve emphasis. Echoing a long line of industrial relations research, the review has pointed to the importance of the structure of collective bargaining in shaping the union impact on rewards (Boraston *et al.* 1975; Clegg 1976). The union mark-up, the dispersion of pay, the gender pay-gap, union influence over IPRP and the harmonisation of benefits are all affected by the structure of collective bargaining. The effect seems most apparent when one considers differences in the union effect on reward between countries. In crude terms, there appears to be a trade-off between a relatively high mark-up for union members secured in countries with fragmented bargaining and a more solidaristic, compressed distribution of pay found in countries with co-ordinated bargaining. The second constraint that has emerged repeatedly through the review is the system of employment law, though in many respects this should be viewed as an opportunity rather than as a constraint. What is striking is the extent to which there is interaction between union attempts to influence reward through joint regulation and the system of legal regulation of pay and benefits. Thus, in many cases the law can operate as a lever for union influence, with unions using equal pay or other legislation to open up negotiations on the shape of pay structures, the operation of pay systems and the distribution of fringe benefits. The direction of influence can flow the other way, however, and it is apparent that unions can play an important mediating role by informing, advising and representing employees when their legal rights to equal pay or a minimum wage are contravened. Unions can use the law to promote joint regulation, therefore, but they can also help enforce the law and ensure legal regulation has genuine effect.

Although much of the review points to the continued effectiveness of unions in shaping reward, it has also pointed to declining influence. Not only has union membership fallen and coverage by collective bargaining contracted, but there is also evidence of unions losing bargaining power where they remain established. There are indications that the union mark-up is eroding: the dispersion of pay is broadening in unionised companies; unions have had to accept contingent pay systems to which they are opposed; and they have experienced difficulty in placing new items on the reward agenda, such as access to training and development. These developments are the concrete manifestation of the 'counter-revolution of our time' referred to in the introduction. It is apparent that with the decline of unions, the system of reward management will become less responsive to the collective interests of employees and will instead be bent to the requirements of employers and their senior executives and shareholders. Individual employees with market power may benefit in a less regulated system, but for the broad mass of employees there are likely to be adverse consequences if union influence over the system of reward continues to decline. On the basis of the preceding review, and other things being equal, these consequences will include:

- downward pressure on the earnings of the less skilled and qualified
- a widening of income inequality and a continuing gender pay-gap
- reduced pressure on employers to eliminate gender discrimination from reward structures and institute systems of gender and ethnic monitoring of pay
- greater use of contingent pay systems which transfer economic risk to employees
- a narrowing of the range and reduction in value of benefit provision
- restricted access to training and a less even distribution of its benefits between employer and employee
- the use of reward procedures that widen management discretion and contain less provision for worker participation, due process and transparency.

In my view, these developments would represent a subtraction, not an addition, to our national economic life.

Acknowledgements

Thanks to Michael Poole and Dave Simpson for helpful comments on an earlier draft.

References

Almond, P. and Rubery, J. (1998) 'The gender impact of recent European trends in wage determination', *Work, Employment and Society*, 12 (4): 675–93.

Arthurs, A. (1992) 'Equal value in British banking: the Midland Bank case', in P. Kahn and E. Meehan (eds) *Equal Value/Comparable Worth in the UK and the USA*, Basingstoke, Macmillan.

Arulampalam, W. and Booth, A.L. (1998) 'Training and labour market flexibility: is there a trade-off?', *British Journal of Industrial Relations*, 36 (4): 521–36.

Bacon, N. (1999) 'Union derecognition and the new human relations: a steel industry case study', *Work, Employment and Society*, 13 (1): 1–17.

Baddon, L., Hunter, L., Hyman, J., Leopold, J. and Ramsay, H. (1989) *People's Capitalism? A Critical Analysis of Profit-sharing and Employee Share Ownership*, London, Routledge.

Bassett, P. (1986) *Strike Free: New Industrial Relations in Britain*, London, Macmillan.

Bassett, P. and Cave, A. (1993) *All for One: The Future of Trade Unions*, Fabian Society Pamphlet 559, London, The Fabian Society.

Batstone, E., Boraston, I. and Frenkel, S. (1977) *Shop Stewards in Action*, Oxford, Basil Blackwell.

Beaumont, P.B. (1995) *The Future of Employment Relations*, London, Sage.

Blanchflower, D.G. and Freeman, R.B. (1992) 'Unionism in the United States and other advanced OECD countries', *Industrial Relations*, 31 (1): 56–80.

Blanchflower, D.G. and Oswald, A.J. (1990) 'The determination of white-collar pay', *Oxford Economic Papers*, 42: 356–78.

Bland, P. (1999) 'Trade union membership and recognition 1997–98: an analysis of data from the Certification Officer and the *Labour Force Survey*', *Labour Market Trends*, July: 343–53.

Blau, F.N. and Kahn, L.M. (1995) 'The gender earnings gap: some international evidence', in R.B. Freeman and L.B Katz (eds) *Differences and Changes in Wage Structures*, Chicago, The University of Chicago Press.

Booth, A.L. (1995) *The Economics of the Trade Union*, Cambridge, Cambridge University Press.

Boraston, I., Clegg, H. and Rimmer, M. (1975) *Workplace and Union*, London, Heinemann Educational Books.

Brown, M. and Philips, P. (1986) 'The decline of piece rates in California canneries, 1890–1960', *Industrial Relations*, 25 (1): 81–90.

Brown, W. (1973) *Piecework Bargaining*, London, Heinemann.

Brown, W. and Walsh, J. (1994) 'Managing pay in Britain', in K. Sisson (ed.) *Personnel Management: A Comprehensive Guide to Theory and Practice in Britain*, Oxford, Blackwell.

Brown, W., Deakin, S., Hudson, M., Pratten, C. and Ryan, P. (1998) *The Individualisation of*

Employment Contracts in Britain, Employment Relations Research Series 4, London, Department of Trade and Industry.

Bryson, A. and McKay, S. (1997) 'What about the workers?', in R. Jowell, J. Curtice, A. Park, L. Brook, K. Thomson and C. Bryson (eds) *British Social Attitudes: The 14th Report*, Aldershot, Ashgate.

Claydon, T. (1996) 'Union de-recognition: a re-examination', in I.J. Beardwell (ed.) *Contemporary Industrial Relations*, Oxford, Oxford University Press.

Claydon, T. (1998) 'Problematising partnership: the prospects for a co-operative bargaining agenda', in P. Sparrow and M. Marchington (eds) *Human Resource Management: The New Agenda*, London, Financial Times/Pitman Publishing.

Clegg, H. (1976) *Trade Unionism under Collective Bargaining*, Oxford, Basil Blackwell.

Colgan, F. and Ledwith, S. (1996) 'Sisters organising – women and their trade unions', in S. Ledwith and F. Colgan (eds) *Women in Organisations: Challenging Gender Politics*, Basingstoke, Macmillan.

Colling, T. and Dickens, L. (1989) *Equality Bargaining – Why Not?*, Equal Opportunities Commission Research Series, London, HMSO.

Colling, T. and Dickens, L. (1998) 'Selling the case for gender equality: deregulation and equality bargaining', *British Journal of Industrial Relations*, 36 (3): 389–411.

Cornfield, D. and Fletcher, B. (1999) 'The US labour movement: towards a sociology of labour revitalisation', in A. Kalleberg and I. Berg (eds) *Sourcebook on Labor Markets*, New York, Plenum.

Crouch, C. (1982) *Trade Unions: The Logic of Collective Action*, Glasgow, Fontana.

Cully, M., O'Reilly, A., Millward, N., Forth, J., Woodland, S., Dix, G. and Bryson, A. (1998) *The 1998 Workplace Employee Relations Survey: First Findings*, London, Department of Trade and Industry.

Cully, M., Woodland, S., O'Reilly, A. and Dix, G. (1999) *Britain at Work*, London, Routledge.

Davies, J. (1998) 'Labour disputes in 1997', *Labour Market Trends*, June: 299–311.

Dex, S., Robson, P. and Wilkinson, F. (1999) 'The characteristics of the low paid: a cross national comparison', *Work, Employment and Society*, 13 (3): 503–24.

Dickens, L. (1989) 'Women – a rediscovered resource?', *Industrial Relations Journal*, 20 (3): 167–75.

Dundon, T. and Eva, D. (1997) 'Trade unions and bargaining for skills', *Employee Relations*, 20 (1): 57–72.

Dunn, S. and Metcalf, D. (1996) 'Trade union law since 1979', in I. Beardwell (ed.) *Contemporary Industrial Relations*, Oxford, Oxford University Press.

Dunn, S. and Wright, M. (1994) 'Maintaining the "status quo"? An analysis of the contents of British collective agreements, 1979–90', *British Journal of Industrial Relations*, 32 (1): 23–46.

Eaton, A.E. and Voos, P.B. (1992) 'Unions and contemporary innovations in work organisation, compensation and employee participation', in L. Mishel and P.B. Voos (eds) *Unions and Economic Competitiveness*, Armonk, NY, M.E. Sharpe.

Edwards, C. and Heery, E. (1989a) *Management Control and Union Power: A Study of Labour Relations in Coal-mining*, Oxford, Clarendon Press.

Edwards, C. and Heery, E. (1989b) 'Recession in the public sector: industrial relations in Freightliner 1981–85', *British Journal of Industrial Relations*, 27 (1): 57–72.

Evans, S. and Hudson, M. (1994) 'From collective bargaining to "personal" contracts: case studies in port transport and electricity supply', *Industrial Relations Journal*, 25 (4): 305–14.

Falkner, G. (1998) *EU Social Policy in the 1990s: Towards a Corporatist Policy Community*, London, Routledge.

Freeman, R.B. (1992) 'Is declining unionisation of the US: good, bad or irrelevant?', in L. Mishel and P.B. Voos (eds) *Unions and Economic Competitiveness*, Armonk, NY, M.E. Sharpe.

Freeman, R.B. and Katz, L.F. (1994) 'Rising wage inequality: the United States vs. other advanced countries', in R.B. Freeman (ed.) *Working under Different Rules*, New York, Russell Sage Foundation.

Freeman, R.B. and Medoff, J.L. (1984) *What Do Unions Do?*, New York, Basic Books.

Gidwell, D. (1977) 'Wage payment systems in the British coalmining industry', *Industrial Relations Journal*, 7 (2): 4–16.

Gilbert, K. and Secker, J. (1995) 'Generating equality? Equal pay, decentralisation and the electricity supply industry', *British Journal of Industrial Relations*, 33 (2): 191–207.

Goodman, A., Johnson, P. and Webb, S. (1997) *Inequality in the UK*, Oxford, Oxford University Press.

Gospel, H. (1998) 'The revival of apprenticeship training in Britain?', *British Journal of Industrial Relations*, 36 (3): 435–57.

Green, F. (1997) 'Union recognition and paid holiday entitlement', *British Journal of Industrial Relations*, 35 (2): 243–55.

Green, F., Hadjimatheou, G. and Smail, R. (1985) 'Fringe benefit distribution in Britain', *British Journal of Industrial Relations*, 23 (2): 261–80.

Green, F., Machin, S. and Wilkinson, D. (1999) 'Trade unions and training practices in British workplaces', *Industrial and Labor Relations Review*, 52 (2): 179–95.

Gunnigle, P., Flood, P., Morley, M. and Turner, T. (1993) *Continuity and Change in Irish Employee Relations*, Limerick, University of Limerick Press.

Gunnigle, P., Turner, T. and D'art, D. (1998) 'Counterpoising collectivism: performance-related pay and industrial relations in greenfield sites', *British Journal of Industrial Relations*, 36 (4): 565–79.

Hastings, S. (1992) 'Equal value in the local authorities sector in Great Britain', in P. Kahn and E. Meehan (eds) *Equal Value/Comparable Worth in the UK and the USA*, Basingstoke, Macmillan.

Hecksher, C.C. (1988) *The New Unionism: Employee Involvement in the Changing Corporation*, New York, Basic Books.

Heery, E. (1984) 'Computers and the industrial relations manager: a case study of the mining industry', *Personnel Review*, 14 (4): 16–21.

Heery, E. (1997a) 'Performance-related pay and trade union de-recognition', *Employee Relations*, 19 (3): 208–21.

Heery, E. (1997b) 'Performance-related pay and trade union membership', *Employee Relations*, 19 (5): 430–42.

Heery, E. (1998a) 'Campaigning for part-time workers', *Work, Employment and Society*, 12 (2): 351–66.

Heery, E. (1998b) 'The re-launch of the Trades Union Congress', *British Journal of Industrial Relations*, 36 (3): 339–60.

Heery, E. and Kelly, J. (1988) 'Do female representatives make a difference? Women full-time officials and trade union work', *Work, Employment and Society*, 2 (4): 487–505.

Heery, E. and Warhurst, J. (1994) *Performance-related pay and Trade Unions: Impact and Response*, Kingston Business School Occasional Paper, Kingston University, Kingston-upon-Thames.

Heyes, J. and Stuart, M. (1998) 'Bargaining for skills: trade unions and training at the workplace', *British Journal of Industrial Relations*, 36 (3): 459–67.

Heywood, J.S., Siebert, W.S. and Wei, X. (1997) 'Payment by results systems: British evidence', *British Journal of Industrial Relations*, 35 (1): 1–22.

Hill, S. (1981) *Competition and Control at Work*, London: Heinemann.

Hirschman, A. (1991) *The Rhetorics of Reaction: Perversity, Futility, Jeopardy*, Cambridge, Mass., Harvard University Press.

Hougham, J., Thomas, J. and Sisson, K. (1991) 'Ford's EDAP scheme: a roundtable discussion', *Human Resource Management Journal*, 1 (3): 77–91.

Industrial Relations Services (IRS) (1991) *Pay and Gender in Britain: A Research Report for the Equal Opportunities Commission*, London, Industrial Relations Services.

Jackson, M.P., Leopold, J.W. and Tuck, K. (1993) *Decentralisation of Collective Bargaining: An Analysis of Recent Experience in the UK*, Basingstoke, Macmillan.

Kelly, J. and Heery, E. (1994) *Working for the Union: British Trade Union Officers*, Cambridge, Cambridge University Press.

Kennedy, S., Drago, R., Sloan, J. and Wooden, M. (1994) 'The effect of trade unions on the provision of training: Australian evidence', *British Journal of Industrial Relations*, 32 (4): 565–80.

Kessler, I. (1994) 'Performance related pay: contrasting approaches', *Industrial Relations Journal*, 25 (2): 122–35.

Kessler, I. (1995) 'Reward systems', in J. Storey (ed.) *Human Resource Management: A Critical Text*, London, Routledge.

Knight, K.G. and Latreille, P.L. (1996) 'Apprenticeship training and day release in UK engineering: some cross-sectional evidence', *British Journal of Industrial Relations*, 34 (2): 307–14.

Lawler, E.E. (1990) *Strategic Pay: Aligning Organisational Strategies and Pay Systems*, San Francisco, CA, Jossey Bass.

Low Pay Commission (1998) *The National Minimum Wage: First Report of the Low Pay Commission*, London, HMSO.

Machin, S. (1996) 'Wage inequality in the UK', *Oxford Review of Economic Policy*, 12 (1): 47–64.

Main, B. (1996) 'The union relative wage gap', in D. Gallie, R. Penn and M. Rose (eds) *Trade Unionism in Recession*, Oxford, Oxford University Press.

Marchington, M. and Parker, P. (1990) *Changing Patterns of Employee Relations*, London, Harvester Wheatsheaf.

Metcalf, D. (1994) 'Transformation of British industrial relations? Institutions, conduct and outcomes 1980–1990', in R. Barrell (ed.) *The UK Labour Market*, Cambridge, Cambridge University Press.

Millward, N. (1995) *Targeting Potential Discrimination*, Manchester, Equal Opportunities Commission.

Millward, N., Stevens, M., Smart, D. and Hawes, W.R. (1992) *Workplace Industrial Relations in Transition*, Aldershot, Dartmouth.

Milner, S. (1995) 'The coverage of collective pay-setting institutions in Britain, 1895–1990', *British Journal of Industrial Relations*, 33 (1): 69–91.

Minford, P. (1985) 'Trade unions destroy a million jobs', in W.E.J. McCarthy (ed.) *Trade Unions*, Harmondsworth, Penguin Books.

Mishel, L., Bernstein, J. and Schmitt, J. (1999) *The State of Working America 1998–1999*, Ithaca, NY, and London, ILR Press.

Nolan, P. and Marginson, P. (1990) 'Skating on thin ice? David Metcalf on trade unions and productivity', *British Journal of Industrial Relations*, 28 (2): 227–47.

National Union of Teachers (NUT) (1999) *It May Be Green, But Is It Good For You?*, London, National Union of Teachers.

Pendleton, A. (1997) 'Characteristics of workplaces with financial participation: evidence from the WIRS', *Industrial Relations Journal*, 28 (2): 103–19.

Phelps Brown, E.H. (1990) 'The counter-revolution of our time', *Industrial Relations*, 29 (1): 1–14.

Poole, M. (1989) *The Origins of Economic Democracy: Profit-sharing and Employee-shareholding Schemes*, London, Routledge.

Price, L. and Price, R. (1994) 'Change and continuity in the status divide', in K. Sisson (ed.) *Personnel Management: A Comprehensive Guide to Theory and Practice in Britain*, Oxford, Blackwell.

Rainbird, H. and Vincent, C. (1996) 'Training: a new item on the bargaining agenda', in P. Leisink, J. Van Leemput and J. Vilrokx (eds) *The Challenges to Trade Unions in Europe*, Cheltenham, Edward Elgar.

Rubery, J. and Fagan, C. (1994) 'Equal pay policy and wage regulation systems in Europe', *Industrial Relations Journal*, 25 (4): 281–92.

Slichter, S.H., Healy, J.J. and Livernash, E.R. (1960) *The Impact of Collective Bargaining on Management*, Washington DC, The Brookings Institution.

Smith, P. and Morton, G. (1993) 'Union exclusion and the decollectivisation of industrial relations in contemporary Britain', *British Journal of Industrial Relations*, 31 (1): 97–114.

Storey, J., Bacon, N., Edmonds, J. and Wyatt, P. (1993) 'The 'New Agenda' and human resource management: a roundtable discussion with John Edmonds', *Human Resource Management Journal*, 4 (1): 63–70.

Strauss, G. (1998) 'Collective bargaining, unions and participation', in F. Heller, E. Pusic, G. Strauss and B. Wilpert (eds) *Organisational Participation: Myth and Reality*, Oxford, Oxford University Press.

Streeck, W. (1992) 'Training and the new industrial relations: a strategic role for unions?', in M. Regini (ed.) *The Future of Labour Movements*, London, Sage.

Terry, M. (1995) 'Trade unions, shop stewards and the workplace', in P. Edwards (ed.) *Industrial Relations: Theory and Practice in Britain*, Oxford, Blackwell.

Thomas, C. and Wallis, B. (1998) 'Dwy Cymru/Welsh Water: a case study in partnership', in P. Sparrow and M. Marchington (eds) *Human Resource Management: The New Agenda*, London, Financial Times/Pitman Publishing.

Thornley, C. and Coffey, D. (1999) 'The Low Pay Commission in context', *Work, Employment and Society*, 13 (3): 525–38.

Trades Union Congress (TUC) (1996) *Part of the Union? The Challenge of Recruiting and Organising Part-time Workers*, London, Trades Union Congress.

Trades Union Congress (TUC) (1997) *Partners for Progress: Next Steps for the New Unionism*, London, Trades Union Congress.

Visser, J. (1988a) 'Trade unionism in Western Europe: present situation and prospects', *Labour and Society*, 13 (2): 125–82.

Visser, J. (1998b) 'The Netherlands: the return of responsive corporatism', in A. Ferner and R. Hyman (eds) *Changing Industrial Relations in Europe*, Oxford, Blackwell.

Visser, J. (1998c) 'Two cheers for corporatism, one for the market: industrial relations, wage moderation and job growth in the Netherlands', *British Journal of Industrial Relations*, 36 (2): 269–92.

Wever, K.S. (1998) 'International labor revitalisation: enlarging the playing field', *Industrial Relations*, 37 (3): 388–407.

Whitehouse, G. (1992) 'Legislation and labour market gender equality', *Work, Employment and Society*, 6 (1): 65–86.

York, C. (1993) 'Bargaining for work and family benefits', in D.S. Cobble (ed.) *Women and Unions: Forging a Partnership*, Ithaca, NY, ILR Press.

4 Grading systems and estimating value

Sue Hastings

Introduction

Classical economists argue that wage rates represent the price at which the supply and demand for labour coincide (Sapsford and Tzannatos 1993). Whilst organisations may position their pay structures in relation to what they perceive as the 'going rate' for the relevant types of work, and structural shortages are likely to lead to increases in salaries for the group in question, the theory is inadequate as a means of explaining pay practice. It does not tell personnel practitioners how to deliver a stable pay structure, nor how to allow for the serious lags and imperfections in the market. Nor does it provide personnel managers with a satisfactory way of grading and paying jobs that are unique to the organisation (Sapsford and Tzannatos, 1993; Jacobsen 1998: 203–342). Macro-economic theorists also have difficulty explaining how economic forces result in discrimination in favour of some and against other groups of employees, apparently regardless of the relative efficiency of these groups.

The reality is that the labour market provides only part of the explanation for pay determination. Individual pay rates are set, not only against the labour market, but also by reference to a system of micro-economic internal relativities – the organisational grading structure.

This chapter examines the background to modern grading systems and the influence of cultural, social and legal factors. In the first section we consider the origins of British grading systems; the second outlines current grading techniques, reviewing competence-based pay (CBP) systems and job evaluation. We then discuss the impact of equal value legislation and its continuing importance for job evaluation. The chapter concludes with a comment on the future of grading.

The historical development of modern British grading systems

British grading systems for 'manual' and 'non-manual' groups have existed and developed, until recently, quite separately. The reasons lie in the origins of the structures for the two groups. The separation has been perpetuated by collective bargaining systems.

The origins of manual pay structures

The origins of manual pay structures lie in the systems established by the ancient craft guilds and perpetuated through the development of trade unions, apprenticeships and collective bargaining in the nineteenth century.

Essentially, manual work, for men at least, was broadly divided into skilled and unskilled, with the skilled work being reserved for those who served apprenticeships, or an equivalent form of work-related training, and became members of the guild or trade organisation. Pay rates were determined according to this broad, skill-based banding system. In many organisations a semi-skilled band was also created and subsequently sub-divided into numerous rates, negotiated individually or collectively, as they were needed.

The social construction of skill discriminated against women. Female workers in manufacturing establishments did not usually have access to guild or craft training. The jobs to which they were allocated were, for the most part, regarded by employers and by skilled male workers as unskilled, on the grounds of women's physical weakness. Women were therefore paid less than unskilled men, regardless of the tasks on which they were actually employed. These lower rates became institutionalised into separate women's rates, usually for different or distinctly separate jobs. The process was reinforced by the Factories Acts, which regulated hours of work for women and young people but not for men; and by the activities of male-dominated trade unions, which did not want women to be able to under-cut their pay rates (Boston 1987).

Skill-based grading structures, with superstructures of allowances and plus payments, prevailed until the 1970s and 1980s, and can still be seen in some smaller organisations. However, large-scale industrialisation led to the introduction of more sophisticated techniques, for example, payment by results (PBR) systems. Such systems generally retained the old skill-based classifications but allowed workers to earn more than the standard rate for their grade of work, essentially by completing designated tasks in a lower time than that allocated.

Women's jobs were also subjected to payment by results. However, some women proved adept at increasing their levels of dexterity and co-ordination, and, thus, their rate of work. Such women could earn more, in spite of the lower base rate for calculations, than the average earnings of men in the grade or grades above them – a point sometimes quoted to the author of this chapter by the managers of relevant employees to show that piecework payment systems are not discriminatory.[1] By the 1980s, however, British industry was moving away from payment by results.

The origins of non-manual structures

Significant numbers of non-manual jobs developed only with industrialisation and with the accompanying growth of employment in the retail and finance sectors, in office and administrative jobs and in state employment. Wages for clerical staff were generally low compared with those for production employees.

Incentives to remain with the employing company were provided by seniority or age-related scales, whereby employees received a small increase on their birthday or on the anniversary of starting with the firm. The underlying assumption was that clerical employees higher up an age-related scale would have more knowledge of the organisation's procedures and thus be able to undertake more demanding work, including supervising less experienced clerical staff. Such service- or age-related pay scales provide the origins of traditional annual incremental scales for non-manual employees, just as skill-related rates of pay provide the origins of flat 'rate for the job' pay systems for manual workers once entry training was completed.

Large corporations and the development of job evaluation systems

Techniques of job evaluation were originally developed in the United States of America before and immediately after the Second World War. The aim was to find methods that would provide for non-manual administrative and managerial jobs in large public corporations a systematic basis for grading and pay similar to that provided by work study techniques for manual and production-related jobs. Practitioners were also interested in identifying the job features that determined labour market rates for white-collar employees – as levels of skill were seen as doing for manual workers (Benge *et al.* 1941; Patton *et al.* 1964). One of these early practitioners was Edward Hay, whose Guide Chart Profile system of job evaluation was refined into its present form in the years immediately following 1945 (Hay and Purves 1954).

Some job evaluation (JE) systems involve developing a job hierarchy, either by putting them in rank order on the basis of information about the jobs as a whole, or by matching them against criteria in a job classification system. Such whole-job rank order and classification systems of JE are much less common than they used to be. They cannot deal with the complexities of modern organisations and may be open to challenge on discrimination grounds, although they are still described in current JE textbooks (Armstrong and Baron 1995: 51–64; Pritchard and Murlis 1992: 51–55).

However, what the Hay System and most other job evaluation techniques had in common, then as now, was (a) the analysis of jobs under a set of factor headings agreed to be suitable for the job population in question; and (b) the assessment of each job against factor scales (usually but not always predetermined) to give a total score for each job. The third feature of these techniques was the weighting of factors, initially to reflect the perceived value placed by the labour market on each, but subsequently modified to reflect organisational values.

Job evaluation techniques were introduced to Britain in the early 1950s to replace the seniority or age-related systems that had predominated for non-manual employees in the pre-war era. Among the early users of job evaluation, often encouraged by union representatives, were companies in the insurance sector, but the techniques spread during the 1950s and 1960s to other large, predominantly white-collar companies in the private sector, and to managerial groups in many organisations.

Job evaluation for manual workers

The use of job evaluation for manual worker groups was rare in Britain until the mid-1960s. Around this time some management consultants, notably in Urwick Orr (subsequently part of Price Waterhouse) and Inbucon (now part of PE), began adapting the techniques for manual jobs – as Urwick Orr did for Ford production workers in 1967.

In 1968 the National Board for Prices and Incomes (NBPI) published a report specifically on job evaluation (National Board for Prices and Incomes 1968). The report recommended the adoption of JE as a mechanism for rationalising the very complex structures that had developed for manual groups in the public sector. As a direct result of this and similar recommendations in sectoral reports, job evaluation schemes were developed and implemented, for example, for ancillary workers in the National Health Service and manual workers in local government (both Urwick Orr schemes).

Following these initial public sector exercises, separate schemes were designed during the 1970s to cover non-manual groups in the public sector – for example, the Administrative, Professional, Technical and Clerical (APT & C) group in local government. There was also an ill-fated exercise in the electricity sector, which took years to complete and was effectively outdated by the time it was implemented.

What was common to all these schemes was the fact that they were developed to match traditional collective bargaining groups. So a single company in the private sector might, by the 1980s, have three or four different job evaluation schemes in operation to cover its distinct bargaining groups. Alternatively they might use job evaluation for some groups and other grading and pay systems for others. In the banking sector, for example, there was a sector-wide job evaluation scheme covering clerical, secretarial and administrative staff. Each major bank had its own grading and pay structures for what were known as the appointed grades (professional, financial and managerial jobs), often using the Hay Guide Chart System of job evaluation; and all had non-evaluated, skill-related structures for their messenger (and other manual) employees.

Current grading techniques

These historical developments have influenced current grading techniques. Within this section we focus on competence-based payment systems and job evaluation.

Competence-based payment systems

There has been growing employer interest in competence-related pay. Personnel practitioners have been developing competence frameworks to cover all employees, (often referred to as skills-based pay for manual workers), as the basis for recruitment, redundancy, promotion and training policies, in order to secure the best return on investment in human resources. Some organisations have linked their competence frameworks to pay. What these have in common is that they reward individuals for the broad competencies (not just traditional skills, or formal qualifications) required for the work, and often also for the acquisition of additional competencies.

Competence-based payment systems can take a number of different forms (Hastings and Dixon 1995), as outlined below.

Competence as the basis for pay progression

In such systems, jobs are graded in accordance with a job evaluation or other conventional grading technique, but pay progression depends on the acquisition of additional competencies – either assessed by the immediate line manager, in a manner akin to a performance-related pay system; or validated against an object-ive standard. As such systems do not affect the basic valuation of the job, they are outside the remit of this chapter and are discussed in Chapter 6.

Competence as the basis for grading

In these schemes, jobs are graded by reference to the overall competencies required, usually by reference to an objective standard, such as National Vocational Qualifications (NVQs) or the Scottish equivalent (SVQs). The difference between this type of grading structure and a traditional skills-based structure is that the former encompasses a wider range of skills. Competencies may include written and oral communication skills, information technology and record-keeping skills, as well as technical and manual skills. They can, therefore, accommodate non-manual as well as manual jobs. Examples of competence-based grading structures are to be found covering the different levels of Healthcare Assistants in some NHS Trusts.

Competence as the basis for both grading and pay progression

Here jobs are graded by reference to the competencies required, as defined by an objective standard, as for the previous category. However, progression up the pay scale or within the pay range also depends on the acquisition of additional com-petencies, often within modules leading towards the next broad competence band. One example is the Scottish Power's Generation (SPG) Wholesale Division, covering all its power station and associated head office staff, from industrial and clerical assistants through craft-trained electricians and qualified electrical engineers to power station managers (Adams 1993). All roles were assimilated into one of six bands depending on the competence levels required, by reference to SVQs for technical, professional and administrative occupational groups (with some additional modules specifically designed for unique power generation roles). Progression within the band salary range for individuals depends on the acquisition of additional competence modules along predetermined pathways for particular occupational groups.

The Scottish Power example illustrates the advantages of competence-based pay (CBP). Management wanted a more flexible workforce, able to increase production without the need to employ more people. Employees and their union representatives wanted the opportunity to acquire additional skills, and to be paid for doing so. This example also illustrates the potential disadvantages and possibly explains why few organisations have adopted comprehensive competence-based pay systems (CBI/Hay Group 1995: 22–3). Linking competence to pay requires substantial investment in training facilities and competence assessment systems, so that all employees have the opportunity to increase competence and pay levels. Even with this investment, it is still necessary to have some sort of rationing procedure, as not all employees can be released for competence-related training at the same time. At SPGW the solution, as part of a broader partnership agreement, was to have joint power station-based committees to prioritise skills acquisition and decide who would be trained first. But the rationing process inevitably leads to anomalies and grievances – and particular care is needed to avoid discrimination on gender or race grounds in the allocation of training opportunities.

Other obstacles, however, to a CBP system for employers may be the difficulties of making sufficiently accurate assessments of competencies (Sparrow 1996); and concerns over whether competency-based pay systems can meet with legal equality requirements (Adams 1996; Gilbert *et al.* 1996).

Job evaluation

By the 1980s, traditional job evaluation techniques were appearing outmoded because of changes in technology and work organisation (Grayson 1982 and 1987). Yet paradoxically, from being recorded in just over 20 per cent of establishments in the Workplace Industrial Relations Surveys of 1980 and 1984 (Daniel and Millward 1983: 204; Millward and Stevens 1986: 252–8; Ghobadian and White, 1995: 18–41), job evaluation systems have spread into new areas, such as the public sector. Although there are no directly comparable figures, one 1995 survey suggests that 44 per cent of responding organisations used job evaluation for executive jobs and 51 per cent for senior management jobs and below (CBI/Hay Group 1995: 19–21). There are a number of possible reasons for this spread.

First, changes in technology and work organisation have in practice led to job evaluation becoming more flexible. Second, job evaluation systems are no longer restricted to traditional collective bargaining groups, but have become broader in coverage, a development which has necessitated re-thinking some of the techniques, for example, making factor-level definitions more generic to cover different families or types of jobs. Third, instead of evaluating tightly defined sets of tasks, job evaluation techniques have been adapted to cover more flexible, sometimes multi-skilled roles (Pritchard and Murlis 1992).

Additionally, job evaluation techniques have been adapted to incorporate the concepts of competency by, for example, placing increased emphasis on broad skill-related factors. An example of this is the Higher Education Role Analysis (HERA) system, developed by a consortium of higher education institutions to cover all jobs in their sector, 'from porter to professor', as their publicity material says (Education Competences Consortium 1998). The HERA scheme elements for analysis are set out in Figure 4.1.

Equal value legislation has encouraged employers to adopt job evaluation for all employees, and, arguably, is increasingly influencing the nature of modern job evaluation. Because this has major implications for grading structures, it is considered in more detail in the next section.

The impact of 'equal value'

As we have seen, jobs typically undertaken by women, whether manual or non-manual, were generally categorised as unskilled or less skilled than those of men. This became institutionalised in separate, and lower, women's rates of pay, which prevailed in many sectors until the mid-1970s. This institutionalisation was a particularly acute problem in Britain. Although women's average earnings are lower than men's in most countries for which statistics are collected, most other EU member states have equal pay provisions written into their constitutions or other fundamental legal framework; and in many member states the gender earnings gap is significantly smaller than in Britain (Jacobson 1998: 350–3).

So, for example, at the Ford Motor Company before a new job evaluated structure was introduced in 1967, there were effectively four grades for produc-

---

1 Communication
2 Teamwork and motivation
3 Liaison and networking
4 Service delivery
5 Decision-making processes and outcomes
6 Planning and organising resources
7 Initiative and problem-solving
8 Investigation, analysis and research
9 Sensory and physical co-ordination
10 Work environment
11 Pastoral care and welfare
12 Coaching, development and instruction
13 Teaching and training
14 Knowledge and experience

Figure 4.1 Higher Education Role Analysis elements

Male – Skilled
Male – Semi-skilled
Male – Unskilled
Female

Figure 4.2 Ford grading structure pre-1967

tion workers if account is taken of the separate grade for women (Friedman and Meredeen 1980: 44). (See Figure 4.2.)

The largest single group of female Ford production workers at that time comprised sewing machinists, who earned 92 per cent of the basic rates of men undertaking unskilled jobs, such as sweeping floors and supplying components to the production line, and 80 per cent of the male semi-skilled rate (*Report of a Court of Inquiry under Sir Jack Scamp* 1968/9: paras 13–15). Similar grading and pay structures prevailed in other motor companies, and indeed in many other manufacturing companies.

Amongst National Health Service ancillary workers in the same period, there existed separate grading structures for men and women, with multitudinous pay rates for each, all agreed at national level. There were, for example, separate rates for matron's maids and for porters. The only area of overlap was in laundries, where women were paid a percentage of the male rates for each job.

British equal pay legislation

The principle of 'equal pay for work of equal value' was embodied in Article 41 of the Constitution of the International Labour Organisation at the end of the First World War (*Report of the Royal Commission on Equal Pay* 1946). However, in the UK there was little progress until Herbert Morrison, then a Minister in the National Government, set up a Royal Commission on Equal Pay in 1944. During the Second World War, as in the First, women had taken over men's jobs in munitions and other manufacturing establishments, often at lower rates of pay.

The Royal Commission concluded that equal pay for equal work, in the sense of the same rate for the job, could be introduced in what they termed 'overlap areas' (where men and women worked interchangeably) for non-industrial civil servants, teachers, and local government officers (*Report of the Royal Commission on Equal Pay* 1946: para. 563). The Commission avoided the issue of 'equal value', by doubting 'whether there is any standard of measurement by reference to which this [equal effort or equal sacrifice in very diverse activities] might be decided, or any serious proposal that remuneration should be based on such a decision'. As a result of these recommendations, equal pay for the same work in the non-manual public sector was achieved gradually and by negotiation with recognised trade unions during the early 1950s. Women teachers, female civil servants and local government employees all received equal pay for the same work as men during this period. There was still no mention of 'equal value' at this stage.

The moves towards equal pay for the same work did not extend into the private sector, nor did they cover manual women workers in the public sector. One of the reasons for this was the very high degree of occupational segregation, and thus absence of 'overlap', in these areas. As a very broad generalisation, women did different jobs to men, so the question of equal pay for the same work arose relatively rarely. But the absence of equal pay legislation was a cause for concern amongst the emerging women's and civil liberties groups of the late 1950s and early 1960s. Their campaigning contributed to the inclusion in the Labour Party Manifesto in 1964 of a commitment to introduce legislation on equal pay.

The Equal Pay Act (EPA) did not become law until 1970. It might never have been passed had it not been for the Ford sewing machinists. In 1966–7, the Ford Motor Company commissioned consultants, Urwick Orr & Partners, to develop and implement a job evaluation scheme covering production and craft jobs. The scheme was typical of those for manual jobs at this time, with twenty-eight factors (called characteristics in the Urwick Orr system) and a relatively small number of levels for each factor. Some of the factors were more heavily weighted than others. The weighting was achieved by computerised regression analysis against a 'felt fair' rank order of jobs (note that in the previous production hierarchy, sewing machinists were at the bottom, on account of the lower women's rate of pay) (*Report of a Court of Inquiry under Sir Jack Scamp* 1968). The scheme was implemented by teams of assessors, who went round the various Ford plants interviewing jobholders, observing their work, and then making assessments on the spot for each factor by comparison with the relevant benchmark job assessments.

The resulting grading structure, introduced from July 1967, had five broad grades, as set out in Figure 4.3.

The job of sewing machinist was one of fifty-six benchmark jobs used as the basis for designing the system. It came out in grade B; however, as this was before the 1970 Equal Pay Act, the machinists were not paid the full grade B rate, but only 85 per cent of it. The sewing machinists were incensed, first because they received only 85 per cent of the rate for men doing work in the same grade as themselves, but second on account of the grade of the job. They thought their jobs should have been in grade C. They took industrial action and, as cars cannot be sold without seat covers, rapidly brought production to a halt (Scamp Report 1968).

The dispute was resolved, following a meeting with Barbara Castle, at the Department of Employment and Productivity in June 1968 (Friedman and Meredeen, 1980). The agreement awarded the sewing machinists 100 per cent of the male grade B rate phased in over two years; and established a public court

---

E – most skilled craft jobs
D – less skilled craft jobs
C – more skilled production jobs
B – less skilled production jobs
A – unskilled jobs

Figure 4.3 Ford grading structure from July 1967

of inquiry to examine the grading of the job. By 1971 they were receiving the full grade B rate, but the Court of Inquiry concluded that the dispute was 'about the grading of sewing machinists, not about equal pay', and recommended an internal review committee with an independent chairman, which ultimately confirmed the grade B rate (*Report of Special Ad Hoc Joint Committee under the Chairmanship of J. Grange Moore* 1968: para. 6).

Barbara Castle hastened preparation of the Equal Pay Bill. By introducing an implied equality clause into the contracts of all employees, the 1970 Equal Pay Act (EPA) had the effect of making separate women's rates of pay illegal.[2] The EPA also provided for those not receiving equal pay for 'like work' to be able to take claims to an industrial tribunal (IT).[3] Employers were allowed until 1975 to eliminate separate lower rates. The response of many was to raise the women's rate to the lowest male rate, regardless of the comparative skill levels. Some employers introduced job evaluation schemes, which often weighted highly factors such as physical effort and traditional skills, thus achieving a similar effect by a supposedly objective means (Ghobadian and White 1995: 9–10).

A further provision of the EPA was to allow those whose work was 'rated as equivalent', but who did not receive equal pay, to take their claims to an IT. It is clear from the Standing Committee proceedings on the Bill that this was a direct response to the situation of the Ford sewing machinists, rather than having anything to do with 'equal value'. However, it was subsequently used by Margaret Thatcher's Conservative government to argue that the UK legislation did provide for 'equal pay for work of equal value'.

European equal pay legislation

In the meantime, the original members of the European Economic Community had signed the Treaty of Rome in 1957. Article 119 provided for 'equal pay for equal work' between men and women,[4] in order to achieve a level economic playing field, given the differences in proportions and working arrangements of women workers in member states. This was amplified in the Equal Pay Directive of 1975,[5] to require 'equal pay for work of equal value', although without definition of the concept, except to say that job classification systems (which are taken in European terminology to encompass job evaluation schemes) should be free from discrimination. The Equal Pay Directive also required member governments to have legislation to provide for national enforcement of its provisions.

The European Commission decided to take the UK government to the European Court of Justice (ECJ) on this issue. In spite of the 'work rated as equivalent' clause of the EPA, the ECJ was satisfied that a significant proportion of women fell outside the scope of 'equal value' (Industrial Relations Law Reports 1982). The result was the Equal Pay (Amendment) Regulations of 1983,[6] which, from 1 January 1994, added a third ground for a complaint to an industrial tribunal – where an applicant considered that her work was of 'equal value' to that of a male comparator in the same employment. The concept of 'equal value' is not defined in the amended Act, except to say that the jobs of applicant and comparator should be compared 'under such headings as effort, skill and decision'.

The impact of the 'equal value' clause of the EPA has been both delayed and diluted by the cumbersome procedures enacted for determining the question of equal value, and by the legal issues raised on behalf of employers apparently aimed at thwarting the intentions of the legislation. These technical issues are largely outside the remit of this chapter, but where they impact on grading and pay structures, they are dealt with below. However, there have been a number of successful cases, which illustrate how work typically undertaken by women has been historically undervalued.

Hayward v. Cammell Laird

Julie Hayward was a cook employed by Cammell Laird in the canteen at their Birkenhead shipyard. Supported by her union, the GMBATU (now GMB), she claimed equal pay for work of equal value with male craft workers – a shipboard painter, a joiner and a thermal insulation engineer – who received higher craft rates of basic pay. The independent expert appointed to the case by the IT determined that Julie Hayward's work was of equal value (*Report of the Independent Expert* undated) and the IT accepted his report (ICR 1985).

The case continued for many years through the appeal courts, although not on the issue of equal value, which was uncontested. A further question arose as to whether the fact that Julie Hayward was on non-manual terms and conditions and so received better sick pay and holiday provisions than the craftworkers could be balanced off against her lower basic pay. The House of Lords eventually decided in her favour (IRLR, 1988).

However, the key issue for the purpose of this chapter was that the work of a City & Guilds qualified cook had been found to be of equal value to that of male apprentice trained craft workers.

Enderby v. Frenchay Health Authority

Dr Pam Enderby was the legal test case for around 1,200 speech therapists, who in 1987 claimed equal pay for work of equal value with clinical psychologists and hospital pharmacists. The claims were delayed by Health Service employers, primarily around the argument that, because the pay of the three groups was determined under separate collective bargaining arrangements (separate Whitley Council sub-committees), this provided a 'genuine material factor' defence to the equal pay claims. This argument was eventually turned down by the European Court of Justice (IRLR 1993: 591).

The question of 'equal value' was not considered by any IT until 1995, when twenty 'lead cases' were referred to a team of independent experts. The first report to be considered by the IT was in the case of Evesham v. West Hertfordshire. The applicant, Margaret Evesham, was in 1987 a district speech therapist, responsible for the speech therapy services for the District Health Authority

(DHA) and with additional responsibilities for co-ordination of para-medical services, including clinical psychology. Her comparator was district clinical psychologist, responsible for the clinical psychology services for the DHA and with additional specialist responsibilities for personally providing psycho-therapy services. The IT followed the independent expert's report and found the applicant's work to be of equal value to that of her comparator.[7] More radically, in two further speech therapist claims, the industrial tribunal went against the conclusions of the relevant independent experts, for different reasons, and found the jobs to be of equal value. In one of these claims, the tribunal considered the question, previously avoided by most tribunals, of 'what is equal value' and effectively found that 'almost equal value' is 'equal value'.[8] The Tribunal concluded (para. 31):

> The Tribunal . . . finds that there is no . . . measurable and significant difference in the demands made upon Mrs. Worsfold as compared to her comparator. It is supported by this in the evidence of Mr. Colville [Independent Expert] to the Tribunal that if he as a manager were grading the job for job evaluation purposes the difference would not lead to a difference in grading in the real world. The Tribunal therefore concludes that the Applicant was engaged on work of equal value with that of her comparator.

The Employment Appeals Tribunal subsequently confirmed this decision.

In these speech therapist cases, the IT found equal value in relation to specialist and professional management posts in a typically female caring occupation, which had traditionally been paid substantially less than the male-dominated medical and related Health Service professions. It is clear that these cases have major implications for all the female-dominated care professions, and indeed for future grading and pay determination for professional groups in the Health Service (Department of Health 1999).

Hayes and Quinn v. Mancunian Community NHS Trust

The applicants in this case were two dental surgery assistants, who having tried and failed to secure regrading to the highest relevant grade, in 1993 submitted tribunal claims for equal pay for work of equal value. Their comparators were a senior dental technician, a senior mortuary technician and a technical instructor, employed by an occupational therapy department to provide and supervise woodworking and upholstery activities to assist in-patient/client rehabilitation. Of these, the best paid was the senior dental technician, followed by the technical instructor and then the senior mortuary technician. The applicants and the three comparators were covered by four separate collective bargaining agreements.

The claims were referred to an independent expert whose report concluded that the applicants' jobs were of equal value to that of the technical instructor, but not to those of the other named comparators. Somewhat unusually, the respondent did not appoint its own expert until after the independent expert had reported, but, in spite of their report from Hay Management Consultants, the tribunal confirmed the independent expert's findings and awarded equal pay with the technical instructor.[9]

This tribunal decision showed that inequities in pay structures apply not only to independent practitioner groups in the Health Service, but also to those who directly assist the practitioners in providing services to patients and clients.

McKechnie & Others v. Gloucestershire County Council

The applicants were nursery nurses employed by the County Council in a number of settings, for example, a special school for children with severe physical disabilities, a family centre, a pre-school opportunity centre for children with communication delay or disability, and an infant school class assisting the class teacher. Under the terms of a national agreement they were employed on a scale equivalent to 2/3 on the local government administrative, professional, technical and clerical (APT & C) structure. Their position on the structure allowed for their reduced hours per week (thirty-two and a half instead of thirty-seven) and weeks per year (term-time) compared to full-time employees, as well as the demands of their work, so their actual job-related grade would probably have been scale 4.

The applicants, supported by their union UNISON, claimed equal pay for work of equal value, on a rate per hour basis, with a waste technician, in the Environmental Health Department, graded and paid on scale 6 of the APT & C structure; and an architectural technician, graded and paid on the next higher grade, Senior Officer (SO)1. After hearing expert evidence, the tribunal effectively re-assessed the jobs themselves on the basis of the evidence they had heard, using the respondent's expert's approach and then comparing this with the applicants' expert's conclusions. They found the work of the applicants to be of equal value to both their named comparators.[10]

Once again, an IT had found in favour of applicants in a female-dominated caring occupation, whose work has traditionally been undervalued and underpaid, arguably because of the association of their work with roles performed unpaid at home. The decision was significant because of the large numbers of women working as qualified nursery nurses in both the public and private sectors, and the consequent cost implications.

Job evaluation and 'equal value': recent developments

There are a number of ways in which the concept of equal value, as applied in the UK, is associated with, and has impacted on, job evaluation in this country. The first is in relation to the law. The obvious legal connection between 'equal value' and job evaluation is that the EPA requires a comparison 'under such headings as effort, skill and decision' – headings which are also often factors, or characteristics, in job evaluation systems. It is clear that those who drafted the Equal Pay (Amendment) Regulations saw this connection. Indeed, they saw it so clearly as to write into the legislation that the existence of a fair and non-discriminatory job evaluation scheme, covering the jobs of both applicant and comparator, would provide a 'no reasonable grounds' defence to an 'equal value' claim.[11] This was on the basis that in this situation the two jobs have already been analysed and compared 'under such headings as effort, skill and decision'.

The consequence of this provision is that, where both applicant and comparator jobs have been evaluated under a reputable job evaluation scheme, the applicant has first to demonstrate that the scheme is fundamentally flawed, either in design or implementation, or both. To date, no job evaluation scheme has been found to be flawed in this way, but some applicants have got round this JES defence by showing that their work has not been correctly analysed or evaluated under the scheme.

The first job evaluation scheme to be considered by an IT was that covering Ford production workers. A number of sewing machinists had submitted 'equal value' claims almost as soon as the Equal Pay (Amendment) Regulations were effective, from 1 January 1984. The preliminary hearing, on the company's 'job evaluation study' defence, took place in April 1984 (IRLR 1984). The majority decision of the tribunal was that the system was widely respected and recognised and that they could find no fundamental flaw in it. They therefore concluded that there was no evidence of bias or discrimination in the Urwick Orr job evaluation study.

Similar conclusions were reached by ITs in other cases where a job evaluation scheme was challenged. For example, in a Northern Irish case, where the applicant domestic assistants were challenging the Health Service Ancillary Staffs Council (ASC) job evaluation scheme, the Belfast tribunal allowed the challenge, but on the grounds that the job evaluation scheme had not been developed for jobs in Northern Ireland. As in the Ford case, the tribunal found that the scheme itself had been developed and maintained by reputable consultants and was fair and non-discriminatory. The respondent health board submitted an appeal against the reference of the claims to an independent expert, and the applicants cross-appealed on the findings in relation to the job evaluation scheme, but neither was heard, as the claims were settled in the meantime.

None of the cases in which job evaluation schemes have been accepted by tribunals as providing 'no reasonable grounds' for equal value claims to be pursued has reached an appeal hearing. There are, however, grounds for considering that these decisions may not meet European requirements.

The effect of this provision and the way it has been interpreted by tribunals is that a number of equal value claims have been defeated at this preliminary stage, without consideration being given to the question of whether the jobs were of equal value. It seems likely that many more claims will have been deterred. The decision in the case of speech therapist Margaret Evesham is notable for the tribunal's comments on the equal value assessment methodologies adopted by the expert commentators. The respondents' experts, who were employed by Hay Management Consultants, used a version of the company's Guide Chart Profile system of job evaluation to make their comparative assessments. The tribunal accepted the criticism made on behalf of the applicant that the scheme was not sufficiently modified properly to reflect the key demands of jobs, especially in relation to interpersonal skills. They also expressed concerns about how the internal scoring constraints within the Hay system impacted on the jobs in question.[12] Hay consultants have responded to these criticisms by pointing out that the system is used as an equal value comparative assessment methodology, rather than as a job evaluation scheme. Yet these criticisms, together with the Hayes and Quinn decision, suggest ways in which job evaluation schemes, put forward as defences to equal value claims, may be subject to challenge in the future.

The impact of the job evaluation study defence has been to contribute to the extension of JE, not just in the private sector, but in the public sector also. Following claims against Lloyds Bank by clerical and secretarial employees who claimed equal pay with higher-paid messenger grades, this bank and all except one of the other major English clearing banks implemented the Hay job evaluation system to cover all employees.

This extension of JE would be no problem if job evaluation schemes were fair and non-discriminatory, and thus delivered equal pay for work of equal value. However, there is considerable evidence that this is not the case, as the case of the Ford sewing machinists demonstrated. When in 1984 the industrial tribunal rejected the equal value claim of the Ford sewing machinists, they did so on the grounds that there was a fair and non-discriminatory job evaluation scheme in place. The Transport and General Workers' Union (TGWU) appealed against this decision, on behalf of the applicants. The sewing machinists also submitted a further internal grading appeal, in accordance with company procedure, at the time of the annual pay negotiations in late 1984. The grading appeal was again rejected by the company; and again the sewing machinists took industrial action.

The dispute was resolved by an agreement to refer the matter to an independent job evaluation panel.[13] The terms of reference required the panel to 're-profile' the sewing machinist job, using the original job evaluation system. The panel effectively re-evaluated the sewing machinist job. This process placed the job in grade C, the grade that they had claimed, and, in fact, quite close to the grade D boundary. The company accepted the panel's report and re-graded the sewing machinists. The view of company representatives appears to have been that the panel's conclusion arose because so many of the original benchmark jobs had changed or ceased to exist. An alternative interpretation would be that the scheme had been implemented in a discriminatory way in 1967. This is only hinted at in the report. There was growing awareness of the ways in which factors can be interpreted in a sexually discriminatory way. The characteristics for which the panel changed the original benchmark assessment, included the following:

- 'visualisation of shapes and spatial relations' (originally the job had been scored 'low' because the machinists did not use engineering drawings or patterns, but they did have to work 'inside out' and were assessed by the panel at 'high');
- 'paced muscular effort' (increased from 'moderate' to 'high' because of the pace of the work, even though it did not require as great a physical exertion as many of the benchmark jobs);

- 'hand/eye co-ordination' (where the panel judged the degree of hand eye co-ordination to be higher than that of even the highest level benchmark job) (*Equal Opportunities Review* 1985: 8–12; Industrial Relations Services 1985: 15–17).

The non-discriminatory finding on the Ancillary Staffs Council JES is also open to question, as the employers subsequently agreed to a review of the job evaluation scheme, which resulted in significant changes to the scheme. However, these have never been implemented because of the introduction of local collective bargaining into the NHS, following the Conservative government's NHS reform legislation.

Concerns about traditional job evaluation schemes have led to reviews, even where schemes have not been formally challenged, as the following case demonstrates. A 1987 report was critical of the Greater London Whitley Council (GLWC) job evaluation system on a number of grounds:

- the 'education' factor, based on qualifications, was 'too narrow' and 'not sensitive to knowledge, skills and expertise acquired in ways other than by formal education';
- the 'experience' factor reflected typically male, managerial career patterns;
- the 'supervisory' responsibility factor was 'outdated' in giving more points to those managing professional staff than to those managing technical or clerical employees, and the scheme failed to measure the supervisory responsibilities of many care jobs for clients or residents;
- the scheme over-rewarded professional status, managerial roles and the position of jobs in the status hierarchy (all more likely to be associated with male-dominated roles);
- it under-rewarded caring and other interpersonal skills, difficult or demanding contacts, work pressures, stress, creativity, skills less likely to be recognised through professional qualification, knowledge gained through experience (e.g. of other cultures), language skills, and supervision of clients (all more likely to be associated with female-dominated roles) (London Equal Value Steering Group 1987: 6–10).

Following this report, this scheme was withdrawn and replaced by an updated version, which dealt with most, but arguably not all, of the defects.

The legislation has led to the development of a small number of schemes designed specifically to move towards 'equal pay for work of equal value', rather than simply providing the employer with a defence to 'equal value' claims. One of the first of these was a scheme covering all employees at the Save the Children Fund (SCF) charity (IRS 1989: 9–10).

Another early 'equal value' job evaluation system was the Local Authorities' Manual Workers' Job Evaluation Scheme (IRS 1987). The features of this scheme are summarised in Table 4.1. The major differences between this scheme and the early predecessor scheme, implemented with the assistance of Urwick Orr in

Table 4.1 Local Authorities' Manual Workers' Job Evaluation Scheme: Summary, 1987

Factor	Level					Weight (%)
	1	2	3	4	5	
Skill/responsibilities	36	72	180	306	360	36.0
People	12	30	90	120		12.0
Resources	12	30	90	120		12.0
Supervision	6	12	54	108	120	12.0
Initiative	6	18	36	60		6.0
Mental effort	8	24	48	80		8.0
Physical effort	8	24	48	80		8.0
Working conditions	6	18	36	60		6.0
						100.0

around 1969, are the 'Responsibilities for People', that is, clients, children and members of the public; and the specific inclusion of references to 'caring skills' in the 'skills factor' level definitions.

With hindsight, there are criticisms to be made of this scheme. The measurement of the 'responsibility for supervision' factor, in terms of numbers of staff supervised, proved problematic in times of competitive tendering (when staff numbers and hours tended to decrease). The scheme undervalued the more extensive work allocation and team-leading responsibilities of school cooks (compared with caretakers supervising cleaners, for example). The 'skills' factor would nowadays probably be sub-divided, to avoid undervaluation of interpersonal and/or physical skills. And the uneven scoring system is difficult to justify. However, of its period it was progressive and certainly raised the basic pay of large numbers of female employees (notably home helps, care assistants, school catering staff, and school crossing patrols) relative to that of traditional male groups, such as gardeners, refuse collectors, roadworkers and roadsweepers. It also influenced other schemes developed to cover groups of manual jobs (IRS 1989).

Some of the key features, of both design and implementation, from the Manual Worker Scheme are also to be found in the more recent job evaluation scheme designed to support the 1997 local government agreement covering both manual and APT & C jobs, the Single Status Agreement (IRS 1998). The scheme factor plan, scoring and weighting are summarised in Table 4.2.

The scheme is innovative because it includes a relatively large number of knowledge and skills factors – intended to ensure that, for example, caring, other interpersonal skills and physical skills, such as dexterity and co-ordination, are all fairly measured. This is in addition to the more conventional knowledge demands. An emotional effort factor is incorporated (to complement the more conventional mental and physical effort factors) and an arithmetic scoring system, with equal numbers of points per level per factor (to avoid introducing an unjustified hierarchical effect into the system).

Table 4.2 Local Government NJC (single status) Job Evaluation Scheme, 1997

Factor	Level								Weight (%)
	1	*2*	*3*	*4*	*5*	*6*	*7*	*8*	
Knowledge and skills									
Knowledge	20	40	68	80	100	121	142	163	16.3
Mental skills	13	26	39	52	65	78			7.8
Communication skills	13	26	39	52	65	78			7.8
Physical skills	13	26	39	52	65				6.5
Effort demands									
Initiative and independence	13	26	39	52	65	78	91	104	10.4
Physical effort	10	20	30	40	50				5.0
Mental effort	10	20	30	40	50				5.0
Emotional effort	10	20	30	40	50				5.0
Responsibilities									
People	13	26	39	52	65	78			7.8
Supervision	13	26	39	52	65	78			7.8
Financial resources	13	26	39	52	65	78			7.8
Physical resources	13	26	39	52	65	78			7.8
Environmental demands									
Working conditions	10	20	30	40	50				5.0
									100.0

The future of grading

There seems little doubt that large organisations will continue to need to value and grade jobs relatively for the foreseeable future. Individual market rates provide an alternative for small numbers of managerial or specialist jobs, but have so far proved impractical for larger numbers and are open to anomaly, legal challenge and upward drift.

CBP systems, or at least competence-oriented job evaluation schemes, seem likely to provide the main alternative to conventional job evaluation. They fit well with the current emphasis on increasing skill levels and role flexibility. However, the investment in comprehensive training and assessment, in addition to the implied additions to the pay bill if the system is effective, may render such CBP systems impracticable for most organisations, other than those with specific skill requirements.

That leaves job evaluation. But as we have seen, job evaluation techniques can be used in a variety of ways for a variety of purposes. There are signs that job evaluation schemes in the future will have to accommodate all the roles in an organisation, rather than being restricted to those within the purview of traditional collective bargaining. A number of questions arise: Will this affect the structure of JE schemes? Will traditional schemes be shoe-horned into organisations and made to fit specialist and indirect roles? Or will new JE techniques be developed, using the sorts of approaches of the local government NJC scheme? Will job evaluation be used only to provide a defence to equal value claims from predominantly female groups? Or will it be developed into a tool for implementing equal pay for work of equal value? Job evaluation and other grading systems appear to be at a crossroads.

Notes

1 See for example, Specialarbejderforbundet I Danmark v Dansk Industri, acting for Royal Copenhagan a/s [1995] IRLR 648, where the European Court of Justice said that it was open for employers to explain pay differentials between men and women undertaking work of equal value in terms of 'choice by the workers concerned of their rate of work and to rely on major differences between total individual pay within each of these groups'.

2 Equal Pay Act 1970 (c 41 1970): s. 1(1) states: 'If the terms of a contract under which a woman is employed at an establishment in Great Britain do not include (directly or by reference to a collective agreement or otherwise) an equality clause they shall be deemed to include one.' s. 1(2) of the Act goes on to describe the situations where the equality clause should apply. In 1970 these were when the 'woman is employed on like work with a man in the same employment'; and where the 'woman is employed on work rated as equivalent with that of a man in the same employment'.

3 Equal Pay Act 1970 (c 41 1970) s. 2 (1) states: 'Any claim in respect of the contravention of a term modified or included by virtue of an equality clause, including a claim for remuneration of arrears or damages in respect of the contravention, may be presented by way of a complaint to an industrial tribunal.' Industrial tribunals were established under the Industrial Training Act of 1964 to deal with disputes over the payment by employers of industrial training levies, but had been increasingly been used for other purposes, such as grievances over 'unfair dismissals'. From August 1998 industrial tribunals became employment tribunals.

4 Treaty of Rome, 1957, Article 119 states:

> Each Member State shall during the first stage and subsequently maintain the application of the principle that men and women should receive equal pay for equal work.
>
> For the purposes of this Article, 'pay' means the ordinary basic or minimum wage or salary and any other consideration, whether in cash or kind, which the worker receives, directly or indirectly, in respect of his employment from his employer. Equal pay without discrimination based on sex means:
>
> (a) that pay for the same work at piece rates shall be calculated on the same unit of measurement;
> (b) that pay for work at time rates shall be the same for the same job.

5 Equal Pay Directive, Council Directive No. 75/117, Article 1 states:

> The principle of equal pay for men and women outlined in Article 119 of the Treaty, hereinafter called 'principle of equal pay', means, for the same work or for work to which equal value is attributed, the elimination of all discrimination on grounds of sex with regard to all aspects and conditions of remuneration.
>
> In particular, where a job classification system is used for determining pay, it must be based on the same criteria for both men and women and drawn up so as to exclude any discrimination on grounds of sex.

6 Equal Pay (Amendment) Regulations 1983 SI 1983/1794.
7 Margaret Evesham v. North Hertfordshire Authority and the Secretary of State for Health: case no. 17844/87: Decision sent to the parties 9 September 1997: 'The Tribunal finds that the Applicant was engaged on work of equal value with that of her male comparator.'
8 Mrs S. Worsfold v. Southampton District Health Authority and the Secretary of State for Health: case no. 18296/87: decision sent to the parties 10 March 1998. Mrs Julie Lawson v. South Tees District Health Authority and the Secretary of State for Health: case no. 17931/87: decision sent to the parties on 27 April 1998. Both these decisions were the subject of appeal at the EAT on the question of what constitutes equal value and have been determined in favour of the applicants.
9 Hayes and Quinn v. Mancunian Community Health NHS Trust and South Manchester Health Authority: case nos. 16977/93 and 16981/93: Decision of the Manchester Industrial Tribunal of August 1996.
10 Mrs M. McKechnie & Others v. Gloucestershire County Council: case nos 12776/96; 1400205/96; 1400207/96; 1400208/96: decision sent to the parties 9 September 1997.
11 Equal Pay Act, op. cit.: s. 2A(1) provides that where there is a dispute over an 'equal value' claim, the tribunal may either:

> (a) proceed to determine that question; or
> (b) unless it is satisfied that there are no reasonable grounds for determining that the work is of equal value as so mentioned, require a member of the panel of independent experts to prepare a report with respect to that question.

s. 2A(2) explains that there are no reasonable grounds for determining the question if

> (a) . . . [the woman's] work and the work of the man in question have been given different values on a study such as is mentioned in section 1(5) above [a job evaluation study]; and
> (b) there are no reasonable grounds for determining that the evaluation contained in the study was (within the meaning of subsection (3) below) made on a system which discriminates on grounds of sex.

Subsection (3), rather meaninglessly from a job evaluation perspective, states that

> An evaluation contained in a study such as is mentioned in section 1(5) above [a job evaluation study] is made on a system which discriminates on grounds of sex where a difference, or coincidence, between values set by that system on different demands under the same or different headings is not justifiable irrespective of the sex of the person on whom these demands are made.

12 Evesham v. North Hertfordshire HA, op. cit.: paras 36–38.
13 ACAS: Independent Job Evaluation Panel Report and Award on a Dispute between the Ford Motor Co. Ltd. and the Transport and General Workers Union: ACAS 2C/107/85: 25 April 1985: p. 1, para. 3.

References

Adams, K. (1993) 'Scottish Power post-privatisation: using competencies to achieve top performance', *Competency* 1 (2) Winter: 13–20.
Adams, K. (1996) 'Competency: discrimination by the back door?', *Competency* 3 (4) Summer: 34–9.
Armstrong, M. and Baron, A. (1995) *The Job Evaluation Handbook*, London, Institute of Personnel and Development.

Benge, E.J., Burk, S.L.H. and Hay, E.N. (1941) *Job Evaluation Manual*. New York, Harper Brothers.

Boston, S. (1987) *Women Workers and the Trade Unions*. London, Lawrence & Wishart.

CBI/Hay Group (1995) *Trends in Pay and Benefits Systems, 1995 CBI/ Hay Survey Results, 1995*. London, CBI.

Daniel, W.W. and Millward, N. (1983) *Workplace Industrial Relations in Britain. The DE/PSI/ ESRC Survey, 1983*. London, Heinemann Educational Books.

Department of Health (1999) *Agenda for Change, Modernising the NHS Pay System*. London, Dept. of Health.

Education Competences Consortium Ltd (ECC) (1998) *Higher Education Role Analysis (HERA): Submission to the Independent Review of Higher Education Pay and Conditions*. London, ECC.

Equal Opportunities Review (1985) no. 2 July/August: 8–12.

Equal Pay (Amendment) Regulations (1983) S1 1983/ 1794. London, HMSO.

Friedman, H. and Meredeen, S. (1980) *The Dynamics of Industrial Conflict. Lessons from Ford*. London, Croom Helm.

Ghobadian, A. and White, M. (1995) *Job Evaluation and Equal Pay*, Policy Studies Institute, Research Paper no. 58. London, Dept. of Employment.

Gilbert, K., Lawrence, V. and Mitchell, J. (1996) 'Equality and competency in payment systems'. Paper presented to Conference on Equal Pay in a Deregulated Labour Market, 7 June, Middlesex University, London.

Grayson, D. (1982) 'Job evaluation and changing technology'. ACAS Work Research Unit. Occasional Paper no. 23. September. London, ACAS.

Grayson, D. (1987) 'Job evaluation in transition.' ACAS Work Research Unit. Occasional Paper no. 36. January. London, ACAS.

Hastings, S. and Dixon, L. (1995) *Competency: An Introduction*. Oxford, Trade Union Research Unit.

Hay, E.N. and Purves, D.D. (1954) 'A new method of job evaluation – the guide chart profile method', *Personnel* (US) 31 (1) July.

Industrial Cases Reports (ICR) (1985) *Hayward v. Cammell Laird Shipbuilders Ltd*. London, Incorporated Council of Law Reporting for England and Wales.

Industrial Relations Law Reports (IRLR) (1982) *Commission of the European Communities v. United Kingdom of Great Britain and Northern Ireland 333 ECJ*.

Industrial Relations Law Reports (IRLR) (1984) *Neil and Others v. Ford Motor Company Ltd 339 IT*.

Industrial Relations Law Reports (IRLR) (1988) *Hayward v. Cammell Laird Shipbuilders Ltd 257 HL*.

Industrial Relations Law Reports, (IRLR) (1993) *Enderby v. Frenchay Health Authority and Secretary of State for Health 591 ECJ*.

Industrial Relations Services (IRS) (1985) 'Ford and Smales', *Industrial Relations Review and Report* 345 (4) June: 15–18.

Industrial Relations Services (1987) 'Equal value in local authority job evaluation', *Industrial Relations Review and Report* 388 (17) March: 8–12.

Industrial Relations Services (1989) 'Job evaluation: the road to equality?' 'Employment Trends' section of *Industrial Relations Review and Report* 448 (26) September: 8–10.

Industrial Relations Services (1998) 'From status quo to single status: job evaluation in local government'. 'Employment Trends' section of *Industrial Relations Review and Report* 663 September: 4–11.

Jacobsen, J. (1998) *The Economics of Gender*. 2nd edn. Oxford, Blackwell.

London Equal Value Steering Group (1987) *Job Evaluation and Equal Value – A Study of White-collar Job Evaluation in London Local Authorities*. September, London, LEVEL.

Millward, N. and Stevens, M. (1986) *British Workplace Industrial Relations 1980–1984, the DE/ ESRC/ PSI/ ACAS Surveys, 1986*. Aldershot, Gower.

National Board for Prices and Incomes (NBPI) (1968) Job evaluation report no 83. Cmnd 3772. London, HMSO.

Patton, J.A., Littlefield, C.L. and Self, S.A. (1964) *Job Evaluation – Text and Cases*. 3rd edn. Homewood, IL., Richard D. Irwin, Inc.

Pritchard, D. and Murlis, H. (1992) *Jobs, Roles and People: The New World of Job Evaluation*. London, Nicholas Brealey.

Report of a Court of Inquiry under Sir Jack Scamp into a dispute concerning sewing machinists employed by the Ford Motor Company Limited. (1968) (the Scamp Report). Cmnd. 3749, August. London, HMSO.

Report of the Independent Expert, case number 5979/84 (1984): Miss J.A. Hayward (Applicant) v. Cammell Laird Shipbuilders Limited (Respondent), attached as appendix to Decision of Industrial Tribunal, available from Central Office of Industrial Tribunals.

Report of the Royal Commission on Equal Pay, 1944–46 (1946) Cmd. 6937: October, Appendix II. London, HMSO.

Report on the Proceedings of a Special Ad Hoc Joint Committee under the Chairmanship of J. Grange Moore Esq. TD (1968) 5 September. London, Ford.

Sapsford, D. and Tzannatos, Z. (1993) *The Economics of the Labour Market*. London, Macmillan.

Sparrow, P. (1996) 'Too good to be true', *People Management*, 5 December: 22–7.

5   Wages systems

Janet Druker

The divide between salaried and waged workers has been a fundamental and significant feature of payment systems within the UK. This chapter focuses on the position of 'waged' workers. This opening section sets the framework for discussion by identifying the ways in which 'waged' workers are differentiated from those who are salaried, with reference both to workplace rules and to the composition of the wage packet. The second section points to the limited scope of state regulation and the importance of employer discretion on wages. The third considers the significance of the hourly rate of pay as a basis for wage calculations, including overtime. Incentive schemes are considered in the fourth section with particular attention to the decline of payment by results. Skills-based pay and single-status working are discussed in turn in the fifth and sixth sections of the chapter, which concludes with a comment on the future of wages systems.

The differentiation between 'salaried' and 'waged' workers can be seen as marking a social and status divide within the enterprise with important implications for the way in which people are managed (Price and Price 1994). It is a distinction that appears to run counter to 'New Pay' ideas, which emphasise paying the person, rather than paying for the job (Lawler 1990; Schuster and Zingheim 1992). Within traditional pay arrangements, salaries are calculated on an annual basis and are normally paid monthly, whereas wages systems are characteristically distinguished by hourly rates of pay, normally for a specified number of weekly hours, paid at intervals of less than one month – normally weekly or fortnightly. Under wages systems, earnings may be composed of many elements including a basic rate, shift or overtime premia, bonuses and allowances – not all of which will count towards earnings-based benefits such as pensions. Workers who are receiving 'wages' are more likely than salaried employees to fall within the ranks of the low paid (White 1999a).

The discussion of wages systems in this chapter is concerned particularly with the position of manual workers, who constitute a large proportion of hourly or weekly paid workers in manufacturing and construction. It also embraces wages systems for lower-paid employees in the service sector – in retail, hotels and catering, and in cleaning, as well as in lower-grade clerical or administrative occupations – since some of these workers may also receive hourly or weekly 'wages' rather than salaries. Some of the growing number of employees engaged in telesales in customer services or in call centres, for example, may be hourly paid. Yet there is no clear occupational classification that determines which categories of employee receive hourly or weekly based wage payments. Information is limited because both of the two major sources of data on pay, the *New Earnings Survey* (NES) and the *Labour Force Survey* (LFS) collect information about total gross earnings. This information is then converted to weekly and to hourly earnings (Low Pay Commission 1998, appendix 2, para. 26: 174). Within all of the groups mentioned there are workers who are covered by salary systems, and the distinction that is made between wages and salaries may be blurred – and is increasingly blurred – over time.

The divide between wages and salaries reflects and reinforces the principles of job-based pay which, in turn, is associated with organisational status. The promise of pay is made against a commitment of work to be delivered, while the choice of wage or salary system provides a means of mediating authority relations within the workplace to ensure that work is actually performed (White 1981). Workplace rules tend to be stricter and working hours longer for waged workers, who are less likely than salaried employees to identify with the company (White 1981; Cully *et al.* 1999a: 19). The division between salaried and waged workers may have as much to do with mechanisms of control as with the payment systems (Price and Price 1994: 528). Wages systems are intended to reinforce industrial discipline by associating pay with controls over time to assert discipline, for example, for lateness or unauthorised absence. Waged employees in manufacturing at least are more likely to be required to clock in and out at the commencement and at the end of the working day – a requirement which is less commonly applied to salaried employees (Millward 1994: 107). Payment by results (PBR) systems have been designed to motivate workers and to reinforce employer control over output. Variations in PBR and in overtime pay mean that earnings are prone to fluctuate from week to week. The unpredictability of earnings has been a central feature of the experience of many waged workers by contrast with the relative security and regularity of income for salaried employees. The more tenuous nature of the relationship between the organisation and the waged worker is reflected in the brief notice period that is applied by comparison with those with 'salaried' status. Historically a perception of transience within the employment position of waged workers was suggested by their more limited access to key organisational benefits such as sick pay or pension schemes and by longer working hours.

The decline in manufacturing industry and the growth in service sector employment means that some traditional areas of 'waged' work have disappeared whilst new ones have emerged. Many new jobs have been created on a part-time basis in low-paid sectors such as wholesale and retail employment, or in hotels and restaurants (Cully *et al.* 1999a: 24). The use of non-standard workers – for example, fixed-term contract workers and agency 'temps' – has increased over the last decade (Department of Trade and Industry 1999a). Pay for many temporary agency workers may be calculated on the basis of hourly rates, rather than annual salaries. These factors tend to boost the numbers of insecure 'waged' workers, sometimes in industries or enterprises that are fostering 'customer care'. On the other hand, the changing business dynamic may challenge the traditional definition of the 'waged' worker since 'functional flexibility' is likely to break down the barriers between jobs. The 1998 Workplace Employee Relations Survey found that, in around a quarter of workplaces, workers in the largest occupational groupings were trained to tackle jobs other than their own (Cully *et al.* 1999a: 9). The restructuring of commercial relations and closer links with suppliers and subcontractors may also require a reconfiguration of work processes, with a premium on team-working that may be incompatible with individual payment by results.

The evidence points then to a shift away from output-based payment systems with a decline in the use of payment by results for waged workers. There is some (though partial) evidence of more explicit concern by employers with inputs – both in terms of skills and attitudes – reflected in the emergence of skills-related grading schemes and skills-based pay. Skilled manual workers and supervisors have increased job discretion (Gallie *et al.* 1998: 38) and are increasingly likely to be assimilated into salaried grades, or employed on single-status conditions. Employer interest in single-status working or harmonisation of terms and conditions has eroded some of the distinctions between waged and salaried workers. However, these initiatives are often partial and piecemeal. Traditional distinctions between waged and salaried workers have by no means been eliminated and inevitably there is variation between industries and between employers. There may well be a contrast in the experience of men and women, given the history of employment segmentation, women's greater role in the service sector and changing notions of social equity. If wage systems have historically been constructed to reinforce employer control, we also have to remember that this has often been constrained by collective bargaining, with regard both to the composition and to the level of wages. Whilst collective bargaining is less widespread now than in the past, employers cannot easily change wage systems. They must weigh up the nature and direction of changes in the light of the way in which they may be received by the workforce and by workforce representatives and against the possibility that they will be challenged.

Employer discretion and state regulation of pay

Employers have historically had considerable discretion with regard to the form, level and frequency of pay in the UK. Arrangements may be decided unilaterally or through collective bargaining. State regulation has been limited in the past and was further eroded in the 1980s and early 1990s with the repeal of three laws governing wages and wage payments. The Truck Acts, passed in the nineteenth century requiring payment in cash for manual workers, were repealed with effect from 1987; pay by credit transfer, rather than cash, has become the norm since then. The proportion of manual workers receiving cash-based pay in the trading sector declined from 80 per cent of workplaces in 1980 to 35 per cent by 1990 (Millward 1994: 105). The Fair Wages Resolution, dating from 1891, which required employers on government contracts to pay the recognised wage for an industry or occupation, was revoked. Wages Council rates, with origins in the same period, established to provide a minimum wage in specific industries and for particular grades of employee, were modified in the late 1980s and finally abolished in 1993. Because of positive support from employers, the Agricultural Wages Boards, which set basic rates for workers in the agricultural sector, were the sole survivors. Only in 1999 was a National Minimum Wage established in the UK.

The key areas of legislation governing wages are currently

- the 1970 Equal Pay Act
- the 1983 Equal Pay (Amendment) Regulations
- the 1996 Employment Rights Act, which includes provisions on guaranteed pay (requiring the employer to provide a fall-back payment where normal working has been interrupted other than by a trade dispute) and on rights to an itemised pay statement
- the 1999 National Minimum Wage Act.

Outside of these statutory obligations, employers retain considerable discretion in determining the form, the frequency and the level of pay which, with the exception of unmeasured work and output-based pay, are specified in the individual employment contract.

Hourly based pay

Hourly based pay is a fundamental feature of wage systems, providing arrangements which are normally straightforward and unambiguous both in terms of rates of pay and (expressed as a weekly wage) of earnings calculated on the basis of hours worked (Goodridge 1989). Time-based payment was traditionally the lever through which job time rates were linked to grading structures. Differentials were intended, typically, to underline the notion of skill, with higher time rates for those who were perceived to be the most skilled, and lower rates for the semi-skilled or unskilled.

The social construction of skill placed a lower premium on trades or occupations that were filled by women. Historically, claims to skilled status were often reinforced by trade union organisation; moreover women's skills, particularly interpersonal and caring skills, have been undervalued (Edwards and Gilman 1999). Despite the provisions of the Equal Pay Act (passed in 1970 and introduced from 1975), and the requirement ten years later that there should be equal pay for work of equal value, women's pay remains well behind that of men. The law supports women's case for equal pay only to the extent that comparisons are made with men working in the same organisation. Average gross hourly earnings for women manual workers in 1998 stood at only £5.23 as compared with a figure of £7.30 for male manuals (NES 1998). Some of this difference is accounted for by differences in occupations and working hours. However, the nature of the workplace and gender segregation between different establishments are also important, with women in female-dominated workplaces being more likely to be low paid (Cully *et al.* 1999b: 159–61). The question of equal pay is discussed more fully in Chapter 4.

Under time-based payment systems, employer control over pace and performance is reliant either on direct supervisory controls or on the willingness of the employee to engage fully with a task or range of tasks on the basis of 'responsible autonomy' (Friedman 1977). For these reasons time-based pay is most likely to apply where the pace of work is not the key to optimisation of performance or where the rate of output is controlled by the machine or the process rather than by the operator – for example, on production lines or in some call centres (Fernie and Metcalf 1998: 34).

Hourly based pay provides the baseline from which other dimensions of the wage system are developed. The use of discretionary merit pay or output-based payment by results may accompany hourly based payment. Payment by results or piecework may itself be related back to the hourly rate, where it is calculated on the basis of time saved in doing a particular job. Extending working time provides a mechanism for increasing output and enhances earnings through overtime pay. In many cases, employers pay for overtime at premium rates which range, typically, from time and a quarter through to double time. Employers have no legal obligation to make premium payments, although since 1998, they must observe the provisions of the Working Time Regulations, which limit the average working week to 48 hours. Despite the scope for 'opt-outs' from this stipulation, employers are required to monitor working hours and to keep records.

The National Minimum Wage (NMW), which was introduced in April 1999, hinged around the notion of hourly based payment and was expected to be of greatest relevance to women workers, who feature disproportionately within the low paid. It was set at a rate of £3.60 for adult workers, that is those aged 22 or over (with a recommendation subsequently accepted by the government that with effect from November 2000 the rate should rise to £3.70 an hour) with lower rates for younger workers and for those in training (Low Pay Commission 1998: 11; IDS 1998b, 3; Metcalf 1999). Significantly though, the Low Pay Commission decided that the NMW does not have to be assessed for each hour worked. Rather, it is averaged over the pay period – which for waged workers is likely to be weekly or fortnightly. Some of the other components in the wage package – for example, payment by results and output-based payments – 'count' towards the calculation of the NMW. Lower-paid workers are, in general, less likely than their higher-paid counterparts to receive additions to basic pay. Where workers receive incentive payments, or where they are paid tips or gratuities which are paid centrally through payroll, these payments can be taken into account in deciding whether the NMW has been paid (Department of Trade and Industry (DTI), 1999b). The time-based calculation may therefore set a guaranteed fall-back for workers who – as in the clothing industry – rely on payment by results.

Overtime premia are not included within the calculation for the NMW, which takes account only of the basic rate that is paid. This is important because overtime constitutes the largest single addition to pay that affects the earnings of lower-paid workers (White 1999a).

Overtime payments are more likely to be recorded for manual workers than for non-manual and for men rather than for women. Table 5.1 shows that this situation has prevailed for a number of years, even though overtime working is likely to fluctuate according to the economic situation. Where overtime is costly, employers may seek alternative arrangements which align working hours more closely with operational needs. This may include recruitment of more temporary or part-time workers, encouraging time-off in lieu rather than paying overtime premia, introducing new shift arrangements or moving to annualised working hours (IDS 1997, Study no. 617, January). In the retail sector, for example, Sunday and evening opening has been accompanied by increased use of part-time workers, who are often paid at plain time rather than at premium rates. Despite the range of alternatives, the *New Earnings Survey* data indicate that the proportion of manual employees receiving overtime increased between 1991 and 1995 although it declined slightly from that date. It seems likely that the shift to single-status working is associated with consolidation of overtime premia, a point to which we shall return in the discussion on single status below.

Overtime payments continue to be a more significant component within overall earnings, for manual workers than for non-manual and for men's earnings as compared with women's. Expressed as a percentage of average gross earnings, overtime payments in 1998 were 14.2 per cent for male manual as compared with 2.7 per cent for male non-manual earnings, and 6.8 per cent for female manual as compared with 1.8 per cent for female non-manual employees.

Extra payments are often made for shift-working too. Some of the difference between men's and women's wages may be explained by the fact that men are more likely to work overtime and shifts and so to receive these extra payments. Women are more likely to work part-time, with a lesser possibility that extra hours worked will attract premium rates of pay.

Table 5.1 Employees who receive overtime (%)

Type of worker	1991	1993	1995	1997	1998
Male manual	52.1	51.9	54.8	54.5	53.1
Male non-manual	21.0	19.4	19.0	20.2	19.0
All male	35.4	34.0	35.2	35.4	34.2
Female manual	25.5	28.1	29.3	29.7	30.9
Female non-manual	17.1	16.3	15.9	16.6	15.4
All female	18.6	18.3	18.4	18.9	18.1
Male and female manual	47.3	47.6	50.0	49.8	49.1
Male and female non-manual	19.2	17.9	17.6	18.6	17.4
All	29.5	28.3	29.1	29.3	28.3

Source: *New Earnings Surveys*

Incentive systems

Variable pay is a central feature of the 'New Pay' ideas associated with the writing of Edward Lawler III (1990) and Jay Schuster and Patricia Zingheim (1992). Individual variable pay, group variable pay, gain-sharing and lump sum awards were identified by these writers as providing the flexibility that is required by employers to match complex and dynamic change in the business environment (Lawler 1990; Schuster and Zingheim 1992). Yet despite the interest in performance-related pay for professional, managerial and other white-collar staff in the 1980s and early 1990s the most notable feature of recent UK pay developments for manual workers has been the decline of traditional payment by results.

Employer concern to maximise performance or output has led to intense debate, spanning decades, about the application and value of incentive systems that link a part or all of the pay package to individual or group performance. The interest in incentive systems is explained by the view that effort and output will increase if a worker perceives that this will lead to improvements in earnings – a view that has been often challenged (e.g. Behrend 1959) but which continues to inform management thinking (Heywood *et al.* 1997). Payment by results may be linked to individual or to group performance. Individual incentives are unlikely if the individual contribution cannot be measured or where group norms are important. Team incentives may be practicable if team output can be readily identified and quantified. Group incentive schemes tend to work on the same principle as individual schemes, either through measurement of physical output or through additional payments for time saved on tasks (IPD 1996).

Incentive schemes encompass a broad range of payment systems and some clarification of terminology is necessary because of the variability in usage. Historically, piecework was used in the textile and clothing industries on the basis that payment was made by the task completed or by the 'piece'. Nowadays incentive systems tend to be based upon measurement of output – normally in terms of units of time – with a bonus paid to the worker against the amount of time saved. Production-related wage incentives of this type are often termed 'piecework' but, following the work of Marriott (1971) and for the purposes of this discussion here, we will refer to such arrangements as payment by results (PBR).

The analysis of work method is central to the operation of individually based PBR schemes. The measurement of effort and time involved in a job leads to norms for particular tasks. In theory at least, this enables management to predict, to cost and to manage the production process with a clear understanding of the time which each task – and therefore the total process – will take (Brown and Walsh 1994).

Weekly based PBR can work in four ways:

- Payment can rise in direct proportion to output – as it does under simple piecework
- Wages may increase but at a lesser rate than output

- Wages may increase proportionally more than output
- Wages may increase in proportions which differ at different levels of output.

(Brown and Walsh 1994; Marriott 1971)

At the core of the debate about PBR schemes are different approaches to the motivation and incentivisation of the workforce. On one hand, there is the view that was articulated by Taylor and others such as Gilbreth, that the prospect of improved earnings stimulates additional effort and output (Taylor 1913). The principles of 'scientific' management or the 'one best way' of doing a job (Gilbreth 1911) are associated with clear definitions of work method and with forms of work organisation based upon division of labour and task specialisation. The need for supervision is reduced, since the reward system is expected to encourage the individual worker to maximise output (Marriott 1971).

An alternative view points to the importance of effective human relations as a motivational lever. The value of payment by results is challenged by the belief that it is effective work organisation and workplace communication, rather than incentive payments, which encourage high performance (Behrend 1959; Brown 1962). Improvements in work method may precede or accompany the introduction of PBR and productivity gains may mistakenly be attributed to the payment system rather than to work organisation, it is argued. Conversely, PBR schemes may have a negative impact on quality of output. They can also encourage resistance to change where adverse effects on earnings are suspected. Payment by results alone will not significantly benefit performance, say critics, although it will influence behaviour and remove some obstacles to communication and performance.

In a classic analysis, Brown reported on the ending of payment by results at the Glacier metals plants in the 1960s, pointing out that a move away from incentives did not result in diminished output (Brown 1962). He and other commentators point to the ways in which incentive payments may hamper innovation, locking an organisation into particular work methods where pay is geared towards the established production systems (Thorpe 1989).

One of the most common comments about PBR schemes is that they must be readily comprehensible and make a clear link between performance and pay (Smith, 1983). Yet in some cases schemes are complex and obscure, making it difficult for workers to predict earnings, to check their validity or to establish more than a generalised level of understanding of arrangements (Marriott 1971: 131).

Job analysis – involving the measurement and timing of tasks – is central to the operation of individual PBR. Job analysis is often seen as 'scientific', but there is inevitably an element of subjective judgement involved in the measurement of performance. There are questions about the choice of subjects which should be measured; in what conditions and over what time period; what allowances are to be made – for example, for learning new tasks or for handling interruptions? How should an 'average' performance be defined? Inconsistencies and discrepancies in measurement undermine the scientific credibility of such measurement. Some individuals may hold back on effort when they are under observation, with the view to enhancing the ease with which work targets can be met. Whether the scheme is to be based upon individual or group performance decisions about performance norms is open to question and to challenge. Group norms may be established to govern output, and the close links between work organisation and payment arrangements may in some circumstances become an impediment to change.

In general it seems that large establishments are more likely than smaller firms to use incentives (Brown 1990). In part this is explained because of the economies of scale which can be achieved when incentive schemes are applied to a large number of people (Heywood *et al.* 1997). Incentive pay is more common in routinised jobs and, not surprisingly, there is less use of incentive pay and greater use of standard rates in jobs where duties are variable (Brown 1990).

From the employer's perspective, PBR may reduce the need for direct control of workers. It is interesting that its use has declined in a period when technology is offering employers new types of control accompanied, paradoxically, by workers experiencing increased task discretion (Gallie *et al.* 1998). Drawing on earlier research, Fernie and Metcalf suggest that the choice of wage form is a question of 'control by incentives' or 'control by foremen' (NBPI 1968, para. 87, quoted in Fernie and Metcalf 1998). Payment by results may require fewer supervisors, particularly in a larger workplace where supervisors have a wide span of control (Heywood *et al.* 1997). Payment by results is more common for manual workers where employment contracts are shorter – long-term employment contracts are assumed to work within the internal labour market, creating opportunities for progression or deferred compensation which are not available in the shorter term (Heywood *et al.* 1997).

In practice the industry and its production requirements have a significant bearing on the choice and effectiveness of PBR schemes. PBR remains significant in manufacturing – for example, the clothing industry in the UK, which faces serious overseas competition, still relies heavily on PBR. The industry is labour-intensive – machining garments has not been subject to the process changes that have affected some other industries. Work output is easily measured. Negotiations for the multi-employer collective agreement for the clothing industry are premised on the notion that employers pay piece rate – and that percentage increases agreed at national level will flow through into earnings for the individual. In the textile industry, by contrast, which is more capital intensive, payment by results is less common.

Incentive schemes must be understood in a historical context as part of the apparatus of management control. In the tight labour market of the post-war years, incentive schemes were widely used. In 1949 some 38 per cent of workers in manufacturing and 29 per cent of all workers in industry were in receipt of PBR (Marriott 1971: 51). The processes of work measurement and rate fixing were subject to challenge from below. In the 1960s, despite the prevalence of multi-employer, industry-level collective bargaining, PBR was a significant determinant of earnings. Given the potential for variability in earnings if jobs were re-timed or rates were revised, it is not surprising that PBR was increasingly the focus for conflict between shop-floor union representatives and line management, generating problems for employers in terms of controlling wage levels and wage drift (*Royal Commission on Trade Unions and Employers' Associations, 1965–68* 1968: 104, para. 388). PBR was associated then with Taylorist work methods and with adversarial traditions of industrial relations. Attempts to reform PBR, through the introduction of Measured Day Work (MDW) in the early 1970s had only limited success.

PBR systems are far less important today than they were in the 1960s and, contrary to the forecasts of the 'New Pay' writers, it seems that variable pay may be less rather than more important where employers have moved manual workers into single-status type pay structures. The growing interest in HRM encouraged employers to cultivate – or to claim to cultivate – techniques of high-commitment management, with greater emphasis on intrinsic, rather than extrinsic, motivators (Wood 1996). PBR declined steadily during the 1990s. However, government sources show that manual workers are still far more likely to receive PBR payments than are non-manuals. They also show the decline in payment by results amongst manual workers – from 35.5 per cent to 24.1 per cent of male manuals and 26.2 per cent to 15.9 per cent of female manuals between 1991 and 1998 (see Table 5.2).

The reasons for this trend are clear. PBR encourages speed rather than – and sometimes at the expense of – quality. It may encourage group and trade union norms that tend to inhibit change and to challenge employer decision-taking (Wood 1996: 71). In the face of employer interest in changing forms of work organisation, including team or cellular operations, PBR may reinforce traditional ways of working (Cannell and Long 1991). Higher capital investment may impact on the nature and significance of the labour component in work processes. Changing technology and work organisation challenge traditional definitions of skill and encourage employers to re-assess grading structures and to move to single-status working. Employers may turn to high day rates. They may also look to single-status working to break down the complex array of additions to basic pay that make up earnings. There is some evidence of arrangements that focus on group- or team-based performance pay or on other aspects of performance

Table 5.2 Employees in receipt of payment by results (%)

Type of worker	1991	1993	1995	1997	1998
Male manual	35.5	30.9	29.5	25.6	24.1
Male non-manual	16.0	15.6	16.5	13.3	13.1
All male	25.0	22.4	22.4	18.7	18.0
Female manual	26.2	24.1	21.6	17.3	15.9
Female non-manual	12.0	11.9	12.2	10.5	9.5
All female	14.6	14.1	13.9	11.7	10.6
Male and female manual	33.8	29.6	28.0	24.0	22.6
Male and female non-manual	14.2	13.9	14.5	12.0	11.4
All	21.3	19.4	19.3	16.1	15.3

Source: *New Earnings Surveys*

including skills and behavioural attributes – for example, performance-related pay for individual employees and skills-based pay (Cannell and Long 1991).

The growing interest in group- or team-based PBR seems to support the general direction of the research of 'New Pay' writers' since it rewards team performance when effective team-working is increasingly vital to business performance. Team-based PBR is most likely where group performance can be measured and where it is central to work organisation. Incentive schemes may be used to encourage team-working and to foster co-operation within and between work groups. It is clear that this approach has benefits, but the extent of team-based pay in application is less apparent. Multi-factor schemes build a range of considerations into the bonus calculation – which may be concerned then not only with the volume of output but also with issues such as customer service, cost management, waste disposal and zero fault rates (IDS 1999: Study no. 665, March: 2–3).

Gain-sharing schemes may accompany and reinforce changing working practices, with the intention of distributing efficiency savings within a group or between workers at a particular plant. Traditional schemes, such as the Scanlon Plan, provide a form of gain-sharing whereby productivity (output, total sales or operating profit) is calculated against unit labour costs, so that if unit labour costs fall, the workforce receive a proportion of the savings that accrue. Similarly, the Rucker Plan measures the 'added value' that derives from labour efficiency and distributes some of the benefits within the workforce. Incomes Data Services report on gain-sharing for shop-floor workers at Philips Components in Durham, where payment reflects three criteria – first, local labour market rates; second, technical performance (through gain-sharing); and third, to provide an annual bonus or return on company profitability. The gain-sharing plan is operated on a production team basis and is triggered by factors that are specific to the team as well as by factors that are plant based (such as controlling absence). Teams are ranked on a weekly basis in accordance with 'league tables' and bonus is set accordingly (IDS 1999: 11–13).

It is not easy to chart trends with regard to incentives and performance-related pay since pay levels or pay progression within time-based systems may relate to performance and so changes are not recorded separately within the NES. It is clear though that performance appraisal for manual workers has not been widespread and skills-based pay is more common (IDS 1993: Study no. 543, December). Kinnie and Lowe (1990) studied eight private sector companies where performance-related pay had been applied for manual workers. They suggested that more attention needs to be paid to context (the use of performance-related pay was just one component amongst a number of changes being made) and that manufacturing planning and control systems and total customer service were also important (Kinnie and Lowe 1990). It is a point to which we shall return in the discussion of change below.

Skills-based pay

Whereas incentive schemes have diminished in importance, skills- or competency-based pay has become more widely used in the context of the rapid innovations in technology and work organisation during the 1980s and 1990s (Kessler 1994: 471). The terms 'skills-based pay' (SBP) and 'competency-based pay' are often used interchangeably, although some writers (e.g. Armstrong 1996) suggest that skills-based pay is the preserve of waged workers, whilst competency-based pay is concerned more with white-collar workers. Competency-based schemes are more likely to incorporate behavioural traits such as individual capacity to tackle a task or range of tasks – a definition that is important to high-commitment management practices (Cross 1992).

Skills-based pay seems, at one level, to reward the person, rather than to pay for the job – a distinction that encourages the view that SBP fits readily within high-involvement companies and with a participative management style (Lawler 1990). Discussions of skills-based pay can be confusing however, since there is nothing really new about the notion that employers are paying for skill. Traditional grading structures – for example, in the engineering industry – were founded on a concept of skill that was based very largely on formal systems of apprenticeship training (Gospel and Fuller 1998). This provided a route through which employers accessed intermediate level skills that were traditionally recognised in simple grading systems, often defended by unions and endorsed through collective bargaining. It was a peculiarly male preserve that sustained fixed skill demarcations, with few opportunities for progression – for example, from semi-skilled to skilled status. Grading and pay structures under these arrangements required employers to pay for a skilled worker even if the full range of skills was not regularly deployed. This principle was fundamental to the organisation and defence of craft interests and craft unionism. Employer interest was in standardising and deskilling the work process – or in disaggregating particular skills that were more regularly and routinely required – and paying less for them.

Traditional apprenticeship systems have, of course, declined, though there are attempts to revive employer-based entry training through modern apprenticeships (Gospel and Fuller 1998). The old-style concept of 'skill' has been challenged by technological change. The current interest in skills-based pay must be seen against a background of wider changes which challenge the union controls that were linked to training and grading structures. The shift away from such arrangements is associated with new forms of training, with a revised approach to training standards (in the form of NVQs), and a reconstitution of the meaning of 'skill'. Inherent in these changes is a move away from tight job definitions and the application of broad-based grading schemes that require employees to be functionally flexible within their range of competence. The new grading structure that has been agreed for the heating, ventilating and domestic engineering industry, for example, simplifies grading arrangements and links more closely with NVQ and SVQ occupational standards. Similarly, Sony's manufacturing plants at Bridgend and Pencoed use broad grade descriptions that are essentially skills-based (IDS 1999: 19).

Under traditional arrangements, employers may buy an element of flexibility, for example, through payment of a supplement, typically to a semi-skilled worker, for using a particular machine or piece of equipment. Skill supplements almost invariably relate to manual workers who are placed on a single grade but receive plus payments for operating specific machinery or specialist skills (IRS 1996a). Broad-banded and competence-based grades eliminate the need for such payments. There is a trend to consolidate additional payments (for example, shift pay and overtime discussed earlier in the chapter) into an overall basic pay rate through arrangements which involve multi-skilling and cellular working or which emphasise flexible work across traditional craft lines (IRS 1996a).

Skills-based pay varies more fundamentally by linking pay to the skills that are required within the enterprise. SBP is based on the principle of skill assessment, either through NVQs or on some other basis – for example, a company bespoke scheme. The formal assessment of skills is used by employers in order to locate employees on a skills-based salary scale. SBP provides, in theory at least, for progression within the pay system by rewarding the acquisition and application of additional skills (Armstrong and Murlis 1998).

Employer interest in SBP may be generated as a consequence of wider interest in change and concern to enhance the efficiency and the adaptive capacity of the workforce. The main reasons for using SBP are to communicate and emphasise input factors in the determination of pay, to dilute the task emphasis of the pay system. SBP promises a supply of skilled workers for higher-graded jobs to cope with new technology and changing job requirements. It appears to encourage learning; to reward acceptance of change; to support and to reward attitudinal and behavioural compliance; to link jobs in such a way that team-working or multi-skilling is encouraged; and to remove demarcation between jobs (Cross 1992: 16). The application of new technology requires both the capacity and the willingness of workers to adapt and to update work performance. By focusing on inputs rather than on outputs, SBP is intended to encourage this process (Lawler 1990; Cross 1992). In theory SBP encourages workers to respond to new demands. SBP is seen as more likely to encourage organisational commitment and culture change too, since employees have a prospect of career development (Armstrong and Murlis 1998).

SBP works on the basis of business need. Although some studies (e.g. Armstrong 1996) have referred to it as being people-based rather than job-based, it may more usefully be thought of as serving employer needs in the process of change. SBP is not an unlicensed opportunity for employees to enhance their skills and, in doing so, to improve their pay. Rather, it defines skill or clusters of skills in relation to the operations of the business. Skills blocks are arranged in sequence with break points between different skill levels. Additional pay is awarded for completion of blocks or for the achievement of skill levels – but this incremental progression is dependent first on business need and second on skills acquisition.

There is a lack of convincing evidence about the extent to which SBP has been incorporated into pay arrangements in Britain. There is no doubt that, on the basis of importation of American-based approaches to HR practice, such initiatives have been talked up by management consultants. However, the scope and the coherence of SBP initiatives may be open to question. In 1991 nearly one-quarter of employers responding to an IPM/NEDO survey said that they had introduced changes to their payment systems aimed at encouraging new skills and breaking down traditional job boundaries (Cannell and Wood 1992). The same survey indicates that SBP has been particularly important for non-management grades (Cross 1992: 9). The 1995 CBI/Hay survey indicated that only a quarter of organisations were using or considering using a skill- or competency-based approach to the management of pay (CBI/Hay Group 1995). Industrial Relations Services research found that most employers take account of skills in setting pay – that is, the individual is allocated to a grading structure in accordance with existing skills or competencies. Gallie *et al.* (1998), drawing on data from the Employment in Britain research programme, suggest that, even when account is taken of age, sex and occupational class, where skills increase, these have been rewarded with increased pay. However, this does not equate to SBP.

There are constraints as well as benefits in the use of SBP. It requires a careful analysis of skill needs and a clear commitment to training opportunities. Whilst skills-based payment systems seem to facilitate an open-ended commitment to upward mobility, employers are concerned with the application as much as with the acquisition of skill. There is a concern to avoid paying for skills that are not used. The scope for advancement through skills acquisition is likely to be inhibited both by the training budget and by employer willingness to accommodate increased wage costs, unless it is an integral and necessary aspect of organisational change.

Harmonisation and single status

The blurring or the erosion of distinctions between salaried and waged employees has been seen as a distinctive feature of the ideas associated with 'human resource management' since the 1980s (IRS 1996b, *Employment Trends* no. 600; Torrington and Hall 1998). Harmonisation of grading and working conditions across the traditional divide between waged and salaried workers can be seen as one facet of employer initiatives to encourage high commitment on the shop-floor (Wood 1996: 60). The harmonisation of terms and conditions of different groups is associated with changes in the form of pay (from cash to credit transfer), changes in the frequency of payment (from weekly paid to monthly paid) and changes in grading arrangements which erode or eliminate the practice of differential treatment. It has further implications for associated terms and conditions of employment, including the distribution of working hours, the length of the working week, additional payments such as overtime and shift premia, and pensions. Clearly, it is possible to rationalise some aspects of the employment package without embracing the full implications of harmonisation. For example, pay by cheque or credit transfer has become more common for manual workers, as we show above. The simplification of grading and pay arrangements has been encouraged by successive waves of downsizing and business restructuring in many organisations (IRS 1996a: 7). Equal value legislation has hastened the pace of change, as employers have turned to job evaluation as a means of withstanding legal challenge over the question of equal pay.

Changes in technology and in workplace organisation have tended to erode distinctions both between waged workers (e.g. craft and process operators) and across the divide between waged and salaried employees (IRS 1998). In manufacturing industry lean production methods and just-in-time working rely on group or plant performance rather than on individual effort, whilst team-working and multi-skilling tended to erode distinctive job titles and payment systems and to encourage harmonised working arrangements in manufacturing. The most recent WERS data show that single-status working is strongly associated with team working and with job security (Cully *et al.* 1999a: 11). Brown *et al.* point out that these changes – so often seen as part of the trend to individualisation of the employment contract – in fact represent a standardisation of non-pay terms of contract (Brown *et al.* 1998).

Because of the complexity of changes to shift arrangements, overtime and working hours, harmonisation tends to be introduced in phases, as happened at the Rolls-Royce aircraft engine plant in Derby. The agreement that was reached there with the four unions representing skilled, semi-skilled and unskilled manual workers followed a move to cashless pay, on the condition that there would be 'no significant loss of earnings' associated with 'factory staff' status. Harmonisation was implemented in five stages to take account of changes to shift premia. It began with the abolition of clocking-in and the establishment of staff terms for periods of sickness, for holidays, for lay-off pay, and for notice. At the second stage an element of shift pay was consolidated into the basic rate (although without being incorporated into pensions since shift premia had not previously been used to calculate pensionable pay); shift premia were reduced on a tapering basis and overtime pay was standardised. Stage three brought further downward adjustments to shift pay and additional incorporation of shift premia into the basic rate. Stage four saw a reduction in the working week for dayshift employees with an entitlement to accrue time-off in lieu up to six days a year. The final stage gives employers the benefit of greater flexibility in the distribution of working hours, since employees could be requested to transfer to temporary shift patterns if requested in the event of 'unpredictable business requirements' (IDS 1998: 14–15).

Comparable pressures have emerged within the public sector, with employer interest in developing quality or customer care. It is often the lower-paid and lower-graded workers who are key to the provision of customer service. The 1997 agreement for local authority workers reflected this by providing for single-table bargaining and for single-status pay and grading for administrative, professional, technical, clerical and manual grades within local authorities (UNISON 1998).

Within this process of change, the craft worker has become an 'endangered species' (IRS 1998: 2–7). Harmonisation between craft and process operators may involve the simplification of grading structures in many establishments, with a reduction in the overall number of grades and a rationalisation of conditions between different categories of the waged workforce.

There are many aspects to the social distinction between waged and salaried employees and it is clear that moves towards harmonisation are not the same as the achievement of harmonisation. A shift from weekly cash payments to monthly credit transfer simplifies administration and carries cost benefits for the employer. A reduction in working hours is more complex, since unit costs may increase unless other gains are made – for example, in terms of productivity or flexibility of working arrangements. Pay structures have been harmonised more slowly than methods of payment or key benefits such as pensions, sick pay and holiday entitlement (IRS 1993).

Yet these changes – like many in British industry – have not been thorough-going. New costs are involved for employers as well as new opportunities. Wages systems survive. It is to the uneven processes of change and continuity that we turn in our conclusion.

Change and continuity in wage systems

Employers may be encouraged by human resource management and by 'New Pay' ideas to question and to review pay practices and to seek to bring wages systems into line with business strategy and process. There is strong evidence of employer interest in maximising the use of plant and equipment in manufacturing industry and in extending service hours to customers in the service sector. Changes that support these objectives have had repercussions for pay arrangements. Taylorist work organisation and controls have not been abandoned but may be applied in new work situations, underpinned by a culture of 'customer care'. Traditional incentive schemes, overtime and premium rates – introduced to enable employers to buy an element of flexibility – have been seen as too cumbersome and too costly. Employer interest is in standardisation of cost with scope for variability in working practice to meet business targets. The changes described above are designed to provide both. The move to annualised working hours minimises the need for overtime payments. The growth in skills-based pay reflects employer interest in harnessing the capabilities and the loyalties of workers to the realities of technological innovation, to team-working and to multi-skilling. The distinction between waged workers and salaried employees has in this context been increasingly open to question. Grading systems have been rationalised, and harmonisation and single-status working have become more commonplace.

Yet 'New Pay' ideas cannot be seen as fundamental to changing pay structures and practices for waged workers. The form of wages as well as their level have historically been the subject of conflict between workers and employers. Trade unions officers and union workplace representatives have sought to shape incentive schemes and to improve wage levels (Brown 1973). The effect of their presence is examined in Chapter 2, which shows that the 'union effect' is greater for wages systems and for manual workers than for salary systems or non-manual workers. It is greater too (at least in the US context and it seems likely in the UK too) in medium-sized workplaces than in the largest workplaces (Brown and Medoff 1989).

One of the debates about human resource management since the 1980s has been concerned with its impact on the role of trade unions. The continuing decline in collective bargaining and in trade union membership suggests that human resource management has served to by-pass trade unions. However, it is also the case that trade union recognition is more common in firms that have taken positive initiatives to foster human resource management (Martinez Lucio and Weston 1992; Kelly 1996). In concluding this discussion about the form and structure of wages, it is relevant to note that in the post-war years, incentive systems opened up opportunities for workplace bargaining and, in doing so, tended to foster and to reinforce union workplace controls (Brown 1973). The decline of PBR, the growth of broad-banded, competence-focused grading structures, the introduction of skills-based payment systems and the moves to single-status working seem to reflect and to reinforce workplace arrangements in which unions have less influence. Paradoxically, they also reflect union successes, since they carry the advantage of higher status and of the associated, wider range of benefits. In relation to the work of the 'New Pay' writers, we must note that whilst allowances may disappear, earnings are less subject to fluctuation – and there is less 'at risk' pay, rather than more.

Incentive systems created a rationale for union intervention at the level of the workplace both in connection with the process and equity of rate-setting and in connection with the level of rates. Whilst unions may be involved in the establishment of skills- or competency-based payment arrangements in unionised workplaces, the context and organisational culture are likely to be very different, with less manifestation of overt conflict and more attention to the benefits that can be gained from co-operation and partnership. Employer interest in change may, in part at least, be associated with attempts to contain or to neutralise the effects of trade union organisation. Moves away from measured systems of PBR to merit pay leave more scope for decision-taking by team leaders and both reflect and reinforce a shift in the balance of power away from the shop-floor.

Wages systems have been fundamentally affected by changes in business structure and organisation. Innovation in work organisation and processes are critical to the reformulation of pay and benefits. The growth in the number of smaller firms and the decline in manufacturing industry weigh against the likelihood of incentive schemes and of unionised workplaces. The introduction of lean production in manufacturing and the focus on customer care in the service sector make new demands on the ways in which people are managed and skills are deployed. Changes to the traditional supervisory role may play a part too, where team-working relies on a changing approach to communication and control, with closer and more direct relationships between team leader and team members.

Yet it is easy to overstate the extent of change. There is remarkable continuity in the operation of wages systems in spite of all the initiatives identified. Many of the prescriptions of the 'New Pay' writers were directed at the service sector workforce or at 'knowledge workers' – professional, managerial and technical employees. What is interesting is that they said so little about status differences and segmentation within internal labour markets. Gallie *et al.* (1998) highlighted the importance of the employee's experience and the difference in that respect between men and women. Payment 'for the job' failed to deliver equal pay for women workers but, given a legacy of workplace gender discrimination, there is a risk that payment 'for the person' will counter rather than advance the cause of pay equity. The weighting between change and continuity must be affected by considerations of gender, by women's historic exclusion from many skilled areas of manual work, and by the growth in women's labour market participation. Moreover the status difference between the waged workforce and salaried employees in the UK has not disappeared. Where there is evidence of change, it often reinforces employer control in a changed work environment. Moves to harmonisation are sometimes partial and piecemeal and many of the fundamental features of wages systems remain in place. The account of changes in payment arrangements that tends to accompany discussions of human resource management and 'New Pay' initiatives must be balanced by a reference to new categories of lower-paid work and to continuity in the experience of many waged workers.

Acknowledgements

Thanks are due to Nick Kinnie and to Anna Pollert for comments on an earlier draft of this chapter.

References

Armstrong, M. (1996) *Employee Reward*. London, IPD.

Armstrong, M. and Murlis, H. (1998) *Reward Management: a Handbook of Remuneration Strategy and Practice*. London, Kogan Page. Published in association with Hay Management Consultants. 4th edn.

Behrend, H. (1959) 'Financial incentives as the expression of a system of beliefs'. *British Journal of Sociology* 10 (2): 137–47.

Bowey, A. and Lupton, T. (1989) *Salary and Wage Systems*. Aldershot, Gower. 3rd edn.

Brown, C. (1990) 'Firms' choice of method of pay'. *Industrial and Labor Relations Review* 43, special issue, February: 165-S–182-S.

Brown, C. and Medoff, J. (1989) 'The employer size-wage effect'. *Journal of Political Economy* 97 (5): 1027–59.

Brown, W. (1962) *Piecework Abandoned: the Effect of Wage Incentive Systems on Managerial Authority*. London, Heinemann.

Brown, W. (1973) *Piecework Bargaining*. London, Heinemann Educational Books.

Brown, W. and Walsh, J. (1994) 'Managing pay in Britain'. In Sisson, K. (ed.) *Personnel Management: a Comprehensive Guide to Theory and Practice in Britain*. Oxford, Blackwell. 2nd edn, 437–64.

Brown, W., Deakin, S., Hudson, M., Pratten, C. and Ryan, P. (1998) 'The individualisation of employment contracts in Britain'. Department of Trade and Industry. Research paper. London, DTI.

Cannell, M. and Long, P. (1991) 'What's changed about incentive pay?' *Personnel Management* October: 58–63.

Cannell, M. and Wood, S. (1992) *Incentive pay: Impact and Evolution*. London, IPM and NEDO.

Confederation of British Industry (CBI) (1995) *Trends in Pay and Benefits Systems: 1995 CBI/Hay Survey Results*. London, CBI/Hay Group.

Cross, M. (1992) 'Skills-based pay: a guide for practitioners'. *Issues in People Management* 3. London, Institute of Personnel Management.

Cully, M., Woodland, S., O'Reilly, A., Dix, G., Millward, N., Bryson, A. and Forth, J. (1999a) *The 1998 Workplace Employee Relations Survey: First findings*. ESRC, ACAS and PSI. London, DTI.

Cully, M., Woodland, S., O'Reilly, A. and Dix, G. (1999b) *Britain at Work: as Depicted by the 1998 Workplace Employee Relations Survey*. London, Routledge.

Department of Trade and Industry (DTI) (1999a) *Regulation of the Private Recruitment Industry: a Consultation Document*. London, Department of Trade and Industry. URN: 99/774.

Department of Trade and Industry (DTI) (1999b) *A Detailed Guide to the National Minimum Wage*. Crown copyright, London, DTI.

Edwards, P. and Gilman, M. (1999) 'Pay equity and the national minimum wage: what can theories tell us?' *Human Resource Management Journal* 9 (1) Special Issue: 20–38.

Fernie, S. and Metcalf, D. (1998) '(Not) hanging on the telephone: payment systems in the new sweatshops'. Centre for Economic Performance. Discussion paper 390.

Friedman, A. (1977) *Industry and Labour: Class Struggle at Work and Monopoly Capitalism*. London, Macmillan.

Gallie, D., White, M., Cheng, Y. and Tomlinson, M. (1998) *Restructuring the Employment Relationship*. Oxford, Clarendon Press.

Gilbreth, F.B. (1911) *Motion Study*. New York, D. Van Nostrand.

Goodridge, M. (1989) 'Payment by time'. In Bowey, A. and Lupton, T. (eds) *Salary and Wage Systems*. Aldershot, Gower. 3rd edn, 301–26.

Gospel, H. and Fuller, A. (1998) 'The modern apprenticeship: new wine in old bottles?' *Human Resource Management Journal* 8 (1): 5–22.

Heywood, J., Seibert, W.S. and Xiangdong Wei (1997) 'Payment by results systems: British evidence'. *British Journal of Industrial Relations* 35 (1) March: 1–22.

Incomes Data Services (IDS) (1993) 'Performance appraisal for manual workers'. *Study* 543, December.

Incomes Data Services (IDS) (1997) 'Overtime'. *Study* 617, January.

Incomes Data Services (IDS) (1998a) *Report* 753, January.

Incomes Data Services (IDS) (1998b) *Report* 771, October.

Incomes Data Services (IDS) (1999) 'Bonus schemes'. *Study* 665, March.

Institute of Personnel and Development (IPD) (1996) *The IPD Guide on Team Reward*. London, IPD.

Industrial Relations Service (IRS) (1993) *Employment Trends* 548, November.

IRS (1996a) *Pay and Benefits Bulletin* 391, January.

IRS (1996b) *Employment Trends* 600, January.

IRS (1998) *Pay and Benefits Bulletin* 448, May: 2–7. Craft pay: 1998 survey.

Kelly, J. (1996) 'Union militancy and social partnership'. In Ackers *et al.* (eds) *The New Workplace and Trade Unionism: Critical Perspectives on Work and Organisation*. London, Routledge.

Kessler, I. (1994) 'Performance pay'. In Sisson, K. (ed.) *Personnel Management: a Comprehensive Guide to Theory and Practice in Britain*. Oxford, Blackwell. 2nd edn, 465–94.

Kinnie, N. and Lowe, D. (1990) 'Performance-related pay on the shop-floor'. *Personnel Management*, November: 45–49.

Lawler, E. (1990) *Strategic Pay: Aligning Organizational Strategies and Pay Systems*. San Francisco, Jossey-Bass.

Low Pay Commission (1998) *The National Minimum Wage: first report of the Low Pay Commission*. Cm 3976. London, Stationery Office.

Marriott, R. (1971) *Incentive Payment Systems: a Review of Research and Opinion*. London, Staples Press. 4th edn.

Martinez Lucio, M. and Weston, S. (1992) 'HRM and trade union responses: bringing the politics of the workplace back into the debate'. In Blyton, P. and Turnbull, P. (eds) *Reassessing Human Resource Management*. London, Sage, 215–32.

Metcalf, D. (1999) 'The British national minimum wage'. *British Journal of Industrial Relations* 37 (2): 171–201.

Millward, N. (1994) *The New Industrial Relations. Based on the ED/ESRC/PSI/ACAS Surveys*. London, Policy Studies Institute.

National Board for Prices and Incomes (1968) 'Payment by results systems'. *Report* 65, Cmnd 3627, May, London: HMSO.

New Earnings Survey (1998). Part A: streamlined analysis; description of survey. London, Office for National Statistics.

Price, L. and Price, R. (1994) 'Change and continuity in the status divide'. In Sisson, K. (ed.) *Personnel Management: a Comprehensive Guide to Theory and Practice in Britain*. Oxford, Blackwell. 2nd edn, 527–61.

Royal Commission on Trade Unions and Employers' Associations, 1965–68 (1968) Chaired by the Rt. Hon. Lord Donovan. Cmnd 3623. London, HMSO.

Schuster, J.R. and Zingheim, P. (1992) *The New Pay: Linking Employee and Organizational Performance*. New York, Lexington Books.

Smith, I. (1983) *The Management of Remuneration: Paying for Effectiveness*. London, IPM and Gower.

Taylor, F. (1913) *The Principles of Scientific Management*. New York and London, Harper and Brothers.

Thorpe, R. (1989) 'Payment by results'. In Bowey, A. and Lupton, T. (eds) *Salary and Wage Systems*. Aldershot, Gower. 3rd edn, 283ff.

Torrington, D. and Hall, L. (1998) *Human Resource Management*. London, Prentice Hall. 4th edn.

UNISON (1998) *Single Status in Local Government: a National Agreement for the Future*. UNISON, http:\\www.unison.org.uk/local-govt/singlest.htm.

White, G. (1999a) 'Pay structures of the low paid and the national minimum wage'. *Labour Market Trends* 107 (3): 129–35.

White, G. (1999b) *Pay Structures and the Minimum Wage*. Low Pay Commission Occasional Paper 3. London, Low Pay Commission.

White, M. (1981) *The Hidden Meaning of Pay Conflict*. London, Macmillan.

Wood, S. (1996) 'High commitment management and payment systems'. *Journal of Management Studies* 33 (1) January: 53–77.

6   Salary progression systems

Marc Thompson

Salary progression payment systems have traditionally been a notable feature of white-collar employment, particularly for those in large public and private sector organisations. The nature of these systems has, however, been subject to change in the last twenty years. The rise of 'New Right' rationalist economics, with the election of the Conservative government in 1979, marked a major change in public policy, with special implications for the management of public sector salary systems. Furthermore, faced with increasing global competition, private sector employers embarked on wide-scale organisational restructuring which had implications for the traditional systems of pay and reward. The purpose of this chapter is to analyse and explain the rationale, nature and context of these 'New Pay' progression practices and to consider the degree to which they have been adopted. Because of the wide range of occupations covered by the term 'white-collar', we concentrate on the concept of salary progression payment and how it has changed over the last twenty years, making distinctions where appropriate between developments in the public and private sectors.

We begin this chapter by introducing the concept of pay progression and its use. We then consider the context for change and the theoretical basis for the new practices before going on to consider the evidence for change. We look at the spread of performance-based progression systems and, in particular, consider the more recent phenomenon of competency-based systems. The impact of these new practices upon the employment relationship is then discussed before a final summary and conclusion looks towards the future.

This chapter is not concerned with the technical and operational specificities of salary progression payment systems, as these aspects are well covered by a growing number of prescriptive texts (e.g. Armstrong and Murlis 1998). Where appropriate, however, it draws upon specific examples to illustrate more general points. The overall aim of the chapter is to situate developments in salary progression systems within a number of wider perspectives. New Payment systems are more likely to be introduced for a host of complex reasons and in this chapter we seek to understand why organisations have been changing their salary progression systems and with what consequences.

The concept of pay progression

The concept of pay progression originates in the development of salaried employment within organisations in the late ninteenth century. In contrast to wage workers, salaried status implied a long-term employment relationship and the potential for career development. Employees therefore tended to be rewarded for seniority and their growing experience and hence value to the organisation. Salary progression payment systems, in traditional terms, consist of a number of basic elements: a number of levels of work organised around a grade structure, often determined by a job evaluation methodology, together with a series of steps or pay points enabling incremental progression within these grades. The means of progression through these scales was, until recently, based upon length of service or age. When an employee's skills or potential outgrew the limits of the grade, there was often an opportunity for promotion to a higher grade. In addition, white-collar staff also typically enjoy a range of employee benefits that differentiate them from manual employees. Typically, white-collar employees have occupational or company pension schemes, shorter working hours, longer holidays, and access to a range of perks dependent on their grade and status. These salary systems supported the internal labour market structures of the large private and public sector organisations that dominated the economy in the 1960s and 1970s.

White-collar employment today covers a heterogeneous range of occupations (i.e. professional, managerial, technical, clerical and administrative occupations) and this is reflected in the diversity of employment practices and arrangements for these groups. This broad area of employment accounts for nearly two-thirds of all jobs in the UK and has grown significantly over the last twenty years, from 49 per cent in 1981 to 54 per cent in 1986 and now stands at just over 60 per cent (*Labour Force Survey* 1998) with further growth projected (Institute for Employment Research 1999). While not all white-collar workers are salaried, one implication of the growth of white-collar employment is that salary progression systems now have much greater coverage than wages systems.

In order to understand why employers have restructured their salary progression payment systems, we need to understand why such systems are used in the first place. What advantages accrue to firms in providing salary progression systems? Internal labour market theory provides a helpful theoretical lens through which we can understand both the development of salary progression systems and their changing nature and content. In this section, the nature and rationale of internal labour markets are discussed and the linkages with salary progression systems explored. We pay particular attention to employer strategies for control, especially for key workers. The consequences of internal labour market rules for embedding a specific type of employment relationship are also discussed.

An internal labour market is characterised by a number of specific features. First, there are likely to be one or two jobs into which the majority of staff are recruited. These 'ports of entry' are at a reasonably low level but are likely to require high levels of educational attainment (Osterman 1994). A typical example would be the banking sector, where access to the company has traditionally been at school-leaver or graduate level and qualification levels determine the scale of labour flow into the organisation. Once inside the firm, the individual progresses up through a hierarchy of jobs or grades. Progression through grades can be based on a range of criteria but traditionally seniority has tended to predominate. Progression between grades is possible when vacancies are available at higher levels, which implies that such systems depend on growth or reasonable levels of staff turnover (in a steady state environment) in order to open up opportunities and thereby maintain the incentives of such a structure.

Indeed, in reality such structures have existed primarily in large organisations in the public and private sector, where there is scope for such progression. Internal labour markets are much weaker outside of these types of business (Eyraud *et al.* 1990). Therefore, most of the discussion of salary progression systems and internal labour markets relates to large organisations. Internal labour markets are seen as beneficial by some economists because they minimise transaction costs, maintain organisational stability through the use of efficiency wages and can also resolve so-called 'principal-agent' contractual problems (Williamson 1975; Doeringer and Piore 1971). Efficiency wage theory suggests that the higher wages available in the organisation's internal labour market will have two main effects. First, it will prevent employee turnover because employees will not be able to command the same salary levels in the external market. Therefore, the losses associated with leaving the firm will encourage employees to exert more effort on behalf of the organisation. This is based on the assumption that an employee's skills are generally firm specific, such as familiarity with a particular working environment, a group of colleagues and the organisation's systems and processes (Stevens 1999). This can be clearly seen in the financial services sector, where organisations have had quite distinctive and discrete administrative systems.

In Williamson's transaction costs theory (Williamson 1975), firms rationally choose seniority-based pay systems because the information and system costs of specifying and monitoring individual performance contracts are considered too high. Internal labour markets are also seen as beneficial by human resource theorists, who argue that they enhance employee commitment through increasing employee identification with the firm (Benson 1995; Cappelli 1995). Furthermore, this increased commitment leads to positive economic benefits for the firm in the form of higher levels of productivity, better quality and customer service, as well as lower levels of employee turnover. Therefore, internal labour markets are seen as integral to a high commitment and high performance organisation.

Another important dimension of internal labour markets is that the administrative rules that govern their operation contribute to a set of expectations and psychological behaviours amongst employees. These rules underpin and help develop customs and norms about wage structures, promotion and progression arrangements as well as other aspects of work (Doeringer and Piore 1971). Internal labour markets can therefore help create a stable environment of mutual expectations and obligations – a high trust environment. As a consequence, any change in the administrative rules will have a serious knock-on effect for the psychological dimension of the employment contract.

The reference to administrative rules in the operation of internal labour markets can help us understand developments in salary progression payment systems. While the analytical distinction between internal and external labour markets has been criticised for its utility (Arrowsmith and Sisson 1999), because employer strategies and processes within the firm do not necessarily conform to a 'market' paradigm, the importance of administrative rules, customs and norms in explaining the operation of internal labour markets is a useful and dynamic analytical framework.

It is argued that we are witnessing a shift in the nature of the psychological contract away from a 'relational' model based on long-term obligations and reciprocity to a 'transactional' model where both parties' expectations of the employment relationship are short-term and instrumental (Rousseau 1990). The implications of these shifts in the psychological contract for New Pay systems are discussed later.

So to what extent have the rules governing internal labour market pay progression changed? What evidence is there for a shift towards systems based more on contractual relationships and individual value?

The pressures to change

There were two main sources of pressure for the changes in pay progression systems. On the one hand there was a distinct shift in government policy, especially in the public sector which it could influence most easily. There was also pressure within the private sector from increasing global competition. This forced organisations to restructure their businesses and to question many of their existing practices. In both private and public sectors, changes in business practices led to the increasing contractualisation of the employment relationship, either physically through the reorganisation of work and the subcontracting of key functions, or through an increasing emphasis on individual contracts and external labour markets for employees.

Political pressures

The rise of New Right ideology with the election of the Conservative government in 1979 saw the erosion of the post-war consensus on wages and employment. The collective institutions that had regulated the employment relationship and held together a consensus (albeit with varying success) on pay determination were identified as barriers to efficiency and economic dynamism. The notion of a 'fair wage' and the 'going rate' were seen as irreconcilable with ideas of free markets. Pay was seen as just another factor of production, the level of which was to be set by the interplay of market forces. Gone was any idea of norms, of equity or of best practice.

There were two main thrusts in the Conservative policy towards pay determination – decentralisation and individualisation. The institutional structure that underpinned and sustained established pay structures was steadily eroded over the

1980s and 1990s. Any legal impediments to the working of market forces in the labour market were a target for reform or abolition (as in the case of the Wages Councils). This reform of institutional arrangements governing pay and employment was accompanied by a government rhetoric which emphasised (a) the creation of a link between pay processes and (b) performance and an organisation's ability to pay. The protection afforded by traditional institutions and their effect in creating norms and beliefs about pay levels and differentials evaporated. The Lawson boom of the late 1980s, with its chronic labour shortages in particular parts of the country, saw a pay explosion and a widening dispersion of incomes, leading to the greater disintegration and the fragmentation of established pay structures.

The government embarked on a process of 'marketising' state employment (Pollitt 1993) through compulsory competitive tendering and privatisation. The logic of the market was then diffused from the provision of goods and services into the determination of civil servants' pay. Experiments with pay flexibilities (regional pay variations) for civil servants were tried during the over-heated labour markets of the late 1980s (supporting the principle of decentralisation) but were unsuccessful. From 1990, however, the Major government continued to push forward both the notion of decentralised pay determination and performance-based payment systems for the public sector through initiatives such as the Citizen's Charter (1991: 7), which stated: 'Pay systems in the public sector need to make a regular and direct link between a person's contribution to the standards of the service provided and his or her reward.' By the mid-1990s all civil servants' pay encompassed some performance-based element. The shift to more individualised pay systems was less successful in other parts of the public sector, where it remained the preserve of mainly management and professional grade staff.

The key thrust of government policy has been, and continues to be, even under 'New Labour', to make the pay of public servants contingent on performance, preferably individual performance. Proposals to reform teachers' pay are based on this principle, while the assessment of individual teachers' classroom performance, as well as exam results, continues the reforms started under the previous administration. Interestingly, the lessons learned by the private sector in its longer-term experimentation with these payment systems have not been necessarily taken on board by the government. The CBI has recently (*Financial Times*, 23 April 1999) advised that the government should separate pay and performance appraisal and furthermore that it should not seek to link pay to performance until the performance management system has had time to settle down. The extent to which such pragmatism will be listened to by a government keen to demonstrate that it is 'fixing' education within an electoral cycle is open to question.

Pressure from organisational change

The other pressure for change in pay progression systems came from the global competition facing private sector organisations. Organisational restructuring has led to the fragmentation of firms' internal labour markets and, with it, the emergence of a new paradigm for white-collar employment. In particular, the move by large corporations to what Lash and Urry (1987) have described as 'disorganisation', has had a profound effect on employing organisations' structures and processes. This embodied a move away from functional interdependence, vertical integration and centralised bureaucratic control towards functional autonomy and horizontal integration through network structures.

Employers have made decisions to externalise activities that can be provided more cost-effectively by the market. Typically these have covered ancillary services (catering, cleaning and security) but firms are increasingly outsourcing functions such as IT and administration, key sites of white-collar employment. We are seeing, furthermore, the development of new forms of white-collar employment, most notably the dramatic growth in employment in 'call centres'. These are estimated to employ just under half a million people (or 2.5 per cent of the working population) and are anticipated to more than double in the next five years (Fernie 1998).

The effects of the 1992 recession combined with the growing diffusion of information technology to reshape white-collar employment. Information technology enabled firms to restructure and to reduce the levels of management previously required to monitor and calibrate larger, more bureaucratic organisations. Layers of middle managers were removed and those remaining managers' roles were changed and extended. Spans of control widened, team-working (or at least the rhetoric) became more commonplace, and managers were encouraged to adopt managerial styles that complemented these changed working practices.

This process of delayering had two major implications. First, internal labour markets were fragmented and reshaped according to a new logic. In the old hierarchical structures, career development happened through functional 'silos'. However, in the new organisation work is increasingly cross-functional, done in teams and with much greater delegation of responsibility for targets and objectives. This is supported by evidence from WERS 1998, which found that 65 per cent of workplaces had formal team-working for most employees and 61 per cent operated a system of team-briefing (Cully *et al.* 1999). Career development moved from a vertical and functional logic to a horizontal one entailing the broadening of skills and responsibilities. As a result, promotions are fewer and the steps between levels much steeper. The move to flatter structures has considerable implications for payment systems; moreover the failure to 'thoroughly overhaul performance-management and reward systems' (Quinn *et al.* 1996) has been identified as one of the reasons why flatter organisations experience difficulties in gaining the full efficiencies from these new organisational forms.

Skill and responsibility levels have grown significantly as a result of this restructuring. One important feature of employers' response to technological change and competition has been the raising of skill levels through job enrichment and redesign. The increasing skill demands in work can be seen in a number of areas. First, employers are demanding higher levels of educational attainment for entry-level jobs, with 'A' levels becoming more important as a minimum requirement for many white-collar occupations. Employers requiring at least 'A' level qualifications rose from 25 per cent to 35 per cent between 1986 and 1992 (Gallie *et al.* 1998). Furthermore, these increased skill levels also worked their way through into higher pay: 'Within every occupational class those whose skills had increased received higher gross hourly earnings than those whose skills had remained unchanged ... the effect appears to have been virtually identical for men and women' (Gallie *et al.* 1998: 35).

Organisational strategies and changes have driven the fragmentation and reconstitution of white-collar internal labour markets. These pressures have seen the rise of a white-collar proletariat at one end of the spectrum (i.e. in the 'light satanic mills' of the call centres) and the growth of employment among highly skilled, knowledge workers at the other (in high-tech industries, consultancy and the professions). These diverse, recursive and inter-related developments have served to question the assumptions underpinning salary progression payment systems, and have led to their fundamental reform in a number of key respects.

The period saw a growing experimentation with payment systems at firm level as the constraints of national- and industry-level collective agreements were cast off. With the absence of strong industry pressures and deregulation of the collective bargaining environment, this provided a permissive context in which employers have had unparalleled freedom to experiment with new pay arrangements. This suggested a move to organisation-based payment systems away from industry-based ones, as firms were able to take more account of their particular operating environment and managerial objectives in order to develop their own approach to payment systems.

So what are the theoretical implications of these changes?

The diffusion of 'New Pay' ideas

Whilst internal labour market theory provides the frame for salary progression payment systems and underlines the importance of administrative rules in the pricing of labour, other perspectives are helpful in taking account of the changes in these administrative rules (i.e. away from seniority to performance). We need to understand not only the factors that might explain emerging managerial strategies, but also how the practices related to these strategies are diffused and spread throughout the economy.

Managerial strategies are shaped by a range of constraints and choices that are shaped by both internal and external forces (Purcell and Alhstrand 1994). The internal labour market structure and the rules governing a salary progression payment system, whilst fitting the organisational circumstances of stable markets and steady growth, might not be as appropriate in rapidly changing markets and discontinuity. Changing the rules then becomes an imperative, and managerial rhetorics are likely to concentrate on the inefficiencies of these rules and the need for change. Often these rhetorics are articulated through 'new' approaches to organisational management.

One of these approaches has been the notion of strategic reward management. The so-called 'New Pay' paradigm implies that a new set of choices should now feature in any organisation's approach to payment system design. The distinguishing feature of the 'New Pay' paradigm is that competitive advantage can be achieved through the better fit of reward policies and practices to business needs. If a characteristic of the 'New Pay' is the desire to relate reward more closely to the objectives of the organisation, what does this mean for pay practices? One of the defining features of this new approach is the drive to link reward to measures of organisational and individual performance. Kessler and Purcell (1992) argue that organisations' use of performance-related pay is being shaped by objectives that are no longer traditional (i.e. the desire to recruit, retain and motivate labour). Their detailed case study work in both public and private sector organisations found that managerial strategies for these pay schemes reflect motives such as culture change or organisational transformation. Performance-related pay was seen to play more of a symbolic role, communicating to employees a new strategic intent and model for the future. Performance-related pay was therefore part of building aspirations amongst the workforce and management.

The contradiction in the concept of 'New Pay' is that it not only marks a departure from how firms traditionally think about pay but also prescribes the adoption of quite distinctive payment systems and practices. It has come to be strongly associated with developments in performance pay, such as linking pay to competencies, using team-related bonuses and, in terms of grading systems, adopting approaches such as broad-banding. The central assumption underpinning the 'New Pay' is the link between business strategy and pay choices. Far from determining the adoption of a specific group of pay practices, this suggests that firms appraising their pay would be as likely to choose so-called traditional payment systems (i.e. piece-rate or indeed incremental salary progression systems) as newer systems such as competence-based pay.

In the words of one of the leading exponents of the strategic reward, 'The New Pay is not a set of compensation practices at all but rather a way of thinking about the role of reward systems in a complex organisation' (Lawler 1995: 16). An important differentiating characteristic is that the New Pay will also seek to align employee interests with those of the firm. This is often seen to operate through the closer integration of organisational performance, individual performance and rewards. Gomez-Mejia (1993: 43) argues that:

> The emerging paradigm of the field is based on a strategic orientation where issues of internal equity and external equity are viewed as secondary to the firm's need to use pay as an essential integrating and signalling mechanism to achieve over-arching business objectives.

The implication of the strategic pay perspective is that we would expect considerable and growing diversity of pay policies and practices within firms as they seek to achieve higher levels of competitive advantage. In theory, we might therefore expect to see two firms in the same product market seeking differentiation not only through traditional means such as technology, protected markets, economies of scale, etc. but also through how they configure and manage their internal payment systems (as well as their total human resource management approach). Thus, broadly similar groups of white-collar employees in two different firms in the same product market may be subject to different pay policies and practices. Unfortunately there is little or no research to date that can help us establish whether this is indeed the case.

It has also been suggested that pay systems design can form part of a distinctive approach to human resource management that is important in conferring competitive advantage. It is argued that to replicate and imitate pay systems is inherently problematic because of the causal ambiguity and different configurations of organisational capabilities that underlie the design and implementation of these pay approaches. These properties of payment systems make them sources of competitive advantage (Gerhart *et al.* 1996).

Another theoretical perspective suggests that we may see greater conformity and similarity in firms' choice of payment systems. Institutional theorists (Di Maggio and Powell 1983; Scott and Meyer 1994; Tolbert and Zucker 1983), argue that organisations respond to pressures in their environment by conforming to accepted ways of doing business, so that they will appear legitimate to customers, investors and other agents who provide important resources to the firm or with whom there exist important relationships (i.e. regulatory bodies, the state). The norms about how businesses should be managed or structured are products of the interplay of cultural, historical, social and other environmental pressures arising from the dynamics of sources such as professions, government, unions and the administrative legacies of firms themselves.

The end product of these interactions and iterations is that we are likely to see more similarity than difference in terms of the structures and practices of organisations. So, for example, as New Pay practices (such as linking pay to individual performance) come to be seen as more acceptable ways of doing business, an increasing number of firms from across a range of industries will adopt this practice.

Three mechanisms have been identified by which organisational practices may become more diffused and institutionalised as new norms. First, firms may be forced to adopt new practices because of political or legal pressures. We might interpret the diffusion and adoption of performance pay schemes in the public sector from this perspective. Second, firms may imitate what other organisations are doing because they are unsure about how they should respond to environmental pressures. Therefore, they look at what they regard as successful benchmark firms and seek to adopt their practices. Quite often these 'best practices' are promulgated by consultant firms, academics and professional bodies. Consultancy firms, in particular, mindful of future income streams and the need to develop new products to generate market demand for their services, are also influential in encouraging the adoption of specific practices. This diffusion is aided by their regular presentations at conferences on pay and reward. Furthermore, these conferences often have the same line-up of companies promoting their particular approaches. Indeed, any conference of competence-based pay would be incomplete without organisations such as ICL, Bass Brewers and Glaxo-Wellcome.

The third mode through which new approaches become institutionalised is by normative processes. A particular pay practice may be endorsed by an influential body that has a high reputation amongst employers. For example, the CBI (Confederation of British Industry) or IPD (Institute of Personnel and Development) may advocate certain practices and this creates a norm which organisations feel under pressure to conform to.

These three mechanisms and the wider framework of institutional theory are useful in understanding the dynamics and pattern of diffusion of New Pay practices. Whereas employer interest and take-up of New Pay forms (such as performance-related pay) can be seen to have been encouraged by these mechanisms, the decision by firms to drop or modify such schemes is likely to be a product of their experience with other practices. One specific characteristic of these New Pay arrangements is the emphasis on employee assessment, which raises a complex set of issues around the measurement of individual performance.

So what is the evidence? To what extent have firms restructured their payment systems for white-collar employees in order to take account of changes in organisation strategy, structures and processes? How widespread is the 'new order' – a salary progression system based on performance assessment or some other market-based criterion rather than one based upon seniority or age?

How prevalent are New Pay progression systems?

A major problem in assessing the growth of salary progression systems linked to performance is the lack of data using consistent measures. The government's annual *New Earnings Survey* (NES) provides information about the composition of employee earnings (i.e. overtime pay, shift pay, payment by results and profit-related pay) over time for different occupational groups. Unless an employee receives a separate merit payment (which can be identified as payment by results), there is no way of determining how an employee is paid. The category called 'all other pay' (which includes basic pay) does not distinguish between the method of progression for salaried workers (seniority, age, performance, skills acquisition or competence). This does not help us understand the extent to which salary progression systems for white-collar employees have shifted from using rules based on seniority to rules based on performance. Addressing these specific weaknesses of the NES, Casey *et al.* (1992) found that individual performance-related pay was indeed of growing importance in a survey of over 200 firms in two local labour markets (Leicester and Reading).

The Workplace Industrial Relations Survey (WIRS) conducted in 1990 (Millward *et al.* 1992) found that around 45 per cent of workplaces had merit or individual performance-related pay and this tended to be higher in larger firms in the private sector. A further study in 1991 conducted for the Institute of Personnel Management (IPM) and National Economic Development Organisation (NEDO) (Cannell and Wood 1992) was able to differentiate between manual and non-manual employees and between a number of different forms of performance-based pay. Around 40 per cent of the 372 organisations covered in the survey used 'merit pay' for white-collar employees, a figure broadly comparable with WIRS. This survey found that just over a quarter of individual performance-related pay schemes had been introduced in the previous five years, which gives an indication of the growing take-up of such practices. It is also noticeable, however, that a third of all firms had schemes that were over ten years old, which suggests that some firms had been long-term users of these payment systems and management staff were more likely to be covered (58 per cent of firms) than secretarial, clerical and administrative staff (45 per cent).

The IPD conducted a follow-up survey in 1997 (IPD 1998) which looked at more recent experiences with performance pay. Based on a 23 per cent response rate (and 1,158 responses), it is the most up-to-date survey on such payment systems (at least until further analysis based on WERS 1998 is published). Like previous surveys, however, it is skewed towards larger organisations and its repre-sentativeness has been questioned (IDS 1998). The benefit of this survey is that it has concentrated specifically on individual performance-related pay and (when published in its entirety) may provide a very useful insight into the workings of these pay systems. Overall, the 1998 survey found that 43 per cent of organisa-tions 'operate at least one form of performance pay scheme for either their managers or non-managers', whereas the 1991 survey recorded that 47 per cent of private sector companies had performance-related pay for non-manuals. Whilst the design of the two surveys does not help with comparability purposes (e.g. different measures of pay and occupational classification are used), there is prima facie evidence that performance pay may not be diffusing as widely as might have been expected.

Furthermore, the 1997 survey suggests that 40 per cent of firms have individual performance pay for managerial staff compared to 58 per cent in the 1991 IPM/ NEDO survey (Cannell and Wood 1992). Once again the coverage appears to have fallen. This may be due to different measures adopted by each of the surveys and it may indeed be the case that the 1997 survey is more precise in its definition of individual performance pay. However, the magnitude of the change (given that we were expecting a shift in the other direction) is what is of interest.

If we look at non-managerial staff, the picture is even more confusing. Whereas the 1991 survey found that 56 per cent of organisations had individual perform-ance pay for their secretarial, administrative and clerical staff, in the 1998 survey only 25 per cent of organisations had performance pay for non-managerial grades. Even if we allow for some occupational blurring, this does appear surpris-ingly low.

There is some consistency between the two surveys in the proportion of organ-isations that have introduced individual performance pay in the last few years. The 1991 IPM/NEDO survey (Cannell and Wood 1992) put the figure at 27 per cent for organisations introducing such schemes in the previous five years, where-as the 1997 IPD survey places it at 24 per cent (a slight fall in the rate of diffusion of this New Pay practice). This slowing down in the take-up of individual per-formance pay schemes is also echoed by Industrial Relations Services. It states that:

While merit pay remains an important feature of the UK remuneration landscape – in our 1996 annual review of pay prospects, six in ten respondents paid at least one group of employees for individual performance – its spread has been checked. In the twelve months to September 1993, there were 218 merit-based pay awards listed on the IRS pay databank. By September 1996, this number had grown to only 227.

(IRS 1997)

One striking difference, and one that may help in understanding the figures from the two IPD surveys, is the number of firms that have dropped individual performance pay schemes. The IPM/NEDO survey (Cannell and Wood 1992: 44) concluded 'that there is virtually no evidence of PRP schemes being withdrawn, although the survey discovered that, like all payment schemes, they are reviewed and substantially revised from time to time'. However, several years later quite a different picture emerges – nearly one in four organisations (23 per cent) had dropped their PRP scheme since 1990 (IDS 1998).

Commenting on the number of firms dropping PRP revealed in the IPD survey results, the specialist pay organisation, IDS said:

This is a striking revelation because it is a far larger number than any previous survey has revealed. To an extent it reflects dissatisfaction with performance pay in some public sector organisations, such as local authorities and NHS Trusts, which are well represented in this survey. However, it also points to one unavoidable conclusion. There has been a great deal of flux over the past few years. Many organisations have adopted a new system, found it unsatisfactory and moved on, often reverting to their old approach – or a modified version of it.

(IDS 1998: 8)

One explanation for the slow-down in the diffusion of individual performance pay may be related to internal labour market structures. Given that these surveys predominantly report the activities of much larger public and private sector organisations which have been the traditional home of internal labour markets, it may be the case that those firms that have easily changed (or been forced to change because of government pressure) their seniority-based salary progression systems to performance-based ones have done so. Either other firms do not have the same incidence of internal labour structures and therefore have no need to reform payment systems along these lines or they have changed their payment systems in other ways. For example, they may have introduced organisation-wide profit bonus schemes or experimented with team- or group-related bonuses.

In summary, the evidence on the spread of individual performance-related pay is in itself open to scrutiny. Whilst there is evidence of an increasing interest in this form of payment system, there are also indications that employers are not adopting it as widely as we are led to believe. Also, there is growing evidence that a significant minority of organisations have abandoned such pay practices. This raises the inevitable question as to why this should be the case. In the next section we look at the problems associated with performance-based pay progression.

Performance-based pay progression

Incremental, seniority-based salary progression systems relied on the assumption that performance improved with length of service and that seniority was as good a proxy measure for performance improvement as any. The interest in measuring and improving employee performance gave rise to 'performance management' as an influential management paradigm. Although the exact definition of performance management is difficult to pin down because of the diverse range of practice that organisations describe as performance management (Bevan and Thompson 1991a), the assessment of individual performance is invariably a core component of such an approach.

This emphasis on individual performance and assessment and on the development of supporting organisational systems and processes has been seen as one element in the broad thrust of corporate strategy towards the individualisation of the employment relationship (Kessler and Purcell 1992). Firms have been identified as having two main approaches for supporting this strategy of individualisation: (a) reward focused and (b) development focused (Bevan and Thompson 1991b). In some cases organisations use the link to pay to inculcate a new individualist philosophy and culture, whereas others seek to achieve this through an emphasis on the development of skills and abilities.

These two approaches reflect deeper-seated philosophies about the management of people in organisations and find resonance in notions of 'hard' and 'soft' human resource management as well as earlier perspectives on motivation (e.g. MacGregor's Theory X and Theory Y modes of managing). However, regardless of the context of the performance management movement of the latter half of the 1980s, there are specific issues that are raised about the assessment of individual performance and its implications for payment systems. The shift from age- or seniority-based progression systems for white-collar employees meant that organisations needed to develop methods and processes for measuring individual performance. There are in practice two broad approaches that firms can adopt: (a) to measure individual outputs (i.e. the 'what' of performance) or (b) measure individual behaviours (i.e. the 'how' of performance) (Williams 1998).

The evidence on employer use of both sorts of assessment is limited and contradictory. The most authoritative and representative data source is the Workplace Industrial Relations Survey (WIRS). In 1990 it found that subjective managerial assessment for the purposes of awarding white-collar pay increases was much more widespread than the use of output-based incentives. About one-third of establishments used this form of assessment and it was two to three times as common as output-based incentives (Millward *et al.* 1992). However, a smaller-scale survey of performance management practices in the UK (Bevan and Thompson 1991a) found that firms were using objective measures to a greater extent because of the problems with subjective measures.[1] Since both methods are based on discriminating between the relative performance levels of individual employees, albeit on a different basis, there are inherent risks that decisions will be made based on poor or inadequate information. Measurement error is one of the most problematic areas in any consideration of the new basis for salary progression payment systems.

The 'principal-agent' model, which has shaped labour economists' work in the area of incentives, suggests that there is an important role for the clear specification and measurement of the performance output required if incentive schemes are to be effective (Marsden and Momigliano 1995). A growing body of work now questions the ability of managers to specify and measure individuals' performance correctly. A burgeoning literature from the field of work psychology has produced considerable evidence to suggest that manager–subordinate assessments of employee performance can be influenced by a broad range of non-job related factors which, in themselves, may carry disproportionate weight in performance evaluations (Landy and Farr 1983). Various studies of managers' appraisals have demonstrated low levels of inter-rater reliability when evaluating the performance of the same employee. For example, a review by King *et al.* (1980) found that the upper limit for the correlation between appraisals by different supervisors of the same employees was 0.6 per cent.

The potential influences on inter-rater reliability have been identified as falling into three broad categories: organisational factors, managerial characteristics and individual (recipient) characteristics (Landy and Farr 1983). Whilst organisational characteristics such as the profitability and nature of its product market may determine the size of the pot available for performance pay increases, it may also indirectly shape managerial assessment behaviour through the imposition of quotas and a consensus that salary costs need to be contained.

Managers' decisions can also be shaped by other factors. For example, a manager may award higher assessment ratings because the employee has similar characteristics or their own appraisal rating may influence their evaluation of subordinates (i.e. a low personal rating of themselves may encourage them to be harsher on their own staff). Similarly, the supervisor's affiliation needs might encourage them to make little or no differentiation between the performance of their employees.

As for employees, age, gender and ethnicity may all play a role in influencing appraisers' evaluations. In a review of gender bias in twenty-four appraisal-based systems, Nieva and Gutek (1980) found that sixteen demonstrated pro-male bias. Research by Bevan and Thompson (1992) found that managers both look for and value different traits and characteristics in men and women subordinates. For example, they found that women were often rated highly if they conformed to stereotypical 'female' behaviour traits (i.e. being dependable, perceptive and committed) but not if they exhibited archetypal male traits (i.e. dynamic, aggressive, ambitious). Evidence of both race and gender bias in assessment have been found across the civil service. The union IPMS found that appraisal results showed 'ethnic minority staff to have been marked significantly lower than white staff; and women to have been marked significantly higher than men' (Labour Research Department 1992: 9).

This research and the broader body of evidence from the psychology field suggest that it is difficult to eradicate the potential for bias, although the better development of performance criteria, the training of supervisors and close monitoring of the process can all play a part. However, these all increase the costs of using such systems and would appear to contradict some of the tenets of transaction cost theory (Williamson 1975).

Organisations have responded to these concerns about the effectiveness and reliability of the measurement of individual performance by introducing more sophisticated processes (thereby increasing monitoring costs of the employment system). Consequently, there has been a growing interest in peer assessment as a way of broadening the information taken into account when assessing an individual's performance. Typically this has developed in professional organisations where senior managers are too removed from the day-to-day activities of their subordinates to have a rounded picture of performance. At managerial level 360-degree assessment processes are becoming increasingly popular as a means of management development. However, many organisations have shied away from making a direct link between these more rounded measures of performance and pay awards, since they are understandably concerned that it may encourage dysfunctional behaviours (Kettley 1997).

While the spread of performance pay was almost as widespread in the public sector as in the private, there were distinct differences in gauging its success. The 1998 IPD Survey found that 'public sector respondents are much less likely to feel that their schemes are generating beneficial outcomes for their organisation on virtually every indicator' (IPD 1998: 6). Some 51 per cent of public sector respondents believed that individual performance-related pay was having a negative effect on staff morale, compared to 34 per cent of private sector respondents.

This may reflect the fact that the application of performance-related pay to professional groups within the public sector has been seen by some as part of a long-term process to gain more managerial control over these groups (Sinclair *et al.* 1995; Fairbrother 1996). Combined with devolution of pay arrangements to the organisational level and away from occupational or sector level, performance-related pay has been viewed as part of the extension of the managerial prerogative and is helping to erode 'occupational identities' as well as to undermine the public service ethos (Rubery 1996; Thompson 1993). One of the consequences of the greater adoption of performance-based pay is that the shift away from seniority-based rules gives managers enhanced power and also side-steps collective regulation and social norms of fairness and equity enshrined in collectivist institutions.

As Heery found in a study of local government, however, managerial objectives ranged from the traditional ones of motivating, recruiting and retaining employees to ideas of spreading a 'new philosophy of work', such as greater entrepreneurial behaviours and problem-solving (Heery 1998). In other words, local government strategies are not uniform and are characterised more by their diversity, responding as they do to specific internal and external circumstances. Furthermore, there were inconsistencies in the application of performance-related pay in local government:

> Management motives also appear to be contradictory in that performance-related pay was to be used to secure both compliance and commitment for employees and underpin seemingly different kinds of employment relationship, low trust and contractual on the one hand and high trust and diffuse on the other.
>
> (Heery 1998: 77)

The public sector is distinctive both in terms of its high levels of trade unionism and its large share of professional employees (also more likely to be unionised). These features generate their own specific set of constraints and issues for the operation of performance-based progression pay schemes. Furthermore, because the output of the public sector is predominantly in non-traded services, the commercial imperatives experienced by private sector organisations are not experienced to the same degree. However, this is not to say that the budgetary pressures exerted by central government do not impose as difficult a discipline as the market.

Competence-based pay progression

White-collar employment in many of its forms is now increasingly about behaviours and attitudes displayed at work in addition (or indeed instead of) any display of specific sets of analytic skills or skills based on a theoretical understanding (Mayhew and Keep 1999). The importance of social skills has been driven by the growth of the service sector, where the competitiveness of the industry is highly dependent on the ability to deal with people effectively. Gallie *et al.* (1998) reckon that, in 1992, 46 per cent of the participants in their survey were doing some form of 'people-work' (i.e. caring for people, dealing with clients and customers or organising others). The growing significance of these attributes has given rise to the term 'aesthetic labour' to describe these forms of service sector employment. Furthermore, because these skills are not conventional, there have been problems in describing and understanding their development. This has given rise to a greater interest in competencies and the measurement of softer skills through competency-based approaches.

Performance management systems are one means through which employers can seek to shape the nature of this aesthetic labour. This can be seen in the use of service 'scripts' in areas such as call centres and telephone-based support services as well as in the more orthodox retail environments. The formulaic dialogue and enthusiastic attitude are all rehearsed in order to achieve higher sales and customer satisfaction, or 'delight'.

Not only are firms interested in what outputs their staff give, they now want to determine and control 'how' these outputs are generated. So in the case of white-collar employees in a professional organisation with high levels of customer contact and team-working, the organisation may describe the behaviours it expects from its employees in different situations. The growth of 'competencies' (or behavioural traits) as a management tool of control has been one of the interesting developments of the 1980s and 1990s. This has extended from recruitment, selection and development areas into pay. However, the risk of bias and discrimination in competency-based assessment and reward systems has been identified as a potential danger (Strebler *et al.* 1997).

A number of pressures are encouraging employers to experiment with competence-based pay. As firms have delayered and flattened their organisational structures, competence-based forms of development and reward have become more attractive. The old structures supported and reinforced the idea that organisations comprise jobs and these jobs are sets of specific accountabilities, responsibilities and activities. Under these new structures, the job paradigm is seen as less effective because it leads to inflexibility and creates a culture and mindset that resists managerial objectives to adapt continuously to changing organisational circumstances. According to one of the proponents of competence-based organisation,

> [i]n a traditional organisation, the concept of jobs often substitutes for the analysis of work processes and the skills needed to perform them. The challenge in a competency-based organisation is to focus on what individuals need to be able to do in order to make the work processes operate effectively.
>
> (Lawler 1994: 76)

The implication of this new type of organising principle for businesses is that

> the movement from a more static job-based model to a more fluid skills-development/skills-utilisation model raises issues concerning both the motivation and self-concept of individuals and how organisations define the accountabilities of individuals and/or teams.
>
> (Lawler 1994: 79)

These adaptive properties, or organisational competencies, are seen as a key source of competitive advantage in the future (Prahalad and Hamel 1994). Competency-based approaches to human resource management (including pay) are of increasing interest because they appear to address many of the problems that stem from these new organisational realities. First, when vertical career progression is no longer available, competencies are seen as providing a new language to talk about performance and development that is no longer linked to the old structures. Second, it can encourage lateral career moves within the business that might otherwise have been resisted by employer and employee. Third, it is based on the acquisition of skills and competencies, which serves to raise the overall effectiveness of the workforce thereby improving performance and increasing its ability to adjust to changing circumstances. Connected to this last point, companies may also be able to mix longer-term core competencies with shorter-term competencies when they are forced to change very quickly (i.e. through the introduction of a new organisation structure or technology).

In reality, competence-based pay is more written about than practised. Even in surveys of large, sophisticated organisations that have the managerial resources and skills to introduce such systems, the take-up has been very low and a wide variety of approaches are common place (IRS-HRBS 1998). The IPD survey on performance pay (IPD 1998) found that competency-based pay applied to 6 per cent of managers and 11 per cent of non-managers. In the USA, where many of these new trends in pay practice are pioneered, even the journal of US pay professionals, the *Compensation and Benefits Review* stated in an editorial on competency-based pay: 'The applications of true competency pay – as a replacement for merit pay or even job evaluation – are few and far between. It might happen for a couple of years and then go away' (Bennett 1996: 49).

Although competencies are still not that widely used as criteria for determining individual pay progression, there is an increasing interest in their use (Towers-Perrin 1997). There is also considerable confusion amongst practitioners and consultants about the definition and application of competencies to pay (Strebler *et al.* 1997). In a critique of competency-based individual pay schemes, Sparrow (1996c) argued that there are two levels of competency – one that is trait based and not open to change and one that can be developed. These two levels of individual competency are difficult to differentiate and most performance assessment systems, Sparrow argues, are not sufficiently robust to make such a differentiation. This means that 'if organisations want to vary rewards to match different competencies, they need to differentiate in-built behaviour from those that can be developed' (Sparrow 1996c: 24).

The pace of rapid organisational change and the need to improve the performance and flexibility of staff, whilst controlling pay bill costs, suggest that interest and experimentation are likely to continue. This is more likely to be among larger businesses which have a reputation for sophisticated and well-developed approaches to human resource management generally. Smaller businesses, without well-resourced human resource management functions, have a lesser capability to design, implement and manage such approaches. Drawing upon institutional theory once again, we might expect that small and medium sized enterprises (SMEs) would be more likely to adopt competency-based pay when it has become established as a 'norm' amongst successful businesses. As it becomes a norm and the understanding of the transferability of such practices improves, SMEs may be encouraged to imitate these approaches both for legitimacy reasons but also because they are correlated with business success.

Criticisms of competency-based pay have focused on its potential to encourage wage-drift and pay bill inflation, in much the same way that skill-based pay schemes have been found to. Inevitably, the corporate pay technicians and consultants have come up with myriad ways to combat these problems. Whereas the inflationary aspects of competency-based pay have caused concern for some organisations, others have seen it as a way of controlling their pay costs:

A major economic advantage for Unisys UK under the new competency-based system is that pay increases are much better targeted than under the old pay-for-results system. The use of the matrix means that those employees with competence scores in the top 10 per cent and earning the lowest salary receive the highest increases, while the bottom 35 per cent of performers should receive no merit-increase at all. This represents a significant tightening up of performance pay, since under the old pay structure, only 5 per cent of staff did not qualify for performance increases.

(MTI 1997: 59)

The emphasis on rewarding particular behaviours and attitudes is an important characteristic of competency-based pay schemes. This linkage of pay to behaviours in such an overt fashion has repercussions for how employees perceive the employment relationship between themselves and their employer. In the next section we consider the impact of the new pay progression systems upon the employment relationship.

The impact of the new systems

The psychological contract between employer and employee is seen as a set of unwritten reciprocal expectations, beliefs or perceptions which characterise the behaviour of both parties in the employment relationship as well as future obligations or promises. Whereas some writers have seen it in individual cognitive processing terms (Rousseau 1990), others have situated it within broader organisational and social processes (Herriot and Pemberton 1996). Sparrow and Cooper (1998) have suggested that assessment of the psychological contract depends on whether it is seen as a 'state of mind', a 'frame of reference' or an individual difference or 'trait'. The first two definitions lend themselves to the idea that the contract can therefore be managed and that employers have the power to alter policies and practices to change perceptions of the contract. The last definition implies that this is a deep-seated phenomenon and is not amenable to change, but is one of the factors that may shape an individual's reactions to change at the workplace.

The notion of the psychological contract is complex and difficult to operationalise. Guest (1998) suggests that it lacks sufficient theoretical rigour to inform practice but that it is a valuable tool in understanding the consequences of changes in organisational policy and practice. The importance of such an analytic construct for salary progression systems cannot be underestimated, as such payment systems are based on a set of mutually agreed rules, which in themselves generate a set of reciprocal obligations and commitments. As we have noted, this 'deal' has changed significantly with the increasing importance of performance-based reward. The issue at hand is whether pay reforms have damaged the psychological contract, or have had a neutral impact, or have moved it on to a more positive plane. A related issue, but one not dealt with here, is the extent to which pay is a means of managing the psychological contract.

If we consider the various elements of the psychological contract – trust, motivation and commitment – we find that studies that have explored the relative contribution of a variety of human resource management practices (including reward) to these goals have found that payment systems do not play an important role. A longitudinal study, albeit only of manufacturing enterprises (West *et al.* 1997), found that higher levels of commitment and business performance were more strongly related to job design and employee involvement. Work by Guest and Conway (1997) similarly placed a low emphasis on reward systems. Ironically, Guest found that 'contrary to much of the evidence on performance management and performance-related pay, the perceptions of fairness are higher in those organisations that do make some attempt to link pay and performance' (Guest 1998).

The potential for performance-based pay to destroy trust and commitment has been demonstrated most effectively in the public sector. Marsden and Richardson's (1994) study of the operation of performance pay in the Inland Revenue over a five-year period found that employees had low levels of confidence in the fairness and equity of the system. They found that over half of the line managers operating the system agreed that 'performance pay has reduced staff willingness to co-operate with management' compared to a fifth five years before. Furthermore, when they explored lateral trust relations between staff, they found that they were much more likely to agree that it had 'caused jealousies' and 'discouraged team-working'. Most interesting of all, performance pay appears to have increased the instrumental and transactional dimension of the psychological contract, with less than a third agreeing that 'personal satisfaction of my work is enough incentive' compared to nearly two-thirds five years previously. The experience of the Inland Revenue appears to be reflected across the public sector as a study of the Employment Service, NHS Trusts and head and deputy head teachers demonstrated (Marsden and French 1998).

Because most of the studies of the employee impact of performance-related pay have been located in the public sector realm, it may not be possible to generalise these findings more widely. However, there are a number of private sector studies conducted in the UK that have shown similar results (Thompson 1992). Performance management systems operating in the public and private sectors may have been based on a philosophy of constraining and prescribing employee behaviour. Given that the studies of West *et al.* and Guest and Conway have pointed to autonomy and trust as two of the important building blocks of employee motivation and commitment, it may be the case that a poorly designed and implemented performance management system with a pay link can only serve to undermine the psychological contract.

The IPD survey on performance pay found that 40 per cent had changed or significantly modified their schemes over the previous two years (IPD 1998), which can be interpreted in a number of ways and on different levels. From an organisational perspective, it suggests that schemes have been poorly designed and are being reviewed. This suggests that the running costs of performance-based schemes may be quite high if, as the IPD data suggest, so many need to be changed. Another implication of the amount of tinkering and change that is associated with such schemes is that they may be further undermining certain elements of the psychological contract. If, as other evidence suggests (e.g. Thompson 1993; Marsden and Richardson 1994), many of these schemes are not perceived as 'fair' in how they both evaluate and reward performance, it could be that employee trust is being eroded by continual change and modification in payment systems.

If trust is a difficult value to create and sustain within organisations (Fox 1973), fragile by nature (Baier 1986), and takes a long time to create (Gambetta 1988), frequent changes in payment systems may be one (albeit of many) organisational processes that are currently eroding trust relationships in organisations. Given the strong messages sent by pay systems, their importance in changing the basis of the psychological contract should not be underestimated, which is presumably one reason why so many organisations have seen it as a tool to change organisational culture (Kessler and Purcell 1992; Cannell and Wood 1992). However, the evidence seems to suggest that the impact of these changes has been predominantly negative in terms of employee morale and motivation, although managers are often reported as more positive on its operation (Kessler and Purcell 1992). Another interpretation is that the ongoing modification of these schemes is a consequence of employers responding to employee dissatisfaction with various aspects of their operation, often revealed through employee attitude surveys (IRS 1997).

Indeed, several studies of the employee impact of performance pay schemes have found that, whilst employees support the principle that individuals should be rewarded for their performance, most are unhappy with the way it operates in practice (Thompson 1993; Marsden and Richardson 1994). The fact that the principle finds support amongst employees appears to justify the continual redesign of these schemes by personnel practitioners and reward consultants.

Organisations may be overlooking stability in payment systems as a source of competitive advantage and not fully understanding how frequent changes in pay system design can serve to undermine the achievement of prized organisational objectives such as commitment, motivation and trust. If a more positive psychological contract can help organisations to be adaptive and flexible, in the context of rapidly changing organisational circumstances, firms need to understand how changing payment systems can potentially undermine this contract. Furthermore, given that most reviews of reward systems are undertaken with consultancy support, it may prove more cost effective in the long run to make fewer changes. The reality, however, is that firms which have embarked on the pay performance road may be locked into a cycle of review and repair that is difficult to escape. As the IPD data suggest, this may be one of the reasons why some firms have been dropping performance pay completely (IDS 1998).

Summary and conclusion

This chapter has looked at changes in salary progression payment systems over the last two decades. It has located the importance of salary progression systems within the prevailing internal labour market models dominant during this period and has drawn attention to the rules that governed the pricing and allocation of labour. Internal labour markets have changed their form and structure as a result of a broad range of pressures ranging from the dominance of neo-liberal economics, increased competitive pressures forcing organisational re-design, the diffusion of new technologies, and new developments in managerial policy and practice. The rules governing the operation of these internal labour markets have shifted as a result of these pressures and thereby influenced the nature of salary progression systems.

The dominant shift has been away from progression rules based on seniority or age to a consensus that some form of performance measurement should be the main determinant. We have drawn attention to some of the problems associated with defining performance, particularly as employers' demand for skills has shifted strongly (partly reflected by the growth of service sector employment) from what we conceive as traditional skills to social skills or 'competencies'. Difficulties in measuring performance on these dimensions may increase the chances of discriminatory practice and, because of the diffuse nature of performance, may decrease employee confidence and trust in such systems.

The new salary progression systems mean that there is a much greater role for managers. The managerial prerogative has been increased through the introduction of performance-based pay systems where managers exercise some discretion in systems that are centrally designed and monitored but locally managed. This process has supported the increasing individualisation of the employment relationship, a dominant characteristic of employer and government strategy in this period.

One of the features of the new salary progression systems is the frequency with which they have been changed. The decay of such systems would appear to be fast, according to survey and case study evidence. Whereas this may be good news for reward consultants or remuneration managers, the implications for employee morale and trust may not be so rosy. The frequency of change and the growing sophistication of some payment systems may be doing more to harm the psychological contract than to support or renew it. This is because elements of the contract, such as trust, take years to build and, because of their fragility, can be damaged very easily. Furthermore, payment systems are one of the objective correlatives of how an organisation treats and values its employees: poor management of this aspect is likely to rebound very quickly on employee morale.

One of the ironies of the changes in payment systems is that they may be delivering the exact opposite of what firms believe they should be achieving. Instead of higher levels of commitment, employee dissatisfaction with the equity of assessment methods may be generating lower levels of trust and also encouraging less attachment to organisations. In other words, performance-based progression systems may, in some of their forms, be reinforcing transactional relationships between employer and employee with their low levels of reciprocal obligations and commitments. This, in turn, is likely to produce rigidities and internal inefficiencies as firms grapple with organisational change and transformation. These problems are becoming increasingly apparent as employers recognise that greater information sharing in today's leaner, knowledge-based organisations is a key to sustainable competitive advantage.

The political economy was identified as a permissive factor encouraging a climate and legislative environment in which the individualisation of the employment relationship could be actively pursued by employers. The rise to power of 'New Labour', on recent evidence, does not point to any dramatic shift in policy towards public sector pay. The managerialism that characterised the 1980s looks set to continue. Although this approach is part of a wider pattern of public sector reform across OECD economies, the government does have some room to make strategic choices over forms of pay and also the speed with which reforms are implemented and the scale of resources devoted to such changes. There is some evidence that this is happening with government accepting that performance pay in the NHS will be linked to 'team' performance whereas in the education sector it will be based on individual teacher performance.

Whilst our review has pointed to conflicting evidence on the rate of the diffusion of new performance-based progression systems, they are undoubtedly one of the most important developments in salary payment systems in the last two decades. Institutional theory may help us understand the likelihood of the future pattern of diffusion of these practices. However, the effectiveness of such systems remains open to much greater scrutiny.

Note

1   The different results may be explained by the fact that the IPM Survey was skewed towards larger organisations.

References

Armstrong, M. and Murlis, H. (1998) *Reward Management*. 4th edition. London, Kogan Page.

Arrowsmith, J. and Sisson, K. (1999) 'Pay and working time: toward organisation based arrangements?' *British Journal of Industrial Relations*, 37 (1): 51–75.

Baier, A. (1986) 'Trust and anti-trust'. *Ethics*, 96 (2): 231–60.

Bennett, U.J. (1996) 'The editor's comments'. *Compensation and Benefits Review*, 28 (6): 49. November/December.

Benson, J. (1995) 'Future employment and the internal labour market'. *British Journal of Industrial Relations*, 33 (4): 38. December.

Bevan, S. and Thompson, M. (1991a) *Performance Management in the UK*. London, Institute of Personnel Management.

Bevan, S. and Thompson, M. (1991b) 'Performance management at the crossroads'. *Personnel Management*, November: 36–9.

Cannell, M. and Wood, S. (1992) *Incentive Pay*. London, Institute of Personnel Management.

Cappelli, P. (1995) 'Rethinking employment'. *British Journal of Industrial Relations*, 35 (4): 46. December.

Casey, B., Lakey, J. and White, M. (1992) *Payment Systems: A Look at Current Practice*. Research Series No. 5. London, Employment Department.

Citizen's Charter (1991) Cmnd 1599. London, HMSO.

Compensation and Benefits Review 28 (6). editorial.

Cully, M., O'Reilly, A., Millward, N., Forth, J., Woodland, S., Dix, G. and Bryson, A. (1998). *The 1998 Workplace Employee Relations Survey. First Findings. ESRC, ACAS, PSI.* October. London, Department of Trade and Industry.

Di Maggio, P. and Powell, W. (1983) 'The iron cage revisited: institutional isomorphism and collective rationality in organisational fields'. *American Sociological Review*, 48 (2): 147–60.

Doeringer, P. and Piore, M. (1971) *Internal Labor Markets and Manpower Analysis*. New York, Lexington Books.

Eyraud, F., Marsden, M. and Silvestre, J.J. (1990) 'Occupational and internal labour markets in Britain and France'. *International Labour Review*, 129 (4): 501–17.

Fairbrother, P. (1996) 'Workplace trade unionsm in the state sector'. In Ackers, P., Smith, C. and Smith, P. (eds) *The New Workplace Trade Unionism*. London, Routledge.

Fernie, S. (1998) 'Hanging on the telephone'. *Centrepiece*. Spring 1998. Centre for Economic Performance. London, LSE.

Fox, A. (1973) *Beyond Contract*. London, Faber & Faber.

Gallie, D., White, M., Cheng, Y. and Tomlinson, M. (1998) *Restructuring the Employment Relationship*. Oxford, Clarendon.

Gambetta, D. (1988) 'Can we trust trust?' In Gambetta, D. (ed.) *Trust: Making and Breaking Co-operative Relationships*. Oxford, Blackwell.

Gerhart, B., Trevor, C. and Graham, M. (1996) 'New directions in compensation research: synergies, risk and survival'. *Research in Personnel and Human Resource Management*, 14: 142–203.

Gomez-Mejia, L. (1993) *Compensation, Organisation Strategy and Firm Performance*. USA, Southwestern Publishers.

Graham, N. (1994) 'Did Keynesianism work?' In Pollard, S. (ed.) *Jobs and Growth: The International Perspective*. London, Fabian Society.

Guest, D. (1998a) 'Is the psychological contract worth taking seriously?' *Journal of Organisational Behaviour*, 19. Special issue.

Guest, D. (1998b) 'The role of the psychological contract'. In Jardine, S.J. and St John, Sandringham (eds) *Trust, Motivation and Commitment: A Reader*. London, Strategic Remuneration Research Centre.

Guest, D. and Conway, N. (1997) *Employee Motivation and the Psychological Contract*, Issues in People Management Report No. 21. London, Institute of Personnel and Development.

Heery, E. (1998) 'A return to contract? Performance-related pay in a public service'. *Work, Employment and Society*, 21 (1): 73–95.

Herriot, P. and Pemberton, C. (1996) 'Contracting careers'. *Human Relations*, 49 (6): 757–90.

Incomes Data Services (IDS) (1998) 'What's happening to performance pay?', *IDS Focus 85*. London, Incomes Data Services.

Institute for Employment Research (IER) (1999) *Review of the Economy and Employment 1999*. University of Warwick, IER.

Institute of Personnel and Development (IPD) (1998) *Performance Pay: Summary Report.* London, IPD.

Industrial Relations Services (IRS) (1996) 'Team reward: part 2'. *Pay and Benefits Bulletin* 400.

Industrial Relations Services (1997) 'Rewarding competencies in the Bank of Scotland'. *Pay and Benefits Bulletin* 445: 42.

Industrial Relations Services (IRS) – Human Resource Business Strategies (HRBS) (1998) *Competence-based Pay.* London, Industrial Relations Services.

Kessler, I. and Purcell, J. (1992) 'Performance-related pay: objectives and applications'. *Human Resource Management Journal,* 2 (3): 34–59.

Kessler, I. and Purcell, J. (1995) 'Individualism and collectivism in theory and practice: management style and the design of pay systems'. In Edwards, P. (ed.) *Industrial Relations: Theory and Practice.* Oxford, Blackwell, 337–68.

Kettley, P. (1997) *Personal Feedback: Cases in Point.* IES Report No. 326, January. Brighton, Institute of Employment Studies.

King, L., Hunter, J. and Schmidt, F. (1980) 'Halo in a multi-dimensional forced choice performance scale'. *Journal of Applied Psychology,* 65 (2): 507–16.

Landy, F. and Farr, J. (1983) *The Measurement of Work Performance.* New York, Academic Press.

Lash, S. and Urry, J. (1987) *The End of Organised Capitalism.* London, Polity Press.

Lawler, E.E. (1994) 'From job-based to competency-based organisations'. *Journal of Organisational Behaviour,* 15 (2): 3–15.

Lawler, E. (1995) 'The New Pay: a strategic approach'. *Compensation and Benefits Review,* 27 (4): 14–20. July.

Labour Force Survey (1998) London, Office of National Statistics.

LRD (1992) 'The perils of performance pay'. *Bargaining Report,* 191: 7–13.

Market Tracking International (MTI) (1996) *Reward Strategies.* London, Haymarket Business Publications.

Marsden, D. and French, S. (1998) *What a Performance: Performance Related Pay in the Public Services.* London, LSE. Centre for Economic Performance.

Marsden, D. and Momigliano, S. (1995) 'Economic theory of incentives and its implications for the design of public service performance-related pay schemes'. Unpublished paper. London School of Economics.

Marsden, D. and Richardson, R. (1994) 'Performance pay? The effects of merit pay on motivation in the public services'. *British Journal of Industrial Relations,* 32 (2): 243–61.

Mayhew, K. and Keep, E. (1999) 'The assessment: knowledge, skills and competitiveness'. *Oxford Review of Economic Policy,* 15 (1): 1–16.

Millward, N., Stevens, M., Smart, D. and Hawes, W. (1992) *Workplace Industrial Relations in Transition.* Aldershot, Dartmouth.

Nieva, V.F. and Gutek, B.A. (1980) *Women and Work: A Psychological Perspective.* New York, Praeger.

OECD (1993) *Private Pay for Public Work: Performance Related Pay for Public Sector Managers.* Public Management Studies. Paris, OECD.

Osterman, P. (1994) 'How common is workplace transformation and who adopts it?' *Industrial and Labor Relations Review,* 47 (2): 173–88.

Pollitt, C. (1993) *Managerialism and the Public Services.* Oxford, Blackwell.

Prahalad, C.K. and Hamel, G. (1994) *Competing for the Future.* Cambridge, Mass., Harvard Business Press

Purcell, J. and Alhstrand, B. (1994) *Human Resource Management in the Multi-divisional Firm.* Oxford, Oxford University Press.

Quinn, J.B., Andersen, P. and Finkelstein, S. (1996) 'Leveraging intellect'. *Academy of Management Executive*, 10 (3): 7–16.

Rousseau, D. (1990) 'New hire perceptions of their own and their employer's obligations: a study of psychological contracts'. *Journal of Organisational Behaviour*, 11 (2): 389–400.

Rubery, J. (1996) *Trends and Prospects for Women's Employment in the United Kingdom in the 1990s*. Report for the European Commission Network on the Situation of Women in the Labour Market, Working Paper, UMIST, Manchester.

Scott, W.R. and Meyer, J.W. (1994) *Institutional Environments and Organisations: Structural Complexity and Individualism*. Thousand Oaks, CA: Sage.

Sinclair, J., Seifert, R. and Ironside, M., (1995) 'Market-driven reforms in education: performance, quality and education in schools'. In Kirkpatrick, I. and Lucio Martinez, M. (eds) *The Politics of Quality in the Public Sector: The Management of Change*. London, Routledge.

Sparrow, P. (1996a) 'Careers and the psychological contract: understanding the European context'. *The European Journal of Work and Organisational Psychology*, 5 (4): 191–205.

Sparrow, P. (1996b) 'Transitions in the psychological contract: some evidence from the banking sector'. *Human Resource Management Journal*, 6 (4): 75–93.

Sparrow, P. (1996c) 'Too good to be true?' *People Management*, 5 Dec.: 22–9.

Sparrow, P. and Cooper, C. (1998) 'New organisational forms: the strategic relevance of future psychological contract scenarios'. *Canadian Journal of Administrative Sciences*, 64 (2): 356–72.

Stevens, M. (1999) 'Human capital theory and UK vocational training policy'. *Oxford Review of Economic Policy*, 15 (1): 16–33.

Strebler, M., Thompson, M. and Heron, P. (1997) *Skills, Competencies and Gender: Issues for Pay and Training*. Report 333. Brighton, Institute for Employment Studies.

Thompson, M. (1992) *Pay and Performance: The Employer Experience*, IMS Report 218. Brighton, Institute of Manpower Studies.

Thompson, M. (1993) *Pay and Performance: The Employee Experience*, IMS Report 258. Brighton, Institute of Manpower Studies.

Tolbert, P.S. and Zucker, L.G. (1983) 'Institutional sources of change in the formal structure of organisations: the diffusion of civil services reform, 1880–1935'. *Administrative Science Quarterly*, 28 (1): 22–39.

Towers-Perrin (1997) *Learning from the Past: Changing for the Future*. London, Towers-Perrin.

West, M., Patterson, M., Lawthorn, R. and Nickell, S. (1997) 'Impact of people management practices on business performance'. *Issues in People Management*, 22. London, Institute of Personnel and Development.

Williams, R.S. (1998) *Performance Management: Perspectives on Employee Performance*. London, Thomson Business Press.

Williamson, O. (1975) *Markets and Hierarchies*. New York, Free Press.

7 Benefits

Ian Smith

Benefit is a generic word used to describe the components of a substantial element of the total remuneration provided by employing organisations to their workforces. This element is a unique part of the payroll in that it is normally provided in non-cash form, although there are significant exceptions to this. Benefits include a wide variety of provisions variously termed 'fringe benefits', 'perquisites', 'allowances', 'subsidies', 'assistance', 'leave', 'discounts' or simply 'something extra'. These terms cover an extensive range of benefit categories which can be regarded as 'extras' to wage and salary. The words in common use, however are 'benefit', 'perquisite' and 'allowance'.

Perquisite (or perk) refers to something of value which is in addition to payment for work, for example, the company car. An allowance can be a sum of money, usually fixed, given at regular intervals to cover special circumstances, for example, protective clothing allowances for work in potentially unhealthy environments. In recent years 'benefit' has superseded 'fringe benefit' (i.e. elements of remuneration on the fringe of pay) and is used as the word to encompass the wide range of benefits in kind in addition to cash payments which companies provide for their employees. These may include items such as pensions, cars, work-related equipment, training and education, accommodation, loans, childcare assistance, discounts, sick pay and maternity leave with pay over and above statutory requirements.

This chapter questions the rationale for benefits provision and suggests an alternative to current approaches. The first half of the chapter highlights the scale and the cost of benefit provision. We explain something of the history and provide an overview of recent developments in major benefit areas – pensions, company cars, sick pay, family-friendly benefits, holidays and insurance. Benefits can operate as 'hygiene factors' or 'motivators' and the second half of the chapter argues for more attention to the links between benefits provision and performance.

Introduction

Benefits represent a substantial cost for employers and can account for up to 50 per cent of basic salary (see example below). They therefore have a significant, though sometimes unrecognised, value to the employee. Yet the returns on this investment are rarely considered. It can affect recruitment, retention and motivation, and can impact on individual performance or contribution to the organisation. Research by IDS (1999) suggests that there have been significant changes in the provision of benefits over the last twenty-five years, which have added considerably to the cost of such packages. Moreover, as IDS indicates, improvements in benefits tend to be permanent commitments. A retrospective review of Hay surveys of benefits from 1970 to 1998 reveals that the major changes have been in paid holiday entitlement and the spread of eligibility for a company car (IDS 1999: 4).

The example below gives an indication of the importance of benefits within the overall costs of a typical company.

Example: financial services company

In this company, with 850 employees, the benefits package for every one of the company's workers is worth substantially more than the cash given in recognition of performance and contribution. The issues which cause most rancour and debate are concerned with the annual cost of living rises – at less than 3 per cent for the past five years – and the performance-based payments provided in lump sums at the end of the financial year. The substantial benefits 'packages' rarely if ever feature in the debate. Yet benefits are a high cost in relation to basic salary.

The figures below show the cost of benefits as a percentage of basic salary for various employee groups within the company.

Chief executive and main board directors	45%
Senior management	35%
Middle management	30%
Senior professional advisers	35%
Professional advisers	30%
Clerical and administrative	17%

For most groups these benefits have a higher value than the performance-related payments in the company, which range between 5 and 20 per cent of basic salary, depending on employee group. How can we explain this paradox? Reasons probably include the following:

- the failure of management in the past to regard benefit provision as anything other than an irksome but inevitable outlay
- a preference for cash among employees
- the almost automatic provision of benefits to management, professional and white-collar groups in some industries
- short-term preoccupations with pay now rather than future provision and security on the part of employees

- employer failure to communicate the real value of benefits to staff
- benefits as an expected and accepted part of the reward package, causing little or no excitement
- inherited benefits provision which current management feel unable to change
- a view among management that some benefits are unavoidable because of the influence of government policy
- the change and uncertainty now affecting benefits provision.

Whatever the causes, we can conclude that benefits deserve more attention. The history of remuneration provides little evidence of purpose and direction for benefits in employment: short-termism and reactive decision-making dominate some hundred years or more of development, to the point where this has become an entrenched part of the approach to managing benefits.

A brief history of some key benefits

For our purposes here we begin at the end of the nineteenth century. Pensions were provided to army and navy officers from an early date and civil servants were included in the nineteenth century. It was, however, enlightened or philanthropic business owners – the Rowntree family and the Lever Brothers among others – who were the first to develop welfare facilities and benefits for employees. Innovations included sick pay, on-site healthcare, subsidies for meals, and housing for their workforces. Despite these early visionary initiatives, the development of benefits provision in the UK has been a slow affair, usually favouring white-collar groups (Price and Price 1994). Until recently, employers have taken the view that the provision of basic social welfare benefits for the majority of the workforce was government's responsibility. In some cases, government has provided a legal obligation on employers to provide minimum levels of benefit to workers (e.g. sick pay, redundancy pay, maternity pay, lay-off pay).

Pensions

Pensions have their roots in local community provision in the form of relief funds for the elderly, sick and destitute during the reign of Richard II. In the nineteenth century friendly societies and some trade unions provided a form of insurance against need and set a framework for fund management. Yet the majority of working-class people often only had recourse to the workhouse and the Poor Law when incapacity forced them to retire. Working men's societies also played a role in growth at the end of the nineteenth century but records reveal only one, the Northumberland and Durham Miners' Permanent Relief Society, paying significant pension benefit covering some 4,000 workers by 1901 (Hewitt Associates 1991). The increasing cost of subscription put pressure on these arrangements by the beginning of the twentieth century. The company pension emerged in the second half of the nineteenth century and provision by the beginning of this century was greatest in the civil service, banking and among railway managers and clerks. The emphasis upon pension provision for white-collar employees has continued since that time (Torrington and Hall 1987) and only in recent decades has there been a significant growth in provision for manual workers.

State encouragement for individual pensions was extended during the twentieth century. Asquith's Liberal government introduced the first state pension scheme in 1908, which was made more generous and realistic in 1925 by Winston Churchill under pressure from the Labour Party, by then strongly represented in Parliament. For the first time a majority of the poorest two-thirds of the UK population could contribute to and 'draw' from a pension.

Employers responded to these initiatives from the 1920s with many larger companies adopting the elements of Trust Law as a means to introduce and administer occupational pensions funds, a development reinforced by the introduction of tax exemption for employer and employee contributions in the 1921 Finance Act. The growth of occupational pensions was to some extent a reaction to external pressures, particularly working-class militancy during and after the First World War, the presence of a Labour Party strongly represented in Parliament, and the experience of the 1926 General Strike, which prompted large employers to move away from the 'hire and fire' practices of the nineteenth century and seek to create a long-term identity of common interest with their employees (Webb and Webb 1926; Flanders 1965; Child 1969). Company pensions were intended to encourage employee retention and foster long service.

Not until the arrival of a Labour government with a large majority in 1945 did any further developments take place in the pensions scene and again these were government-driven in the form of the 1946 National Insurance Act, which introduced the contributory state pension for all. This was modified by the Boyd Carpenter Plan of 1962. The latter introduced graduated state pensions and first allowed company occupational schemes to contract out of the state scheme, a measure designed to increase company scheme membership but in reality doing so for white-collar employees only.

State pensions have proved persistently expensive. By 1986 Margaret Thatcher's government, concerned at the escalating cost of the State Earnings Related Pension Scheme (SERPS) and, consistent with the policies of privatisation, drastically reduced SERPS. Employees were also permitted to transfer out of occupational schemes and into private personal schemes, allegedly to encourage career mobility and remove the pension 'trap' which reduced the pension entitlement of the individual who changed employer.

The extension of employer (or occupational) schemes from white-collar to blue-collar employees has been a slow process (Torrington and Hall 1987; Taylor and Earnshaw 1995). Company pensions are a high cost benefit intended to encourage employee retention and to reinforce loyalty to the company. At a time when employers are less able to create 'lifetime' employment opportunities, they may question the value and role of this investment.

The importance of pensions

Pensions represent deferred income for employees and occupational or company pensions are usually the most costly supplement to the payroll. Membership of such schemes is estimated to include more than 10 million employees in the UK. Schemes are normally financed by employer and employee contributions to a fund (each contribution defined as a percentage of salary), although the ratio of the two contribution sources can vary considerably with directors and key staff often offered non-contributory pensions. Over the past twenty years, pension arrangements and legislative requirements have changed considerably. The administration of pension schemes requires specialist knowledge usually provided through a trust comprising employer, employee representatives and independent members or trustees. However, company or occupational schemes are only one of three ways for funding pensions: a pension can be derived from contributing to three types of arrangement: state, personal and occupational.

State pension arrangements

State pension arrangements pay the full benefit to a male recipient of 65 years of age who has contributed for at least forty-four years and to a female recipient aged 60 or over who has at least thirty-nine years' contributions. Since 1978 the government has run a State Earnings Related Pension Scheme (SERPS) which took over from the graduated scheme introduced in 1962, although the link to earnings has now been severed in an attempt to contain costs. Membership of an appropriate occupational (company) or personal pension scheme allows for employees to contract out of SERPS. The 1998 state pension was £64.70 for single persons and £103.40 for a married couple.

Personal pensions

Private or personal provision became part of the 'alternative' benefits scene in 1988, as a result of government-inspired changes contained in the 1988 Finance Act, permitting money purchase plans outside of the normal employee route to retirement provision. Employees were allowed to choose whether to belong to an occupational scheme provided by their employer or to make their own arrangements. This was particularly attractive to those employees who expected to have mobile lifestyles and frequent job changes. Employees were also encouraged to move from the SERPS scheme to private personal pension plans, with a financial incentive to do so. These personal pension schemes have not so far greatly helped in improving UK pension provision as a result of misselling, frequent under-provision and excessive administrative charges. They are popular with the self-employed and those employees not covered by an occupational scheme by choice or force of circumstances (because the employer does not offer a scheme). A new form of personal pension is the stakeholder arrangements for 'middle income' groups (Department of Social Security 1998).

Occupational or company pensions

These have been traditionally operated by employers on a purely voluntary basis, although compulsion may well result from the 1998 Green Paper proposals. As mentioned above, they are administered by trusts in compliance with legal and Inland Revenue regulations. Certain favourable tax exemptions for contributions and scheme income have helped promote their popularity, and company pensions take the following forms:

- Defined contribution final salary schemes
- Defined contribution money purchase schemes

Defined benefit or final salary schemes are the most popular; the pension paid is a proportion of the employee's salary on or shortly before retirement, usually half or two-thirds of that salary. A variation on final salary arrangements allows for the member's salary to be increased during a year and then averaged, creating the 'average salary scheme'. The defined fraction of salary that is the actual payment received is the product of the member employee's length of time in the scheme and the amount of pension accrued.

Defined contribution schemes determine pension payments on the basis of the amount actually 'purchased' by the employee. Unlike final salary schemes, the pension cannot be guaranteed because it depends on the performance of the pension fund out of which the pension is sourced and not the level of final salary attained by the employee. Because of this feature, contribution schemes have been seen as less costly to the employer, although not as generous to the pensioner as defined benefit arrangements.

Some large organisations with extensive pension schemes offer a mix of defined benefit and defined contribution arrangements to cater for different age groups, using defined contribution arrangements for younger employees and defined benefit arrangements for older, long-serving employees. The increasing cost of defined benefit or final salary schemes has encouraged this shift, with defined contribution arrangements being offered to new or younger employees. Recent changes in taxation on pension funds may herald an even more substantial move away from final salary schemes to contribution schemes.

Various aspects of tax exemption helped the popularity and growth of occupational pension schemes during the twentieth century. Not least of these exemptions was the right of pension funds to claim the 20 per cent corporation tax payable on the share dividends received from investments, which helped funds to grow and ensured their financial viability or strength. With UK pensions holding more than £500 billion of shares, this tax credit system has been of significant value. In the July 1997 Budget the Chancellor announced the end of the Advance Corporation Tax Credit and the cost to pension funds is estimated at some £50 billion in the period 1998 to 2007. The switch from defined salary to defined contribution schemes may strengthen as a measure to reduce payroll costs in the face of the withdrawal of corporation tax exemption.

Popularity, change and the 1998 Green Paper

Against the background of recent changes introduced by government, company or occupational pensions remain very popular. The 1997 survey by the National Association of Pension Funds revealed that 87 per cent of new employees were joining their employers' schemes (NAPF 1997). Almost half of all schemes provide automatic membership. The absence of compulsion has been criticised by the TUC as it leads to poverty in retirement for lower-paid workers. The same survey found that 70 per cent of schemes excluded all part-time workers and 19 per cent had weekly hour thresholds that must be satisfied for pension scheme membership. This position has been challenged by a succession of rulings on part-timers' employment rights by the European Court of Justice. To respond to the situation the government has introduced proposals for compulsory membership, stakeholder pensions, and a wider shake-up of pension arrangements (DSS 1998).

Compulsory membership of occupational schemes will be reinforced for employees who cannot prove that alternative arrangements will offer comparable or better levels of provision. Stakeholder pensions will not compete with occupational schemes. The government's proposals should significantly increase pension scheme availability for the five million low-paid and part-time employee groups, but provision for lower-paid and peripheral workers will still depend on a state pension rather than the potentially greater benefits of a company scheme. Thus occupational schemes continue as before, but employers will be able to insist on membership by employees who do not possess the same or better pension arrangements.

The government's overall hope is that by the year 2050 the government will fund 40 per cent and private sources (personal stakeholder and company) 60 per cent of pension provision. This would reverse the current state of affairs whereby the state bears the brunt of pension costs. There is a real implication here for the costs associated with company pensions, particularly when coupled to the introduction of compulsory membership.

Pensions as performance lever

The company pension remains the most effective route for employees to secure retirement income. Stakeholder and personal pensions come nowhere near them in terms of provision because there is no employer to make a further contribution to enhance pension earnings. Company schemes provide more than a retirement income; the range of benefits provided is more generous than those deriving from other arrangements, as outlined below.

Early retirement has become popular in the last two decades as organisational contraction and redundancies result in people leaving employment before normal retirement age. This option may be less widely available in future as the age profile of the population changes and fund surpluses reduce. The NAPF (1997) survey found that 55 per cent of company schemes reduce pension benefit for voluntary retirement by 6 per cent for each year not worked beyond the early retirement date. When early retirement is instigated by the employer, the figure falls to 31 per cent of schemes; a further 18 per cent of schemes top up the pension with a discretionary payment. It is not usual for schemes to allow for early retirement below age 50 and it is common for the retirement date to be within ten years of normal retirement. Early retirement through ill health is provided by some 97 per cent of occupational schemes with 34 per cent using permanent health insurance arrangements, according to NAPF (1997).

Death-in-service benefit payable on the death of a scheme member to the spouse and/or dependants can take a variety of forms, as revealed by NAPF Surveys (1993, 1995, 1997):

- spouse's pension (provided by 99 per cent of occupational schemes)
- dependant's pension (not common and discretionary)
- children's benefit (payable in about 70 per cent of schemes)
- lump sum payments (provided by 96 per cent of schemes)
- death in retirement (provided by 98 per cent of schemes).

Death in retirement results in a pension for the spouse in 98 per cent of schemes; it is payable at a rate of one-half of the deceased member's pension in 75 per cent of schemes. Two-thirds of pension is paid in 14 per cent of schemes.

The value of pension payments in occupational schemes is normally increased on an annual basis. The NAPF survey (1997) found that 25 per cent of schemes increase payment on a guaranteed basis; 48 per cent give guaranteed plus discretionary increases; and the remainder give discretionary increases only. Almost all schemes periodically uprate the pension payment and average figures for the 1990s are given in Table 7.1. This range of benefits within company pensions represents substantial potential income for recipients on retirement and at other points in their careers.

We could ask why a pension worth one-half to two-thirds of salary is not as powerful a motivator as a bonus worth 10 to 15 per cent. Pensions are a

Table 7.1 Occupational pension payment, annual increases for year ending December 31

Year	Increase (%)
1990	6.2
1991	7.8
1992	7.0
1993	4.1
1994	2.3
1995	2.3
1996	3.3

Source: Watson's Statistics, 1996

substantial factor of reward with an unrealised contribution to performance, but research reveals that management does not necessarily recognise this potential, let alone ensure its realisation. Rarely do management objectives for pensions go any further than attraction (Casey 1993; Taylor and Earnshaw 1995), if objectives are defined at all (Terry and White 1997). Such short-termism may well cause companies to reduce outlay on pensions in the face of rising taxation and costs. These costs cannot be ignored with employer contributions ranging from 15 to 20 per cent of employee salary (Moore 1987). A performance-based strategy could use pension provision as a 'lever' that could offset costs. Such a development would be a 'sea-change' in many organisations, for performance seems hardly to be considered, as underlined by Terry and White (1997): 'why is it that virtually none of our respondents could furnish evidence to support their assessment of the effectiveness of pension schemes?' For company pension schemes to be a performance-related benefit requires new attitudes from management. Yet issues of short-termism versus strategy surface in the benefits debate in connection with the most expensive benefit provided by employers.

Perquisites

These benefits in kind, which cannot immediately be converted into cash by the recipient, emerged in the sixteenth century as an element of government patronage to reward senior public figures for their services. They were usually given on retirement; persisting (although constantly abused) until William Pitt's introduction of income tax in 1799. Ever since then the taxation of perquisites has been a concern (almost a preoccupation) for governments and the civil service. To this day perquisites provide a means of avoiding taxation, and the uncapping of employer contributions to National Insurance still leaves an advantage to the non-cash compensation known as perquisites. Their provision therefore has for some decades now been moved along by employer reactions to government policies on pay restraint and taxation, leading to the UK having the highest levels of company car provision in Europe plus complex patterns of benefits in kind.

Company cars and fuel benefit

The second most expensive outlay after pensions, namely company cars remains a very popular benefit despite increases in taxation over two decades. The popularity of this benefit or perquisite persists for several reasons, including the availability of vehicles to a higher standard than would be afforded out of salary and the avoidance of running costs and 'hassle' associated with car ownership. Increased taxation for the company car is underway in the first years of the twenty-first century, not on the perk value of the car but the pollutant, traffic congestion and resource consumption elements. From April 2002 taxation will be based on exhaust emissions to replace the current system based on mileage and age of the car.

There is already evidence of moves to cash alternatives. In a recent survey

Watson Wyatt (1998) found that 91 per cent of respondents provided company cars in 1998 compared with 95 per cent in 1995 and 98 per cent in 1993. Slightly more than half of the companies (54 per cent) offered a cash alternative. Take-up of this alternative, at only 14 per cent of eligible employees, is slow however (*Pay Magazine* 1998). In Table 7.2 the substantial value of cars is contrasted with the cash alternative offered to sales staff, where a car is deemed a necessity.

Values and allowances for jobs where the car is not a necessity are for what are termed 'status cars' and the 1998 figures by salary level are outlined in Table 7.3. We can see that the value of a car allowance in Tables 7.2 and 7.3 ranges from 25 per cent of salary at the lowest salary to 9 per cent of salary at the highest salary level. These are significant sums of money exceeding the normal range of any performance-related payments and should and could be realistically defined and used by management to influence employee recipient performance.

Car fuel benefit can similarly represent real value to employees, particularly when extended to private usage. For a driver covering 20,000 miles per year in a car averaging 28 miles per gallon, it is worth some £2,400 over the year. When combined with the value of the company car, these sorts of figures once again provide evidence of what is a substantial potential lever for performance. Even higher levels of taxation on these benefits leave the recipient with a net gain.

Despite increases in taxation, the company car and company fuel remain

Table 7.2 Cars and cash alternatives – necessary usage

Job	Median list price £	Median car allowance £
General sales manager	24,000	6,780
Regional sales manager	20,000	5,780
Sales representative	15,090	4,290
National account sales manager	19,543	5,696
Customer service engineer	16,200	4,920

Source: Watson's Statistics, 1998

Table 7.3 Cars and cash alternatives – status provision

Salary level	Median list price £	Median car allowance £
Director at £150,000 +	44,000	11,160
Director £100,000–150,000	34,485	9,067
Director £50,000–100,000	27,850	7,560
Director below £50,000	24,380	6,634
Salary £40,000–45,000	20,118	5,700
Salary £28,000–30,000	17,175	4,400
Salary £22,000–24,000	15,162	4,080
Salary below £20,000	15,000	3,780

Source: Watson's Statistics, 1998

valuable benefits and the inelasticity in demand will survive government onslaught in the area of taxation in the immediate future at least. If the full value of the company car is worth between £5K and £10K per annum, this deserves consideration as an influence on employee performance. The costs of car owner-ship and the poor quality of public transport should ensure the continuing popu-larity of the company car as a benefit for many years to come. Depreciation costs, insurance costs, servicing costs and fuel costs are daunting. Even if future choice were limited to cars with lower list prices and better fuel economy, the likelihood is that the company car would continue to be a substantial part of company benefit policies and expense. Even without it, employees lose nothing financially because of the cash alternative. Yet even in the low taxation heyday of the 1970s and 1980s, no evidence surfaced on the use of company cars as a performance lever, which represents a massive opportunity lost.

Sick pay

State Sickness Benefit has been provided since the National Insurance Act of 1911. Additional sick pay provided by the company is more likely to ensure security than performance, and might almost be regarded as a 'hygiene' factor, with company provision traditionally underpinned by significant government provision. Over the last decade government policy pushed the financial burden for sick pay increasingly towards the employer, with the introduction of Statutory Sick Pay (SSP) in 1983. While initially employers were allowed to recoup most of the cost from their PAYE receipts, from April 1995 they can do so only where costs exceed 13 per cent of gross National Insurance Contributions.

Employers are now more centrally concerned with the process and the provi-sion of benefit and the 1990s have seen an increase in the provision of Occu-pational Sick Pay (OSP) schemes by employers, initially to top up the minimal amounts of SSP. As long ago as 1988 some 90 per cent of companies offered an occupational sick pay scheme with 93 per cent of white-collar and 88 per cent of manual workers covered (Smith 1989). Harmonisation has been notable over the last ten years, and the majority of companies now have one scheme for all employees.

The costs are considerable with pay-outs through OSP schemes reportedly costing £11 billion per annum with 8.4 days lost per employee in the working year (Confederation of British Industry 1998). In order to control costs, companies impose strict conditions for eligibility, with procedures for notification and certifi-cation sometimes backed up by home visits and telephone calls to verify absence when it is persistent and to a pattern.

Costs will rise as coverage of schemes is extended. Where effective human resource management practice is established, the process of controlling sick pay may rest primarily on pre-empting the causes of absence in the first place. Sick pay may underpin security, but other motivational factors could underpin the process of reducing absence and sick pay.

Family-friendly benefits

Maternity and paternity leave, compassionate leave, holidays and childcare provision are sometimes termed as family-friendly benefits. Legislation in this area is expanding to meet the demands of women's greater labour force participation. The White Paper 'Fairness at Work' (Department of Trade and Industry 1999) dealt with family-friendly employment, particularly employment and parenthood, and covered issues such as financial support for working families, the application of European Union (EU) social and employment policies, parental and family 'crisis' leave, and maternity leave. The proposals were enacted in the 1999 Employment Relations Act. The first of the benefits to be discussed here relates to expectant employees.

Maternity and parental leave

Provisions for maternity leave were initially made by the 1975 Employment Protection Act which was not generous, and some companies therefore improved on the statutory entitlement. Currently, employers are liable to pay Statutory Maternity Pay (SMP) to qualifying employees and to allow maternity absence for a period of 18 weeks. The SMP can be reclaimed in part from National Insurance contributions. The right of the employee to resume employment after taking maternity leave is protected by employment legislation.

The history of developments in the provision of maternity leave reveals ad hoc and piecemeal changes which led to complex and unequal provision across employee groups and organisations. This has been recognised in the 1999 Employment Relations Act and in line with the EU directive (implemented in December 1999) it recommends the following:

- extended maternity leave of 40 weeks after one year of service
- the right to 'parental' leave
- continuation of the contract of employment during extended maternity leave and parental leave unless formally terminated by either party
- 3 months' parental leave for parents adopting a child
- employees on parental as well as maternity leave to have the right to return to their jobs or a suitable equivalent
- time off for family emergencies regardless of length of service
- protection against dismissal for employees taking the above leave arrangements.

The government's proposals establish minimum entitlements to benefits and, as in many areas, this raises important issues for employers about whether they should improve on statutory provision. Parental leave, for example, is currently unpaid and in practice this may deter the take-up of a valuable benefit. A provision of considerable value to young families has now come to the fore of the benefits agenda with an impact on employee security and goodwill and perhaps motivation that could at least equal or exceed any extra cost to the employer. Although this impact may be difficult to measure – particularly for smaller firms – it should not deter interest in the issue.

Childcare provision

A further key element of government policy is a 'National Childcare Strategy' which aims to 'encourage businesses to provide access to good quality childcare for their employees' (DTI 1999: 31). This strategy is to be linked to EU family-friendly policies. There is no doubt that presently childcare provision is limited in comparison with practice in mainland Europe, and its non-availability can inhibit access to work and career development, for working mothers in particular. Childcare is a very recent feature of the benefits scene in the UK as the growth in female employment during the past twenty years begins to impact, belatedly and slowly, on human resource management policies. Survey results collected by the Department for Education and Employment in 1997 revealed that only 10 per cent of companies offer any kind of childcare assistance, with just 2 per cent providing nursery facilities, 1 per cent sponsoring a local nursery and 2 per cent providing vouchers or cash allowances for use in independent nursery facilities.

The limited growth of childcare provision has been concentrated on the parents of the 'under fives', with a few private schemes reported – that operated by the Midland Bank (now the HSBC) being the most notable. The Midland began childcare in the 1980s to reduce female staff turnover, and in 1997 had 900 nursery places for employees, although many are dependent on partnership arrangements with private nurseries (Working for Childcare 1997). Such partnership arrangements for childcare between the private and public sector – particularly local authorities and the National Health Service – are eligible for government and EEC capital funding. The Working for Childcare Report (1997) cites such arrangements in Leeds City, Kingston-on-Thames and Milton Keynes Local Authorities which have linked up with a range of private and other public sector partnering organisations. Other means for supporting employees with childcare include career breaks and government funding of initiatives taken by Training and Enterprise Councils to expand childcare places. In the year 2000 the government will introduce tax credits to help low-paid families afford childcare.

Childcare provision is likely to grow primarily as a result of government initiatives. Therefore this is beginning to look more like a benefit driven by government vision rather than employer policies – a somewhat similar situation to that of state pensions and sick pay during much of this century. It can therefore be usefully asked if childcare will go the same way as these more established benefits and grow as a state provision, to the point where the expense incurred prompts the state to decide that the cost should be absorbed by employers and perhaps even employees in the future. Thinking through the position of childcare benefit in reward strategies could be usefully started now by employers to anticipate such a development. Again this is a benefit requiring clear communication of its value to recipients, both to influence goodwill and to encourage co-operation on the part of employees in accepting change. The removal of a constraint on career development for working mothers could be a motivator impacting more directly on the performance of those employees.

Insurance benefits

Demand for private health cover grew from the 1970s, resulting in limited growth in company-financed schemes and group schemes in which employees enjoy a discount on the normal premium (Smith 1989). Recent growth in private health insurance has slowed down considerably due to spiralling premiums and employer moves to control costs. A 1994 survey by Remuneration Economics and the Institute of Management (RE/IM) found that company-paid schemes cover directors, senior management and executive staff only. There is no sign of a move to company-paid schemes for white-collar and manual groups, although these employees can subscribe to a voluntary group scheme. Take-up for such voluntary arrangements is at low levels, usually well below 10 per cent, and trade unions have been traditionally hostile. The concentration on director and management groups is set to continue given the issue of rising costs. Provision is therefore linked to status with little evidence of any performance dimension, although the issue has not been researched.

Life and death-in-service insurance is widely available to white-collar employees plus long-term disability cover. The insurance provisions are normally within the terms of company pension schemes and usually give four times' salary life cover; long-term disability cover (or ill health cover) provides up to three-quarters of salary when sick pay stops. Insurance cover for employee accidental death and disability at work or on company business is also common for white-collar groups.

Benefits and taxation

As benefits have grown, governments have come to see them as a useful source of tax revenue. Given the almost inelastic demand for benefits such as company cars, the Treasury has been able to accrue ever-increasing revenues from such sources. There are two categories under the heading of taxation: tax free and taxable benefits. It is important to note that taxation relates to benefits in kind which are given to an employee as part of their remuneration package. Taxation on such benefits has increased markedly since the late 1970s and is subject to precise conditions and rules. For directors and employees whose annual income exceeds £8,500 – normally termed P11D employees – tax is levied on the cost to the employer. That the income limit has not changed for over a decade indicates a trend of increasing tax revenues from an increasing number of employees whose pay has risen above the limit. Taxation of benefits is a complex issue requiring substantial knowledge on the part of payroll managers; it is likely to grow as governments look for new ways of increasing tax receipts. The belief that benefits in kind are a 'clever dodge' to reduce an employee's tax liability is no longer appropriate. Such benefits (taxable or tax-free) are still attractive additions to cash rewards that can represent real value to the recipient; and even after paying tax the benefit still represents a net gain.

Paid holidays

Holidays with pay were the exception until 1938 when the Holidays with Pay Act was passed (Clegg 1976: 218). This empowered statutory wage-fixing bodies to establish them and from this point paid holidays also featured in collective agreements. Fixed holiday periods were once popular in manufacturing, called 'waits weeks', when the whole factory closed for a period, but today the factory 'shutdown' is less common as employers prefer to use plant and equipment for fifty-two weeks a year. Outside of manufacturing, holiday arrangements have been more flexible. Only with the introduction of the 1998 Working Time Regulations (incorporating the European Working Time Directive into British law) did British workers gain a statutory entitlement to paid holidays, although minimum entitlement was already common throughout most of the EU.

The growth of benefits provision

The above brief and partial review of the history of some key benefits reveals a process largely influenced by employer reactions to external initiatives. Growth in benefits provision has been noticeable since the beginning of the 1960s. Between 1964 and 1981 benefits increased from 11 per cent of average pre-tax remuneration to 19 per cent in UK manufacturing (Green *et al.* 1985). The uneven distribution of these benefits – with high-paid employees receiving absolutely and proportionately much more than the low-paid – has been a consistent characteristic for some decades (Brown 1989; Legge 1995; Blyton and Turnbull 1998). Until the 1970s, pension provision other than the state pension, and company cars, subsidised meals, and expenses were not normally available to the manual worker on wages, rather they were the preserve of salaried employees (Torrington and Hall 1987).

Two key developments have contributed to changing this situation, both of them driven outside the domain of employing organisations. First, the 1975 Social Security Pensions Act had a significant impact on pension provision in Britain and by allowing employees to contract out from the state pension it provided an impetus for more staff to join company pensions. Second, the repeal of the Truck Acts (of 1831!) in 1986 took away the right of manual workers to be paid cash in hand and enabled payment by cheque or credit transfer – the methods of payment used for salaried groups. The stage was set for some elements of remuneration to be 'harmonised' for all employee groups.

Harmonisation: a performance link

Harmonisation essentially refers to a process of aligning pay and conditions across white-collar and manual (blue-collar) employee groups. The origins of the process can be traced back to the implementation of the (1979) National Engineering Agreement in October 1981, which reduced the working week for manual employees in the industry to provide for harmonisation of hours and patterns of work with white-collar employees. During the 1980s and 1990s the process spread across different industries, initially covering conditions of service, particularly hours of work, overtime working and payment methods. Changes in benefits were driven by more developed forms of harmonisation.

Single-status working was aimed at standardising conditions of employment. Staff status conferred white-collar employment conditions on manual groups, particularly skilled and technically qualified employees (Smith 1989: 412).

Harmonisation, single status and staff status represented different degrees of rigour in the approach to eroding differentials between the two key occupational groupings. The aims in companies making such moves were not concentrated on standardisation alone. This was a short-term objective to enable the achievement of the longer-term, and we should note strategic, objective for improved performance (in terms of productivity), simplification of payroll procedures and enhanced management of remuneration. Overall improvements in employee attitudes were anticipated, with a spin-off in improved recruitment and retention of staff (Kennedy 1988). Benefits that were particularly subjected to the harmonisation process in the 1980s were pensions (in terms of eligibility, contributions and benefit), paid leave, sick pay, redundancy payments, meals and mobility allowances (Price and Price 1994).

These changes were more than simple modifications to payroll systems and content. They were intended to achieve and to draw on employee goodwill to facilitate the acceptance of irksome elements of change, and the associated uncertainty (Kennedy 1988). Employee involvement in new and more flexible work processes, in new technology and advanced production systems was to be facilitated by the changes to conditions and benefit provisions for manual workers. The ultimate outcome of harmonisation was the development of single-status agreements with integrated pay and benefit structures for all employee groups in support of the achievement of high-performance organisational objectives (Mullins 1986). The integrated and salaried workforce was intended to meet flexible production conditions and changing market demand.

The process of harmonisation, and in particular the move to single-status arrangements in manufacturing companies, might be viewed in retrospect as designed to ensure the achievement of substantial improvements in organisational performance. Harmonisation was intended to facilitate change, with benefits used to provide leverage on employee attitudes and goodwill in pursuit of improved organisational performance. However, the process slowed by the beginning of the 1990s.

Benefits and performance

The single-status initiatives provide a precedent for discussion of the more focused use of some benefits. A start can be made by categorising benefits in terms of the employee behaviours they might influence and the human resource management objectives and organisational objectives they may thereby help to achieve. The starting point for this exercise lies in the links between corporate strategy and the human resource management activities, which include reward management and which in turn embraces employer-based benefits provision. These links are said to be at the heart of human resource management in much of the literature on the subject (Lawler 1987; Hendry *et al.* 1988; Murliss 1992).

In Table 7.4 benefits have been categorised either in terms of their influence on HRM activities and outcomes, or their influence on performance, or both. The performance dimension may be achieved directly or be derived from 'goodwill', 'security' and 'motivation'. Some benefits may impact directly on performance; others may have a less direct, or longer-term influence. It is suggested here that 'goodwill' benefits might be viewed as motivators and, as such, can be a basis for enabling employee co-operation in new approaches to performance improvement. Security may not be significant in terms of performance but it can act as a 'hygiene' factor in that its presence does not enhance performance but its absence can cause a fall-off in motivation and performance (Herzberg 1975). The list in Table 7.4 is not comprehensive and the value and effects of different benefits will vary in practice. However, the table is intended to give perspective to the perceived value or potential usefulness of benefits by category as a basis for appraising their position and role within remuneration systems in support of performance-related objectives.

Table 7.4 suggests that the majority of benefits have implications for employee motivation and performance (Friedman 1990; Smith 1991; Gregg *et al.* 1993; Terry and White 1997). Benefits may have a role to play in helping to achieve business objectives. More effective use of benefits may serve to contain escalating costs associated with their provision. Thus an opportunity is provided for the employer to relate the total benefits package to the particular circumstances faced by the company.

A word of caution is needed however, for benefits will link to company performance only if they are valued by the employee recipients (Perkins 1998). Benefit provision should be evaluated in terms of whether it relates to individual need. It is reasonable to ask if the effort required in the introduction of a performance-based evaluation is justified and also what means are available to give effect to this approach. Discussion now turns to these questions.

The argument so far has been based on the assumption that benefits might be better managed in order to maximise their impact on performance. The viability of this approach will depend in practice on the labour market context and the wider business environment.

Armstrong and Murliss suggested that flexible delivery systems might provide a way to 'key in' benefits to a performance model of reward management

Table 7.4 Benefits characterised by effect

Benefit	Contribution to HRM function	Contribution to performance/ goodwill/security	Motivator or hygiene
Pensions	Attraction, retention, motivation	Performance direct	Motivator
Company cars and fuel	Attraction, retention, motivation	Performance direct	Motivator
Work-related equipment (e.g. computers)	Attraction, retention, motivation	Performance direct	Motivator
Training and education provided by employers (linked to career development)	Retention, motivation	(Goodwill) performance derivative	Motivator
Accommodation	Attraction, retention, motivation	(Goodwill, security) performance derivative	Motivator
Various allowances and expenses	Attraction, retention	(Goodwill) performance derivative	Motivator
Low-interest loans and mortgages	Attraction, retention	(Goodwill) performance derivative	Motivator
House purchase and relocation assistance	Attraction, retention	(Goodwill) performance derivative	Motivator
Expenses	Attraction, retention	(Goodwill) performance derivative	Motivator
Childcare provision	Attraction, retention, motivation	Goodwill	Possible motivator or hygiene
Discounts on company services and products	Attraction, retention	Goodwill	Possible motivator or hygiene
Enhanced leave arrangements	Attraction, retention	Goodwill	Hygiene
Sick pay	Attraction, retention	Goodwill, security	Hygiene
Health insurance	Attraction, retention	Security	Hygiene
Life insurance	Attraction, retention	Security	Hygiene

(Armstrong and Murliss 1991). Their approach, in line with that of Lupton and Bowey (1974), suggested a contingency or 'best fit' approach which involves 'the right reward processes . . . which are right for a particular organisation' (Murliss and Armstrong 1996). The major characteristics of a contingency model of reward management include the 'tuning' of remuneration to organisational culture to help achieve organisational objectives while appealing to the workforce.

In principle, a firm that relies on a key group of employees (or 'core' employees in terms of Atkinson's flexible firm model (Atkinson 1984)) is more likely to focus high-cost benefits on this group. Subcontracting and outsourcing may create a distanced labour force, disenfranchised from job security and benefits. This approach has encountered the following obstacles (Smith 1996):

- Company culture and characteristics can be difficult to identify and measure in terms of their impact on employee rewards.
- Even when measured, management may not understand the impacts and may not be capable of appropriately modifying the reward system.
- Management may not want to devote the time and effort to the design of an appropriate reward system.

Additional to these obstacles, the role of benefits within a contingency model is not at all clear and is completely overshadowed by the preoccupation with incentives in one form or another (Smith 1996).

Competency-related pay provides another example of attempts to identify and reward those 'clusters' of behaviour (the competencies) demonstrated by employees which should play a role in ensuring the success of the organisation. These behaviours are deemed to reflect the core values of the organisation – the corporate objectives and the appropriate approach to the market and customers (Wisher 1994; Smith 1998). Competencies are concerned with the performance-linked characteristics of the organisation and may simultaneously ensure the requirements of a contingency and performance-based model for determining remuneration. The use of competencies as measures of employee performance has received some criticism (Sparrow 1996), but the method remains popular with applications across many well-known organisations in the public, service and manufacturing sectors (Armstrong 1997). Irrespective of any debate about the efficacy of competency-related pay, reports of applications of the method include little reference to the value of benefits within a competency-related remuneration system. This is a major disappointment, given the number of companies now claiming to use this approach in determining rewards.

Benefits and the 'New Pay'

This section raises questions about the ways in which benefits arrangements might be changed and suggests that the tidy prescriptions of the 'New Pay' paradigm may encompass neither employee expectations nor organisational needs.

The 'New Pay' paradigm surfaced in the United States during the 1990s and has been presented as something radically different to traditional methods (Lawler 1986). Schuster and Zingheim (1992) provide the defining features of New Pay which embrace the strategic performance issues and the placement of benefits within a reward model aimed at the achievement of corporate success. The main elements of the New Pay are as follows:

- Remuneration practices including benefits are to support the business strategy.
- Remuneration is for the person not the job.
- Remuneration practices are to be appropriate to the organisation's requirements.
- Remuneration should support team-based and flexible organisations.
- Reward should be given for skills acquisition and performance.
- Rewards help shift the employee's focus to key business objectives, including quality and customer care.

Variable pay is an important element of the New Pay and it is intended that performance will be driven by performance-related or merit bonuses which must be re-earned every year (Heery 1995). Variable pay is designed to provide attractive rewards to staff when company performance is good, but offers less attractive rewards in years when performance falls – the assumption being that employees will be willing to accept this arrangement irrespective of the cause. Such an assumption may be overly simplistic given the backdrop of complex behaviour in organisations.

Following this model, variability of reward might be expected to apply to benefits as well as to cash. There is very real interest in companies in the United States in containing the costs of benefits, particularly in healthcare, which many American employees expect from their employers since little state-funded provision is available. Reducing the cost of benefits is a key component within the New Pay. Whilst the New Pay does not overtly seek to reduce levels of security for employees in the areas of health, pensions and sick pay, the implications of reducing costs and making benefit provision more dependent on performance and contribution rather than length of service is that employees will lose out. The availability of benefits becomes dependent on ability to pay, which in turn is driven by some sense of which human resource costs can and should be passed on to the customer and which cannot.

This approach raises many contradictions and questions. Will employees accept reductions in benefits? Will they shoulder the risks inherent in the New Pay approach and will their expectations align or conflict with objectives and performance levels determined by management? Has management thought through the impact of New Pay in terms of lower levels of goodwill linking to reduced motivation and performance? Variable rewards are reported to have created some difficult results, not least of which is a substantial deterioration in the quality of industrial relations (Heery 1995; Walsh 1997).

Would benefits be provided in conditions of poor organisational performance?

How much would be provided even in the good times if benefit outlay is to be diverted into variable cash payments? Additionally, would the employer–employee partnership (requiring employees to shoulder the risk of 'difficult' corporate performance and accept the resultant 'difficult' rewards) create resistance to and problems for pay practice? Perhaps any sharing of risk should be secondary to the sharing of decisions about the actual rewards resulting from the New Pay. In the next section we turn to alternative and possibly more positive approaches.

Flexible plans for benefits

At the heart of discussions about flexibility for benefits is the idea of somehow tailoring benefits provision to the requirements of the individual – although the constraint of cost to the employer limits this tailoring effect somewhat (Woodley 1990). Benefits can be seen as 'contingent upon' employee needs. Hence if targeted delivery of benefits can meet needs, there is some advantage to be derived in terms of the goodwill and motivation of the employee, especially for high value benefits such as company cars, pensions, health insurance and assistance with childcare (Hewitt Associates 1991). The possibility of influencing performance in this way is worthy of note. However, the value of the benefits needs to be communicated clearly and effectively to employees. Flexibility may impact on performance only when benefits cease to be undervalued in the remuneration 'package' (Perkins 1998; Smith 1995; Conoley *et al.* 1993).

Flexible benefit plans include key player rewards, cafeteria remuneration, flex plans and life-cycle plans. Life-cycle plans are so far unique to America, where flexibility has proved more popular and durable than in Europe and the UK (Sparrow and Hiltrop 1994). Take-up in the UK has been poor (Arkin 1997). Causes for this situation include problems of administration, the absence of tax advantages in the UK, fear of the unknown, and perhaps a persistent inability to embrace any real change in the management of remuneration except in the arena of performance-related pay (Smith 1993, 1995, 2000). None the less, new pressures on organisations arising from competitive labour markets and rising costs may yet enhance the attractiveness of flexible remuneration.

The approach to implementing flexibility can take one of the following three forms:

- flexible cash and benefits
- flexible benefits
- life-cycle flexible benefits

Of these three, cash and benefits plans are the most commonly adopted in the UK. The Birmingham Midshires Building Society plan includes an employee option to exchange cash for life assurance; an option to exchange cash for extra holidays or vice versa; and options to exchange cash for dental insurance, health screening and critical illness insurance cover (Arkin 1997). Those not automatically receiving medical insurance and cars in the basic package are able to trade cash for private medical insurance and leased cars. These exchanges between cash and benefits are enabled by a 'flex fund' that accounts for 20 per cent of salary. The Midshires scheme has also reduced status-based benefit provision and is, unusually for the UK, available to all employees of the society (Arkin 1997). Flexible cash and benefits plans are more often confined to senior managers and 'key players' in those UK companies adopting the method (Hewitt Associates 1991; Smith 1995). In the United States it is normal for flexible plans to be made available to all categories of employees in the organisation.

Flexible benefit plans allow employees to choose from a menu of benefit options. Originally limited to healthcare, these benefit plans in American companies now allow employees a choice of benefit provision, including the opportunity to remove certain benefits from their personal flexible plan. One type of benefit can be exchanged with another type with the aim of controlling employer costs (an objective not dissimilar to the New Pay) by increasing employee awareness of the costs of benefits. Employees are then left to decide how much they want to pay for benefits out of total salary. The 'control' is usually achieved through employees selecting the least expensive options or by sharing benefits costs with the employer (Rabin 1994).

Life-cycle benefit plans represent the most significant step forward yet in US reward practices and are aimed at meeting changing employee requirements over the duration of a career. Allowances are provided to employees from which they 'buy' benefits such as childcare, care for the elderly, tuition and school fees, down payments on property and legal services, as well as the more normal benefit provisions. This approach (which covers a wider range of provisions than is common in the United Kingdom) is designed to help employees manage the costs associated with life's developments at different stages of a career. The Xerox Corporation, for example, is reported to provide each employee with a lifetime annual allowance of $10K to spend on the elements of the flexible life-cycle plan (Grant 1995).

In the first instance these benefit plans are a means to:

- distribute employee income in the interests of meeting individual requirements
- impact on employee goodwill and motivation
- reduce costs of benefits to the employer, despite the complexity involved in administering flexible plans.

Flexible plans have not been popular in the UK because of their complexity. UK plans tend to lack the sophistication and coverage of their American equivalents. In an uncertain economic and political climate, radical changes such as the introduction of flexible plans seem unlikely, at least for the time being.

Conclusion: performance revisited

The foregoing overview of factors influencing benefit provision and the character-istics of provision reveal some valuable additions to cash payments which in some instances – particularly pensions and cars – far exceed the financial value of performance-related payments. Given the wide availability of those benefits, it may be concluded that there is a substantial potential motivational role for such benefits as pensions and cars which, given their value, should impact directly on performance. But the issue of benefits and performance does not stop here. The benefits that are concentrated on senior executives and include insurance, low-cost loans, assistance with accommodation and expenses, are also of high value and could be claimed to be motivators for people who are most directly respon-sible for corporate strategy and performance. Benefits such as childcare and parental leave should open up new work and career opportunities. Provision of company equipment such as computers and other cash equivalent or cash allow-ances might be deemed to possess a significance with some effect certainly on goodwill and, deriving from this, on employee performance and thus contribution to the achievement of corporate objectives. That evidence of any link between these benefits and performance is lacking is both a disappointment and an opportunity lost.

An essential ingredient of reward management is the link between perform-ance and pay, yet benefits have not so far featured in the debate to any significant extent. Increasing provision of benefits in response to government policies, increasing taxation and costs give just cause for fuller consideration of the issues with attention to the links, methods, outcomes and advantages for benefits strat-egies that are geared to employee and organisation performance. A major first step towards this will require programmes to ensure that employees recognise the true value of benefits. But this may be the most difficult step. The value of benefits to employees depends on their attitudes to and perceptions of benefits. Management might usefully recognise and respond to employee preferences; for example, the current debate on pensions has revealed that a significant number of people are indifferent to future (i.e. post retirement) income provision, and over-coming this will require real managerial effort in an effective communications exercise.

Perhaps it is unfortunate therefore that current changes to benefits are creating uncertainty that may dampen any managerial enthusiasm for starting a com-munications programme for benefits and performance. There is real confusion currently arising in the broader employment field deriving from the 1999 Employment Relations Act and other decisions which confirm the legal right of part-timers to the same contractual provisions and benefits as full-time employees. The erosion of differential provision between full- and part-time employees must increase global payroll costs for organisations. We can remind ourselves that if employers respond at all to the evolving situation, it will probably involve one of two alternatives: the traditional 'knee jerk' cost reduction by cutbacks in total numbers employed or, alternatively, cost absorption through a performance-based return on the investment in benefits. The latter rationally thought-out response is perhaps overdue in order to 'tap' the potential contribution that benefits can make to performance.

References

Arkin, A. (1997), 'Mutually exclusive', *People Management*, 3 (6): 32–34.

Armstrong, M. (1997), 'Competence related pay', *People Management*, 3 (18): 36–9.

Armstrong, M. and Murliss, H. (1991), *Reward Management: A Handbook of Salary Administration*, London, Kogan Page.

Atkinson, J. (1984), 'Manpower strategies for flexible organisations', *Personnel Management*, August: 28–31.

Blyton, P. and Turnbull, P. (1998), *The Dynamics of Employee Relations*, 2nd edn, Basingstoke, Macmillan.

Brown, W. (1989), 'Managing remuneration' in Sisson, K. (ed.) *Personnel Management in Britain*, Oxford, Blackwell, 249–70.

Casey, B. (1993), *Employers' Choice of Pension Schemes. A Report of a Qualitative Study*, London, HMSO.

Child, J. (1969), *British Management Thought*, London, George Allen & Unwin.

Clegg, H.A. (1976), *The System of Industrial Relations in Great Britain*, Oxford, Blackwell.

Confederation of British Industry (CBI) (1998), 'Survey of absenteeism', *People Management*, 4 (18): 17.

Conoly, M., Nugent, M. and How, M. (1993), *Flexible Benefits*, Kingston-upon-Thames, Croner Publications.

Department of Social Security (DSS) (1998), 'A new contract for welfare: partnership in pensions', Green Paper, London, HMSO.

Department of Trade and Industry (DTI) (1999), 'Fairness at work', Cmnd 2968, London, HMSO.

Flanders, A. (1965), *Industrial Relations: What is Wrong with the System?*, London, Faber & Faber.

Friedman, B. (1990), *Effective Staff Incentives*, London, Kogan Page.

Grant, D.B. (1995), 'Life-cycle flex plans: the future of flexible benefits', *A.C.A. Journal*, 4 (2): 48–55.

Green, F., Hadjimatheou, G. and Smail, R. (1985), 'Fringe benefits and distribution in Britain', *British Journal of Industrial Relations*, 23, July: 261–80.

Gregg, P., Machin, S. and Szymanski, S. (1993), 'The disappearing relationship between directors' pay and corporate performance', *British Journal of Industrial Relations*, 31 (1), March: 1–9.

Heery, E. (1995), 'The "New Pay"', *Pay and Benefits Briefing*, 80, June: 6–8. Kingston-upon-Thames, Croner Publications.

Hendry, C., Pettigrew, A. and Sparrow, P. (1988), 'Changing patterns of human resource management', *Personnel Management*, November: 37–41.

Herzberg, F. (1975), 'One more time: how do you motivate employees?', *Harvard Business Review on Management*, London, Heinemann, 361–76.

Hewitt Associates (1991), *Total Compensation Management*, Oxford, Blackwell.

Incomes Data Services (IDS) (1999), 'Benefits costs and values', *Focus* 89, London.

Kennedy, G. (1988), 'Single status as the key to flexibility', *Personnel Management*, February.

Lawler, E.E. (1986), *The New Pay*, Los Angeles, CED Publications.

Lawler, E.E. (1987), 'The design of effective reward systems' in Lorsch, J. (ed.) *Handbook of Organisational Behaviour*, Englewood Cliffs, Prentice-Hall, 253–71.

Legge, K. (1995), *Human Resource Management, Rhetorics and Realities*, Basingstoke, Macmillan.

Lupton, T. and Bowey, A.M. (1974), *Wages and Salaries*, London, Penguin.

Moore, P. (1987), 'The company pension scheme: a boon or a burden?', *The Journal of General Management*, 13 (1) Autumn: 39–51.

Mullins, T. (1986), 'Harmonisation: the benefits and the lessons', *Personnel Management*, March: 38–41.

Murliss, H. (1992), 'The search for performance improvement', *Public Finance and Accountancy*, February: 14–16.

Murliss, H. and Armstrong, M. (1996), 'Reward management revisited', *Pay and Benefits Briefing*, 104, July: 6–8. Kingston-upon-Thames, Croner Publications.

National Association of Pension Funds (NAPF) (1993, 1995, 1997), *Annual Survey of Occupational Pension Funds*, London, NAPF.

Pay Magazine (1998), 'Company car may be eclipsed by alternatives', GEE Publishing, *Pay Magazine*, June: 12.

Perkins, S. (1998), 'Communication and the reward strategy agenda', *Pay and Benefits Briefing* 151, October: 2–4. Kingston-upon-Thames, Croner Publications.

Price, L. and Price, R. (1994), 'The decline and fall of the status divide?' in Sisson, K. (ed.) *Personnel Management in Britain*, Oxford, Blackwell.

Rabin, B.R. (1994), 'Benefits communication? Its impact on employee benefits satisfaction under flexible programmes', *Benefits Quarterly*, 10 (4): 67–83.

Remuneration Economics and Institute of Management (1994), *Survey of Management Pay*, Remuneration Economics, Kingston-upon-Thames, RE/IM.

Schuster, R.J. and Zingheim, P.K. (1992), *The New Pay: Linking Employee and Organisational Performance*, New York, Lexington Books.

Smith, I. (1989), 'Employee Benefits I and II' in Bowey, A. and Lupton, T. (eds) *Managing Wage and Salary Systems*, Aldershot, Gower Press, 393–422.

Smith, I. (1991), *Incentive Schemes: People and Profits*, Kingston-upon-Thames, Croner Publications.

Smith, I. (1993), 'Reward management: a retrospective assessment', *Employee Relations*, 15 (3): 45–59.

Smith, I. (1995), *Key Player Rewards and Flexible Compensation. Special Report 13*, Kingston-upon-Thames, Croner Publications.

Smith, I. (1996), 'The reality of reward management – retrospect and prospect', *Human Resources Briefing*, 75 (11), December: 9–11.

Smith, I. (1998), 'Financial incentives' in Poole, M. and Warner, M. (eds) *The Handbook of Human Resource Management*, London, International Thomson Business Press, 518–31.

Smith, I. (2000), 'Flexible plans for pay and benefits' in Holman, G. and Thorpe, R. (eds) *Strategic Reward Systems*, London, Financial Times/Prentice-Hall, 373–87.

Sparrow, P. (1996), 'Too good to be true?', *People Management*, 2 (24) December: 22–7.

Sparrow, P. and Hiltrop, J.-M. (1994), *European Human Resource Management in Transition*, Hemel Hempstead, Prentice-Hall.

Taylor, S. and Earnshaw, J. (1995), 'The provision of occupational pensions schemes in the 1990s: an exploration of employee objectives', *Employee Relations*, 17 (2): 38–53.

Terry, N.G. and White, P.J. (1997), 'The role of pension schemes in recruitment and motivation', *Employee Relations*, 19 (2): 160–75.

Torrington, D. and Hall, L. (1987), *Personnel Management: A New Approach*, London, Prentice Hall.

Walsh, J. (1997), 'Bank faces winter of discontent', *People Management*, 3 (24) December: 16–17.

Watson Wyatt (1996), *Watson's Statistics – Pensions*, London, Watson Wyatt.

Watson Wyatt (1998), *Car Survey*, London, Watson Wyatt.

Webb, S. and Webb, B. (1926), *History of Trade Unionism*, London, Longman Green and Co.

Wisher, V. (1994), 'Competencies: the precious seeds of growth', *Personnel Management*, July: 36–39.

Woodley, C. (1990), 'The cafeteria route to compensation', *Personnel Management*, May: 42–5.

Working for Childcare (1997), *Practical Guide to Nurseries for Personnel Managers*, London, The Working for Childcare Organisation.

8 Financial participation schemes

Jeff Hyman

In his 1998 pre-Budget report, the British Chancellor of the Exchequer, Gordon Brown, made a clear if unsubstantiated statement on the factors that enhance employee commitment to their organisations:

> Today, only a fraction of British employees and an even smaller minority of those outside senior management own shares in the companies that they work in and yet the evidence is that employee commitment is a vital strength for companies competing and succeeding in the global economy . . . and I want to remove, once and for all, the old 'them and us' culture in British industry. I want to encourage the new enterprise culture of team-work in which everyone contributes and everyone benefits from success. . . . We will make it easier for all employees . . . to become stakeholders in their company. I want to double the number of firms in which all employees have the opportunity to own shares.
>
> (*Financial Times*, 4 November 1998)

Commitment, communal endeavour between employee and employer with everyone on the same side, and teamwork – all linked by the common factor of employee share ownership. The same pronouncements could have been made, and indeed often were, by any of Gordon Brown's recent Conservative predecessors. Despite such affirmative statements, there are doubts about the impact of financial participation. The purpose of this chapter is to go beyond the bland pronouncements of politicians of all hues and to examine the theoretical positions and empirical evidence for the effects of share schemes and of financial participation generally.

The chapter is in four main sections. The first section looks at the context and rationale for financial participation schemes. The second section looks briefly at the various forms of employee financial participation available while the third section examines the effects of share-based remuneration. The fourth section examines the effects of cash-based profit-sharing.

Introduction

Employee participation in work organisation decisions is acknowledged as a prime factor in influencing employee behaviour, even if the consequences can fall below the expectations of the more sanguine prescriptive commentators. It is a closely related step to argue that employees should be able, directly or indirectly, to influence the patterns of incentives and rewards associated with their work and through this, a connection with the actual performance of work can be made. There are well-established means of accomplishing this connection: individual payment by results schemes which provide a direct and visible link between production and reward have a long history, though their weaknesses in linking employee performance to management objectives have been well acknowledged (see Chapter 5). Individual performance-related pay is also a direct means by which employees 'participate' in their remuneration levels (see Thompson 1993), and full consideration of this approach is offered in Chapter 6. In contrast to this individualised approach and following Vaughan-Whitehead, who defines financial participation as 'all schemes which give workers ... a variable portion of income directly linked to profits or some other measure of enterprise performance' (1995: 1), this chapter concentrates on two organisational approaches to financial participation: share ownership plans and, to a lesser extent, cash-based profit-sharing. The focus is primarily on share schemes because, as mentioned above, these initiatives promise to exert positive effects on employees through removing, or at least blurring, boundaries between employer and employee status by offering the latter 'a stake in the firm' (Creigh *et al.* 1981). As stockholders, in addition to share income and capital gains derived from organisational investment, employees can anticipate a say in the running of the company's affairs as well as revising the relationship with hierarchical superiors. The informational and proprietal effects of shareholder status are popularly assumed to exert positive effects upon employee attitudes, behaviour and consequently, performance.

In the UK, the key to opening up and expanding share-based channels of employee influence over remuneration has been the association between political ideology and product market change. A free-market orientated political agenda located in deregulation and privatisation was expressed by government in a number of linked ways: promotion of individualist and competitive values; performance-driven remuneration flexibility; and a drive for private property ownership and shared corporate identification as the means to enhance national economic success. A substantial component of this political agenda included the encouragement of employee share ownership in order to lubricate the sell-off of publicly owned companies and utilities to the private sector. Increased competitive pressures, coupled with a commitment-seeking and quality-orientated performance requirement, dove-tailed with this political agenda. An additional supply-side motive for employers to introduce share schemes has been provided by chronic shortages of key skills within the economy (see Wilson and Peel 1990).

Within this environment, recent UK governments have used tax incentives to encourage employers to adopt remuneration systems which create stronger com-

mitment among employees to their organisations, both financially and behaviour-
ally, whilst also reinforcing commitment to organisational aims through ownership
links. These linkages have provided the thinking behind the proliferation of both
supportive legislation in the UK for financial participation through employee
share schemes and their adoption by a growing number of employers during the
1980s and 1990s.

The intention of the first part of this chapter is to describe the main types of
employee share scheme which have been adopted and to contrast their stated
objectives with an evaluation and explanation of their effects. Employee share-
scheme financial participation is now universal in application and hence we shall
also draw upon experience from other countries to describe and analyse share
scheme effects.

The context and rationale of financial participation

Employer offers of share ownership and equity-derived contributions to income is
not a new concept. Exploratory approaches were adopted in Victorian England,
often to deter or deflect collectivist employee pressures at times of economic
growth and labour shortages (Ramsay 1977; Church 1971). Union members or
activists were in effect denied access to the financial benefits accruing from participation in a share allocation programme. These aggressive, if unstated, motives
gave rise to opposition to such schemes from social critics and, more pragmatic-
ally, to hostility from trade unions. This hostility has lingered through to the
present day, on the grounds that share schemes act as an ideological and com-
municative constraint upon trade unions by presenting a unitarist collusion of
interests between employer and employee at the expense of a collective employee
identity based on conflict of interests between the parties to the employment
relationship. Specifically, share-based remuneration is presented in positive-sum
terms in which both employees and enterprise seek to enhance company wealth
from which both parties benefit, rather than treating pay as a cost to the employer
over which contractual negotiations are conducted. Unions are also concerned
that employees face a compound risk as employment, income and savings are all
tied to the same institution. The assumed consequences of share schemes, though
potentially harmful to trade union interests, were articulated clearly within the
Thatcherite reform programmes of the 1980s; indeed, it was during this period
that share schemes were given their most significant political impetus.

Both supporters and critics of employee share schemes adopt similar arguments and these can be summarised as follows.

1   Employee share schemes offer property rights to participants.
2   The property nexus positively influences the behaviour of the employee
    towards the organisation, reinforcing unitarist values and loosening collectiv-
    ist ones. For the employer, the consequent benefits of these links are assumed
    to be greater organisational commitment, expressed through criteria like
    quality of work, team-working and task flexibility; recruitment of scarce staff

(e.g. in financial services, where share schemes are universally adopted); retention of employees whose share-scheme participation and full tax-free benefits accrue and optimise only after appropriate qualifying periods.
3 Unilateral management control over the introduction and maintenance of the programme.

Employee share ownership schemes

In Britain share-based schemes can be classified into four different approaches. The first of the extant schemes was introduced in 1978 – the Approved Deferred Share Trust (ADST) programme – under which companies can distribute shares according to a stipulated formula to all full-time employees who satisfy eligibility criteria. These were followed in 1980 by provisions for employees to buy shares in their companies at favourable rates through an Inland Revenue-approved savings institution, such as a building society. Both schemes have subsequently been improved financially and participation has been extended to part-time employees. The much derided (though heavily patronised) and now amended 'discretionary' (or 'executive') share option scheme, which was available only to specified (usually senior) personnel by invitation, was introduced in 1984 and replaced in 1996 by Company Share Option Plans. Finally, in 1989, the first Employee Share Owner-ship Plans (ESOPs) were given statutory approval to go alongside ESOPs founded on a combination of earlier legislation and common law precedents (see Pendle-ton *et al.* 1995, 1998). Details of the four approaches can be seen in Table 8.1.

Many organisations run two or more schemes concurrently. An example is

Table 8.1 Key features of UK employee share schemes

Type	Eligibility	Potential gains
Approved Deferred Share Trust (ADST)	All employees with minimum of five years' service	Distribution from share pool. Shares kept in trust for three years attract tax relief
Savings-related share options	All employees with minimum of five years' service	Shares can be bought at no less than 80% of current market price in 3, 5 or 7 years' time based on accumulated monthly savings
Company share option plans	At company discretion. Usually senior management	Options to buy shares at current market price at future date between 3 and 10 years later
Employee Share Ownership Plans (ESOPS)	All employees	Exemption from income tax if shares retained for minimum five years in trust

Sources: IDS 1998; Pendleton *et al.* 1995

provided by NatWest Bank, which offers an Inland Revenue-approved all-employee share scheme open to all staff with continuous employment between payment dates (IDS 1998). The shares are allocated only if the trigger profits reach £600m. The employee share is calculated as a proportion of salary, representing 2.88 per cent for 1997. Running alongside this approved programme is a cash-paying scheme open to all permanent staff who achieve specified performance levels, with a trigger point of £200m profits. Four per cent of salary was paid through this performance-linked scheme. NatWest also operates an all-employee SAYE scheme for its 47,000 eligible employees.

Inland Revenue data indicate that by April 1996 there were 855 operational ADST schemes, covering about three-quarters of a million participants. At the same time 1,305 approved savings-related (SAYE) schemes were in operation, covering 610,000 employees. SAYE employee participation is lower than for ADST participation because individual employees in companies operating SAYE schemes can decide whether to opt into the scheme or not, and participation rates can vary significantly. The IDS study reports that at Sketchley Retail, for example, only sixty out of 3,000 eligible staff (i.e. 2 per cent) are reported to be participating, whereas at Thames Water the participation rate is 50 per cent with 5,000 participants: even higher proportions are recorded for BAT (85 per cent) and Barclays Bank (83 per cent) (IDS 1998).

Research has shown that participation tends to be skewed towards managerial, professional and higher-paid occupations with more disposable income: far lower participation rates are reported among manual workers and lower-paid employees (Ramsay *et al.* 1990). The number of company share option plans is much higher, though of course the proportions of staff eligible to participate are likely to be highly restricted. In April 1996, 4,486 schemes were in operation with about 400 new approvals granted annually. IDS (1998) reports that whilst very few companies have opened up previously 'discretionary' schemes to all employees, two that have done so are large organisations (Kingfisher and ASDA). Participation by these highly visible public companies may well lead other enterprises to adopt less restrictive company share option plans. The numbers of ESOPs operating in the UK are very limited, perhaps totalling at most one hundred schemes (Pendleton *et al.* 1995). This is in contrast to the USA, where upwards of 10,000 schemes are estimated to be in operation, covering more than ten million employees (Allen *et al.* 1991; Hyman and Mason 1995: 109–12). There is a vital contrast between the objectives of US and UK ESOPs: American ESOPs serve a direct purpose as retirement plans rather than as a means to involve employees (Stevens 1991/2; Hanford and Grasso 1991).

Effects of share-based remuneration

It was noted above that employee share schemes are based upon an assumed association with a number of positive factors for employers predicated on the incentivising effects of owning property in the employing organisation. We now examine the claims made for employee share schemes in greater detail.

Claim 1: Employee share schemes offer property rights to employees

ADST, SAYE and company share option plans undoubtedly offer stock ownership to employees. Two issues are relevant, though. The first concerns the financial value of the shares. The second issue concerns share retention.

Financial value can be examined along two dimensions: in terms of the proportion of total individual income derived from employment represented by share allocations; and as a proportion of the company's aggregate share distribution. With respect to the first dimension, it has been contended that the positive motivational effects attributed to share ownership will only be triggered by 'significant' shareholdings. One American study demonstrated that employee satisfaction and motivation were directly associated with the size of the company contribution to their ESOP. Financial rewards, rather than property ownership *per se*, were regarded as the prime motivational source (Klein and Rosen 1986).

The problem is, of course, that it is impossible to know the pivotal proportion of total remuneration represented by shares which can exert meaningful effects on employee orientations or behaviour. We do know, however, that the value of shares distributed to employees under ADST schemes is not high. Inland Revenue statistics indicate that the average shareholding value per participant was as little as £460 in 1991/2, rising to £640 by 1995/6. Studies show that share allocations represent at most 6 per cent of remuneration (IDS 1990) but proportions of between 2 and 4 per cent have been more frequently cited (Baddon *et al.* 1987: 71; Blanchflower and Oswald 1986: 12). More recently, a study of fifteen companies indicated an average payout of 4 per cent (IDS 1998). The average value under SAYE schemes is higher (£2,900 in 1991/2 and £3,200 in 1995/6) but these figures do not represent remuneration supplements but are derived from voluntary regular savings contributions made by participants and these can be as high as £250 monthly for up to seven years. Also, at the end of the savings period, participants may choose to take accumulated cash savings rather than company shares.

With these modest share allocations, it is perhaps not surprising that research indicates that contrary to management hopes, many employees regard their shares as a gratuity or bonus offered to them by their employers. A study by Bell and Hanson, keen advocates of the motivational potential of employee shares, found that over two-thirds of respondents confirmed that share schemes were popular because 'people like to have the bonus' (Bell and Hanson 1987: 24). Research conducted by Baddon and her colleagues (1989) showed that nearly half of their SAYE respondents viewed their shareholdings in such an instrumental way. Conversely, the proportions of shares held by participants in the study by Pendleton *et al.* of employee buy-outs were 'substantially larger than the norm for employee share schemes' (Pendleton *et al.* 1998: 106). Pendleton and his colleagues admit that whilst expressed feelings of ownership were not overly high, they were stronger than in the extensive 1990 study by Poole and Jenkins (over 1,000 companies) of conventional share schemes, possibly 'due to the higher proportions of equity held by the work-forces' in the buy-out companies (Pendleton *et al.* 1998: 109). A similarly positive finding is reported by Bradley and Nejad (1989) in their evaluation of the orientational effects of employee shareholding in a privatised freight concern. In this company, too, employees held substantial proportions of company stock.

The second dimension of employee share scheme participation can be explored by looking at employee allocations as a proportion of aggregate distributed equity. The higher the proportions allocated to employees, the greater the potential for employees to influence company decisions through their shareholdings, especially if employees can be persuaded to aggregate their allocations. Whilst there are no statutory requirements to limit proportions of employee share allocations, guidelines are offered by the National Association of Pension Funds and the Association of British Insurers, whose Investment Committees commend a maximum limit of 10 per cent aggregate distribution to employees involved in ADST and SAYE universal schemes. Further, in any three-year period, a maximum of 3 per cent of issued stock is recommended. Research has indicated that these levels are rarely encountered. Of 108 companies with universal schemes studied by Baddon *et al.*, sixty (56 per cent) had offered less than 1 per cent of stock to its employees (1989: 65). Similarly, the proportions of aggregated employee shares in privatised concerns are low and declining. Baddon *et al* point out that even at the time of flotation in 1984, BT employees collectively owned a mere 4.6 per cent of issued equity, itself representing a higher figure than for many other privatised enterprises. By 1989, employee shareholding at BT had diminished to a minuscule 1 per cent of issued capital. The average BT employee shareholding amounted to 270 shares, dwarfed by the 1.3 million shares held by just five senior executives (Nichols and O'Connell Davidson 1992: 107) and the 629 institutional shareholders who each hold one million or more shares, representing two-thirds of issued capital in the company (Labour Research 1997: 24). Baddon *et al.* conclude that: 'the very existence of this [Investment Committee's] limit and the desire of institutional shareholders to protect their interests indicates that employee share owning is unlikely to lead to any serious degree of employee-shareholder control' (Baddon *et al.* 1989: 289). There is little evidence that this situation is changing, with individual shareholders generally in decline and wielding little in the way of corporate influence (*Labour Research* 1997).

A further indication of a sense of 'ownership' among employees might be illustrated by patterns of share retention. Those who see themselves as genuine part-owners of the business might be expected to retain their stock, whilst more instrumental or opportunistic motives might be associated with share release, especially after qualifying periods for tax concessions had been achieved. Reports that as many as two-thirds of employees 'cash in their share schemes at the first chance' (*Guardian*, 4 November 1998: 16) has led the government to examine 'ways of redesigning' schemes through further tax incentives (*Financial Times*, 4 November 1998: 14). Evidence from privatised industries indicates a progressive release of shares from employees (see Baddon *et al.* 1989: 290–1). With all-employee share schemes, manual employees are most likely to sell their shares and to do so quickly

(Baddon *et al.* 1989: 206–15). An association appears between patterns of share acquisition and retention and ideological attachment, with managers and other personnel motivated by market dynamics being the most enthusiastic and retentive of share scheme participants (see Nichols and O'Connell Davidson 1992). Manual workers and other lower-grade employees, whose hearts and minds 'popular capitalism' was supposed to capture, appear to be more resistant to the appeals of joint ownership.

From the above we can conclude that employee share schemes do offer property rights to employees, though shares offer only modest increments to total remuneration and provide no means for employees to influence corporate governance. Indeed, employees tend to regard their equity in terms of a bonus rather than as a means to corporate participation. From the employer perspective, a number of advantages can be constructed from these findings:

1   They pose no obvious threat to managerial prerogative.
2   As non-contractual elements of pay, they are under the direct control of management.
3   They do offer tax concessions to both employees and to employer.
4   They may exert some effect on the orientations and behaviour of participants, even if this is through the instrumental nexus of the 'bonus'.

We now examine the evidence for and against the motivational effects of share schemes.

Claim 2: Share schemes exert attitudinal, behavioural and performance effects on employees

There are three main perspectives associated with the effects of share schemes: namely that they exert (a) a positive effect on employees, or (b) a neutral or indeterminate effect, or (c) a negative effect. It has already been shown that politicians are uniformly supportive of share schemes. At first glance, practitioner and academic proponents of positive effects appear equally unequivocal in their support of such schemes. Thus, in an introduction to an international collection on workers' financial participation, Vaughan-Whitehead concludes that: 'the empirical evidence provided in this publication confirms the positive effects of financial participation schemes on the motivation and productivity of workers, as well as on organizational performance and innovation' (Vaughan-Whitehead 1995: 25). In a study comparing 113 publicly quoted share-scheme companies with 301 non-participants, Hanson and Watson were in no doubt that the share scheme companies not only out-performed the non-participants over a range of performance criteria, but that their own performance improved following the introduction of the share scheme programme (Hanson and Watson 1990: 180). Even such enthusiastic endorsements of share scheme effects are tempered with reservations. Thus Hanson and Watson acknowledge that, arising from their statistical analysis, the 'apparent correlation between profit-sharing and superior performance may be *entirely* due to any one of several omitted factors' (Hanson and Watson 1990: 180, emphasis added). Hanson, furthermore, in collaboration with the employee share proponent Wallace Bell, concedes that: '*most* managers we have met in profit-sharing companies have said that, *at least* to a modest extent, profit-sharing, as *part* of their total employee participation arrangements, has had *some* effect' (1987: 6, emphasis added). Caveats are also added to Vaughan-Whitehead's 'confirmation' of the positive consequences of share schemes:

> However, the benefits . . . clearly depend on the economic environment in which firms operate. Financial participation works better when employees adopt a long-term perspective, enjoy a close working relationship with management and are involved in the decision-making process.
>
> (Vaughan-Whitehead 1995: 25)

The importance of these factors is demonstrated in a recent New Zealand study of a share scheme introduced during a period of (external) economic transition and (internal) organisational restructuring. This study found no evidence of positive attitudinal shift among share scheme participants (Keef 1998). In other words, the schemes operate well when the behavioural changes assumed to be associated with share schemes are already in place! We need to probe more deeply into the reasons for these reservations and a good place to start is the USA, where both enthusiasm for employee share schemes and doubts about their effects are prevalent.

Numerous studies have been conducted in the USA over the effects of share ownership. As with the UK, there are various approaches to employee share schemes, including individual preferred purchase schemes, open option schemes, and pension-linked ESOPs. The latter form is by far the most significant element of employee schemes: in 1992, 8,543 ESOPs, covering 19.6 million (or 15.8 per cent) of the labour force, were estimated to be in operation (Conte and Lawrence 1992). Another estimate was of 10.8 million employees in 10,000 companies holding at least 4 per cent of company equity (Blasi *et al.*, 1996). Numerous North American studies, at least twenty seven according to Blasi *et al.*, have examined relationships between different forms of employee ownership and aspects of performance. The findings have been mixed, with co-operative ventures that have high ownership and control offering the most positive findings. For the others, including ESOP studies: 'Few of these studies have individually found strong and statistically significant effects of employee ownership on performance' (Blasi *et al.* 1996: 63). In their own extensive study of 562 companies which had at least 5 per cent employee-owned equity, the authors summarise that their findings are also

> consistent with the mixed findings from prior studies of employee ownership, leading to two conclusions: there is clearly no automatic connection between employee ownership and performance, but where differences do exist, they

tend to indicate better performance by EOFs (employee-owned firms) than by non-EOFs.

(Blasi *et al.* 1996: 78)

This major study seems to reinforce the earlier point about a positive potential relationship between level of ownership and employee orientations.

Theoretically, there are a number of reasons postulated for the lack of impact of all-employee schemes: managers may feel less incentive to supervise, if they feel that they are not receiving the full remunerative benefits of this activity (Alchian and Demsetz 1972; Blasi *et al.* 1996: 63). Unless all employees co-operate, there may be an individual tendency to shirk, as all employees receive an equal proportion of gain irrespective of individual contribution. Even in an enterprise as dynamic as Microsoft (30 per cent annual revenue increases and rapidly declining costs), negative effects can be identified. Greg Maffei, Chief Financial Officer for the company, acknowledges that a fall in the share price would make it much harder to recruit the 'bright young graduates' it needs, as share options have formed a significant proportion of the benefits package. Moreover, 'we have a huge problem ... we have overpaid lots of people because stock options don't differentiate between the really good and the less good employee' (quoted in *Guardian Online* 1998).

Some commentators suggest that co-operation may be enhanced through team-working, communication and other 'supportive human resource policies' (Blasi *et al.* 1996: 63; see also Levine 1995). This latter point also leads to questions of causality and synergy. If share schemes exert positive effects in an environment that supports employees, then the contribution or value added subsequently by share schemes to that environment becomes questionable.

Pendleton and his colleagues have reviewed the American literature and, building on the work of Klein (1987), provide a valuable summary of potential share ownership–employee attitude linkages. First, they identify an *intrinsic* model, premised on the direct positive effects of share ownership on commitment and satisfaction. A second, less direct relation is that of *instrumental* satisfaction, in which 'the capacity of ownership to bring about attitudinal change is critically dependent on the extent to which ownership allows greater participation in decision-making' (Pendleton *et al.* 1998: 101). The third *extrinsic* model suggests a link between ownership and commitment/satisfaction through financial rewards associated with ownership. Strong empirical support is offered for the instrumental and for the extrinsic models, but little for the intrinsic model. A later variant of the extrinsic model emphasises 'feelings of ownership' as an intervening variable for locating employee orientations (Pierce *et al.* 1991; Pendleton *et al.* 1998: 64).

Many of the British studies, it is argued, have rested on an assumption of (and hence have gone on to test) direct intrinsic causality between share ownership and orientations. Using multivariate analysis of attitude surveys conducted in employee-owned bus companies, Pendleton and his colleagues arrive at a number of important conclusions:

1   Employee share ownership produces a 'feeling of ownership' and this intervening variable can lead to positive employee orientations.
2   Support is provided for both intrinsic and instrumental models of satisfaction.
3   Different analytical methods require careful interpretation of findings.
4   'Those employees who feel like owners are those with higher relative levels of share ownership and perceptions of participation, and this feeling is significantly related to relatively high levels of commitment and satisfaction with the organization' (Pendleton *et al.* 1998: 117).

In conclusion, the significance of the work of Pendleton and his colleagues lies in this association between the extent and depth of employee ownership, the perceived potential for influence, and orientations to the workplace. Relatively modest share allocations are more likely to be recognised by employees for their instrumental bonus value and to be utilised as such, and in this context are unlikely to be heavily motivational in impact.

Claim 3: Share schemes support management control over employees

Increasing numbers of enterprises are attempting to increase the flexibility of their operations and especially of their labour. One expression of flexibility is to link pay more directly with measures of company performance and hence the ability of the enterprise to pay. A central aspect of this would be progressively to detach pay awards from determined formulae, for example, based directly on indices such as cost-of-living, or indirectly through joint regulation of pay with representative bodies and trade unions. In Britain, share schemes, as a non-contractual element of remuneration, are independent of other pay determination processes and are designed, introduced and maintained (and can be removed) at the initiative of management. As Baddon *et al.* discovered, share schemes are directed at a distance even from the human resource specialists whose responsibilities embrace company pay policy, tending to be located in the management domains of company secretaries and finance directors (Baddon *et al.* 1989: 22). Less directly, there is evidence, both anecdotal and more empirical, that share schemes can deter or delay quits from the company. One company which introduced a share scheme in 1997 reports that: 'already we are seeing higher staff retention rates among the 50 per cent of staff who have taken up the scheme' (reported in the *Guardian*, 4 November 1998: 16). More substantial evidence for these effects is provided by one study where both absenteeism and voluntary quits were lower than in organisations without employee share and profit-related schemes (Wilson and Peel 1990). By contrast, there were few differences in labour turnover between ESOP and conventional firms studied by Osawa (1989) in Japan, with the exception of non-union concerns, where a tendency for lower turnover rates for ESOP companies was reported.

In the USA, coincidence with manifest management interests has been expressed through the linkage between share schemes and concession bargaining over pay with trade unions (see Mitchell 1995: 159). Employee share ownership is also viewed as a means by incumbent managements to defend their organisations against hostile take-overs. Further, in the majority of ESOP cases, employee shares form the basis of retirement plans. These plans derive directly 'from the financial performance of the sponsoring companies (and) also offer other advantages to these companies in terms of potential control over employees' whose future pensions may be constrained by company performance. Further, current mobility of staff can be curtailed owing to potential adverse effects on future pension rights through share allocation restriction (Hyman and Mason 1995: 110–11; IDS 1989).

Cash-based profit-sharing

Employee share schemes offer property rights to employees and this linkage provides the platform for advocates of share schemes to argue that positive outcomes can derive from the association. Profit-sharing or revenue-sharing, as practised in most capitalist countries, purports to offer a more direct link between incentive, performance and remuneration, in that periodic retrospective cash bonuses are offered to employees upon achieving previously stated criteria of collective performance. These criteria can include profits, added value, sales or other measurable factors, and can relate to the enterprise as a whole or identifiable undertakings within an organisation. Through this, 'profit-sharing' variants can be adopted in non-profit-seeking enterprises, such as universities. In some countries like Japan (see below), profit-sharing has been seen as an integral part of an organisation's approach to employee management.

Two potential benefits for management are ascribed to cash-based profit-sharing. First, that there may be an indirect motivational effect which serves to raise efficiency through its effect upon employee orientations and behaviour to the organisation (Baddon *et al* 1989: 9). Second, they may increase pay flexibility, in that labour costs vary with profitability. One of the stated reasons for the previous Conservative government's promotion of profit-related pay was as a means to loosen wage rigidity and to encourage flexibility in the labour market. This policy drew upon the theoretical work of the American economist Martin Weitzman (see for example, Weitzman 1984, 1985). This work was informed by macro-economic assumptions that, in conditions where the majority of companies adopt flexible profit-sharing, changes in product demand will be met by adjustments in marginal remuneration and not by labour-shedding, thereby helping to resolve potential problems of both inflation and unemployment. Criticisms of Weitzman's propositions have accumulated, nevertheless, particularly in the light of an inability to test the model in the absence of economies that employ a universal flexible approach to remuneration based on profits (see Freeman and Weitzman 1988, Weitzman and Kruse 1990 and below for empirical support. More sceptical perspectives are offered by Wadhwani 1985 and by Blanchflower and Oswald 1986). Nevertheless, Japan employs profit-sharing widely and 'on the face of it, Japan offers the best test of the Weitzman hypothesis' (Baddon *et al.* 1989: 14) and is worth examining in some depth.

Profit-sharing plans (PSP) in Japan are based on establishing links between non-executive pay and company performance. A number of variations exist and in nearly a fifth of cases profit is linked to criteria other than profit (Ohashi 1989). The factor common to many of the schemes is the high proportion of pay taken up by the PSP, about three and a half months on average (Jones and Kato 1995: 128). This compares with a maximum of income tax relief of 20 per cent or £4,000 for approved profit-related pay schemes currently in operation in the UK. Cash-linked profit-sharing is widespread, with nearly all companies with more than thirty employees paying biannual bonuses (Ohashi 1989). According to Freeman and Weitzman (1988), between 42 and 67 per cent of profits are paid out as bonuses. The same writers are convinced that the system helps to account for Japanese economic success 'by automatically helping to stabilise unemployment at relatively low levels', a conclusion contested by a majority of other economists (see Jones and Kato 1995 for a summary).

Nevertheless, data from the Japan Productivity Centre (1989) indicate that the great majority of managers and union officials believe that PSPs contribute significantly both to job satisfaction and to productivity. Even so, doubts persist: in Japan both profit-sharing and employee share schemes are embedded within a complex and possibly unique ideological network which emphasises mutual obligations by both employee and employer. From the employer, a stake in the company and its performance is linked with concepts of lifetime employment, individual development and formal consultation. From the employee, dedication, hard work and company loyalty are anticipated. It would be difficult specifically to identify motivational effects attributable to any one strand of these ideologically informed practices. For this reason perhaps, it is difficult to arrive at definitive conclusions over the motivational impact of these schemes in Japan. This is made clear in a conclusion to a review of these schemes: 'the available evidence suggests that a well-designed scheme, *combined with other forms of employee participation*, contributes to the achievement of substantial improvements in company performance' (Jones and Kato 1995: 138, emphasis added). The qualifying points are remarkably similar to those expressed for European and American schemes of financial participation described above.

American studies on profit-sharing are dominated by Weitzman's claims for enhanced productivity. One researcher argues that positive effects attributable to profit-based remuneration can potentially arise from a number of sources; namely it can act: as a direct financial incentive; as a stimulus to train and to co-operate with colleagues; as an incentive to look after plant and equipment; as an aid to improved information flows; as an encouragement to embrace technological developments (Shepard 1994: 452). The same writer conducted research in twenty American chemical plants over a seven-year period and concluded that profit-sharing does indeed influence productivity, though points out that flaws in the research design and an inability to identify the mechanisms through which profit-sharing operates present significant limitations to the analysis. A similarly positive study of gain-sharing (schemes which resemble current approaches to social partnership being adopted in the UK) also pointed out that whilst part of the gain-sharing experience relied upon profit-based pay flexibility, other collaborative initiatives introduced by management at the same time could also influence employee attitudes, orientations and behaviour (Collins 1996; see also Doucouliagos 1995).

In Britain profit-sharing was given a significant boost by the Conservative government's promotion of cash-based profit-related pay in which income tax relief is offered to schemes that meet Inland Revenue requirements. At present, the maximum level of income tax relief is calculated on the lower of 20 per cent of pay or £4,000. Some 14,500 schemes were active in 1997, with tax relief calculated at £1.5 billion (IDS 1998). The anticipated escalation in the loss of income tax prompted the government to phase out tax relief on profit-related pay, concluding in January 2000 with no further relief. Many companies are looking to convert schemes into share schemes. In the absence of reliable data, it is difficult to estimate the impact the profit-related pay experiment had on employee and organisational performance. Tax relief was regarded as a significant motive for its introduction by a number of employers. There has been no evidence that the pay-flexible schemes impacted upon employment levels (as predicted by Weitzman) and motivational effects remain to be tested. It is doubtful, though, whether any performance effects directly attributable to profit-related pay can be positively identified.

Conclusions

This chapter has examined the claims for financial participation in depth. Its clear message has been that unreserved claims that financial participation in the form of employee share schemes or as cash-based profit-sharing positively influences employee attitudes, behaviour or performance and thereby feeds through into enhanced organisational outcomes, should be treated with caution. Notwithstanding occasional exaggerated claims for financial participation, the bulk of supportive studies tends to conclude with disclaimers as to the reliability of the findings. This is hardly surprising, considering the range of influences, both within and external to the organisation, which can potentially affect performance.

Notwithstanding these reservations, or perhaps because of them, two general conclusions emerge. First, with regard to share schemes, positive behavioural effects attributable to ownership are more clearly identified among schemes where participants have higher levels of share ownership. Whilst no 'trigger point' for ownership can be identified, it is apparent that the low levels of share ownership offered by the majority of approved all-employee company schemes are viewed by employees, and appreciated by them, principally for their bonus or instrumental value and are unlikely to exert either prolonged or significant effects on employee behaviour.

In the meantime, the government has reaffirmed its belief that employee share schemes contribute directly to productivity through bolstering employee commitment. Following the Spring 1999 Budget Statement outlining proposals to double the number of companies in the UK with employee share-holding opportunities, the Inland Revenue has published its plans for the New All-Employee Share Scheme. Employee share acquisition is to be encouraged in three ways by offering: (a) *free* shares to employees from the employer (annual maximum £3,000), (b) *partnership* shares purchasable by employees (annual maximum £1,500), and (c) *matching* shares offered by the employer, with a maximum of two matched shares for each partnership share purchased by employees (Inland Revenue 1999). It is further proposed that an element of individual or group-based performance can be used by employers to determine allocations of free shares to employees above an (as yet unspecified) minimum (Pay and Benefits Briefing 1999). A maximum of £7,000 of shares per employee is therefore proposed. Whether the size of share allocations by employer gratuity and/or through employee purchases will be sufficient to trigger and maintain positive behavioural effects is unclear. There are also questions as to whether the discretionary performance allocation element will exert positive or divisive effects, as it seems to prejudice the 'common purpose' underpinning the share ownership philosophy.

The second point is that many studies, both of share schemes and of profit-sharing, have pointed to 'contaminatory' effects of other progressive and participative arrangements located within the organisations under study and directed at the same employees. Whilst helping to confuse the specific contribution of individual techniques, it does appear that combinations of participatory practices can exert positively synergistic effects. In particular, the opportunity for employees to exercise a 'voice' in organisational affairs can be associated with positive behavioural effects (Wilson and Peel 1990; Freeman and Medoff 1984). Offering shares to employees as part of this process could be associated with similarly favourable outcomes (Pendleton *et al.* 1995), especially when trade unions act in what Bradley and Gelb term as a 'loyal opposition' to management (1983).

At the present time, the concept of 'social partnership' between management and employees assumes that such a coalition of interests can be established and in practice is gaining acceptance in many workplaces. Whilst the parameters of this participative approach to employee relations are still under exploration, it is clear that financial participation, especially through share schemes, can and does provide a significant pillar alongside representative decision-making, communication and employee development, to support the partnership approach. Nevertheless, as with any employee relations policy initiative, this route has its pitfalls. A study of the sell-off of a publicly owned railway maintenance company demonstrated that: 'share ownership on paper is no guarantee of the participation and industrial citizenship needed to rekindle British economic success' (Wills and Myhill 1997: 131). The negative consequences in this instructive study were attributable to management secrecy and continuing mistrust between managers, unions and employees, further exacerbated when extra effort was demanded of employees, followed by redundancies and large pay increases for the top managers. Under those circumstances, the ESOP failed to improve the poor relations between the parties. For financial participation to succeed as part of a broader partnership ideal, it appears that both managers and employees need to believe in and to act upon the goodwill and positive intentions of each other. The government and employers following the employee share ownership route would be well advised to bear this caution in mind.

References

Alchian, A.A. and Demsetz, H. (1972), 'Production, information costs, and economic organization', *American Economic Review*, 62 (5), December: 777–95.

Allen, C., Cunningham, I. and McArdle, L. (1991), *Employee Participation and Involvement in the 1990s*, Stockton, Jim Conway Foundation.

Baddon, L., Hunter, L., Hyman, J., Leopold, J. and Ramsay, H. (1987), 'Developments in profit-sharing and employee share ownership', Survey Report, University of Glasgow, Centre for Research into Industrial Democracy and Participation.

Baddon, L., Hunter, L., Hyman, J., Leopold, J. and Ramsay, H. (1989), *People's Capitalism? A Critical Analysis of Profit Sharing and Employee Share Ownership*, London, Routledge.

Bell, D.W. and Hanson, C.G. (1987), *Profit Sharing and Profitability*, London, Kogan Page.

Blanchflower, D.G. and Oswald, A.J. (1986), *Profit-sharing: Can It Work?*, London, New Bridge Consultants.

Blasi, J., Conte, M. and Kruse, D. (1996), 'Employee stock ownership and corporate performance among public companies', *Industrial and Labor Relations Review*, 50 (1), October: 60–79.

Bradley, K. and Gelb, A. (1983), *Worker Capitalism: The New Industrial Relations*, London, Heinemann.

Bradley, K. and Nejad, A. (1989), *Managing Owners: The National Freight Company Buy-out in Perspective*, Cambridge, Cambridge University Press.

Church, R.A. (1971), 'Profit-sharing and labour relations in England in the nineteenth century', *International Review of Social History*, XVI, Part 1.

Collins, D. (1996), 'How and why participatory management improves a company's social performance', *Business and Society*, 35 (2), June: 176–210.

Conte, M.A. and Lawrence, H. (1992), 'Trends in ESOPs', in Turner, J.A. and Beller, D.L. (eds), *Trends in Pensions 1992*, Washington DC, GPO.

Creigh, S., Donaldson, N. and Hawthorn, E. (1981), 'A stake in the firm: employee financial involvement in Britain', *Employment Gazette*, May: 229–36.

Doucouliagos, C. (1995), 'Worker participation and productivity in labor-managed and participatory capitalist firms: a meta-analysis', *Industrial and Labor Relations Review*, 49 (1), October: 58–77.

Freeman, R. and Medoff, J. (1984), *What Do Unions Do?*, New York, Basic Books.

Freeman, R. and Weitzman, M. (1988), 'Bonuses and employment in Japan', *Journal of the Japanese and International Economies*, 1: 168–94.

Hanford, T.J. and Grasso, P.G. (1991), 'Participation and corporate performance in ESOP firms', in Russell, R. and Rus, V. (eds), *International Handbook of Participation in Organizations*, Vol. II, Oxford, Oxford University Press.

Hanson, C. and Watson, R. (1990), 'Profit-sharing and company performance: some empirical evidence for the UK', in Jenkins, G. and Poole, M. (eds), *New Forms of Ownership*, London, Routledge.

Hyman, J. and Mason, B. (1995), *Managing Employee Involvement and Participation*, London, Sage.

Income Data Services (IDS) (1989), *Employee Share Ownership Plans*, Income Data Services, Study No. 438, July.

Income Data Services (IDS) (1990), *Profit-sharing and Share Options*, Income Data Services, Study No. 468, October.

Income Data Services (IDS) (1998), *Profit-sharing and Share Options*, Income Data Services, Study No. 641, January.

Inland Revenue (1999), *A New Employee Share Scheme: A Technical Note*, London, HMSO.

Japan Productivity Centre (1989), *Survey of Institutions Concerning Leisure, Job Satisfaction and Productivity*, Tokyo, Japan Productivity Centre.

Jones, D. and Kato, T. (1995), 'Japan', in Vaughan-Whitehead, D. (ed.), *Workers' Financial Participation*, Geneva, International Labour Office.

Keef, S.P. (1998), 'The causal association between employee share ownership and attitudes: a study based on the Long framework', *British Journal of Industrial Relations*, 36 (1): 73–82.

Klein, K.J. (1987), 'Employee stock ownership and employee attitudes: a test of three models', *Journal of Applied Psychology*, 72: 319–32.

Klein, K.J. and Rosen, C. (1986), 'Employee stock ownership in the United States', in R.N. Stern and S. McCarthy (eds), *International Yearbook of Organizational Democracy*, Vol. III, New York, Wiley.

Labour Research (1997), 'Thank you Sid, and Goodbye!', *Labour Research*, March, 23–24.

Levine, D.I. (1995), *Reinventing the Workplace: How Business and Employees Can Both Win*, Washington DC, Brooking Institution.

Mitchell, D. (1995), 'The United States: flexibility first?', in Vaughan-Whitehead, D. (ed.), *Workers' Financial Participation*, Geneva, International Labour Office.

Nichols, T. and O'Connell Davidson, J. (1992), 'Employee shareholders in two privatised utilities', *Industrial Relations Journal*, 23 (2): 107–19.

Ohashi, I. (1989), 'On the determinants of bonuses and basic wages in large Japanese firms', *Journal of the Japanese and International Economies*, 3: 451–79.

Osawa, M. (1989), 'The service economy and industrial relations in small and medium sizes firms in Japan', *Japan Labor Bulletin*, 1 July.

Pay and Benefits Briefing (1999), 'The new all-employee share scheme', *Pay and Benefits Briefing*, No. 164. London, Croner.

Pendleton, A., McDonald, J., Robinson, A. and Wilson, N. (1995), 'The impact of employee share ownership plans on employee participation and industrial democracy', *Human Resource Management Journal*, 4 (4): 44–60.

Pendleton, A., Wilson, N. and Wright, M. (1998), 'The perception and effects of share ownership: empirical evidence from employee buy-outs', *British Journal of Industrial Relations*, 36 (1): 99–124.

Pierce, J.L., Rubenfeld, S.A. and Morgan, S. (1991), 'Employee ownership: a conceptual model of process and effects', *Academy of Management Review*, 16 (1): 121–44.

Poole, M. and Jenkins, G. (1990), *The Impact of Economic Democracy*, London, Routledge.

Ramsay, H. (1977), 'Cycles of control', *Sociology*, 11 (3): 481–506.

Ramsay, H., Hyman, J., Baddon, L., Hunter, L. and Leopold, J. (1990), 'Options for workers: owner or employee?', in Jenkins, G. and Poole, M. (eds), *New Forms of Ownership*, London, Routledge.

Shepard III, E.M. (1994), 'Profit-sharing and productivity: further evidence from the chemicals industry', *Industrial Relations*, 33 (4): 452–66.

Stevens, B. (1991/2), 'Employee ownership and participation in the USA', *Industrial Participation*, Winter: 16–19.

Thompson, M. (1993), *Pay and Performance: The Employee Experience*, Institute of Manpower Studies, Report 258, Brighton, Sussex.

Vaughan-Whitehead, D. (ed.) (1995), *Workers' Financial Participation*, Geneva, International Labour Office.

Wadhwani, S. (1985), 'The macro-economic implications of profit-sharing: some empirical evidence'. Discussion Paper No. 220, London, Centre for Labour Economics, London School of Economics.

Weitzman, M. (1984), *The Share Economy*, Cambridge, Mass., Harvard University Press.

Weitzman, M. (1985), 'The simple macro-economics of profit-sharing', *American Economic Review*, 75: 937–53.

Weitzman, M. and Kruse, D.L. (1990), 'Profit-sharing and productivity', in Blinder, A. (ed.), *Paying for Productivity: A Look at the Evidence*, Washington DC, Brookings Institution.

Wills, J. and Myhill, T. (1997), 'Stakeholding: can employee ownership play a part?', Official Proceedings, Fifth International Industrial Relations Association Conference, Dublin, Oak Tree Press, 115–34.

Wilson, N. and Peel, M. (1990), 'The impact of profit-sharing, worker participation, and share ownership on absenteeism and quits: some UK evidence', in Jenkins, G. and Poole, M. (eds), *New Forms of Ownership*, London, Routledge.

9 International reward management

Paul Sparrow

This chapter explores some implications for reward strategy of the increasing globalisation of business organisations. A neglected area of research is the problem of how organisations take account of national characteristics and contexts in the design of reward systems. In considering pay design within an international context, we have to engage the debate about convergence and divergence in the rewards field. There are pressures to alter the level at which pay determination takes place, and there is an attack on the collective process in Japan and sector-wide agreements operated in Germany. Many tensions, however, are faced by organisations as they attempt to harmonise reward packages, notably the influence of national culture on pay systems. Rather than focus attention on the management of expatriate compensation and benefits, which has been a traditional focus in the international IHRM literature, this chapter analyses the factors that international organisations should consider when they make decisions about how to manage their rewards systems across national boundaries. A number of psychological factors, such as national value orientations, distributional justice, the concept of socially healthy pay, and the role of pay as a motivator, are considered.

The issue of international convergence in rewards systems has taken centre-stage. Depending on the level of analysis adopted, different conclusions may be drawn about the desire for and actual level of convergence in rewards systems. Certainly at the level of HR philosophy, the convergence argument can find some support. Even at the beginning of the 1990s, organisations (especially MNCs, but also large domestic organisations) around the world could be seen to be converging managerial attention around the need to improve the link between pay and performance. Analysis of data from the Towers Perrin/IBM study of 1991 for twelve countries (Sparrow *et al.* 1994) showed that the issue of individual performance-related pay was one of the philosophies that all HR managers saw as being central to the achievement of competitive advantage. It was anticipated that it should be reflected in actual practice. However, depending on the level at which we analyse rewards systems, the evidence of international convergence around best practice has to be tempered by an increasingly sophisticated awareness of the distinctive nature of rewards policies and behaviour across countries (Sparrow 1998).

This chapter notes a range of cross-national factors that influence reward practices in organisations, but gives particular attention to the role of national culture. Why is a consideration of national culture so important? Naisbitt and Aburdene (1990) point out that whilst the lifestyles of managers around the world are becoming more homogeneous, the faster the pace at which this happens, the more steadfastly they shall cling to and cherish the traditions that spring from within. We might expect that deeper values will predict responses to new reward initiatives. Although ultimately the forces for convergence might prevail, the harder organisations push for convergence in rewards practice, the bumpier their ride to convergence will become. What pressures then are making our worlds more similar, perhaps at a pace too fast for some?

Is there convergence around pay flexibility?

Rewards systems in Germany, Japan and China are facing radical change. There are also high levels of reward failure in the US and UK, where a shift from jobs-based to people-based systems is currently taking place (Sparrow and Marchington 1998). The pursuit of flexibility in human resource management (HRM) has led to calls for more pay flexibility (Thierry 1998). The drive towards flexibility requires more ease with which employees' or managers' pay can be adjusted, especially to reflect the correlation between:

- pay level and the organisation's success (or otherwise)
- pay focus and general strategic policy objectives
- risk-sharing between the organisation and the employee
- pay level and the individual effort.

Flexibility is intended to deliver greater differentiation between individuals, teams or units within an organisation and requires greater market sensitivity of rewards.

The German Kostenkrise *debate*

Europe has seen calls for more wage flexibility. The *Kostenkrise* in Germany has become the centre of much attention. The Bundesverband der Deutschen Industrie (BDI) argues that German enterprise is blighted by high tax, wages and welfare costs and there is pressure to break up the 42,000 '*tarifverträg*'. These are the conventional contracts that cover not just wage rates, bonuses and sick pay, but also training, part-time work, and sometimes longer hours in return for job security. They regulate German pay and compensation negotiations. Until recently firms operating outside the system actually ended up paying wages at least as high, if not higher, than those within the system. This is now changing. The number of individual contracts with unions has increased from 2,500 in 1990 to 5,000 by 1997: for example, the IG Chemie trade union in Germany agreed in June 1997 to allow Hoechst, Bayer and BASF to cut wages by up to 10 per cent in difficult economic periods; while in Eastern Germany twenty firms have official permission to pay below the '*Tarif*' whilst many employers shun the system and negotiate on-site with workers. Although productivity has increased in Germany by 8.5 per cent and unit labour costs have fallen by 10 per cent (*Economist*, 1999a), it is argued that high labour productivity (partly the result of a highly skilled and functionally flexible workforce and harmonious plant- or company-level industrial relations) is not sufficient to compensate for the labour cost disadvantage (Tüsselmann 1999).

The accumulated unit labour cost (ULC) disadvantage for Germany from the period 1989–96 amounted to 18 per cent. Of this disadvantage, 33 per cent can be attributed to internal (non-currency value) labour cost factors, and of this, non-wage labour costs (which amount to 80 per cent of direct wages in Germany) have accounted for much of the increase. Social security contributions, paid for jointly by the employer and employee, have risen from 26.5 per cent of gross wages in 1970 to 36 per cent in 1989, and now stand at 42 per cent. Germany is actually at the mid-point in terms of social costs. Social costs (as a percentage of gross average pay adjusted to reflect purchasing power relative to the US) range from as low as 22 per cent in the US, to 26 per cent in the UK, 83 per cent in Germany, 122 per cent in Sweden, 127 per cent in Switzerland and 128 per cent in Japan (*Economist*, 1999a). Table 9.1 shows that the cost and burden factors in Germany compare unfavourably to other major OECD countries in the 1990s.

It is argued that the result of this is an exodus of capital in a globalising market and that this will force domestic organisations to reform wage systems. Certainly, German outward foreign direct investment (FDI) did increase substantially during

Table 9.1 Comparison of selected location cost factors in manufacturing sector

	WG	EG	USA	J	UK	F	NL	B
Labour costs on DM basis, 1996, WG = 100	100	66	55	69	47	65	74	75
Labour productivity, 1996, WG = 100	100	59	76	85	58	98	109	99
Labour unit cost change, 1989–96, national currencies, %	20.1	–	11.4	6.8	24.3	7.5	2.8	16.2
Annual working time, 1996, WG = 100	100	105	121	117	112	112	109	110
Effective marginal tax burden of joint stock companies, 1996, WG = 100	100	76	51	111	36	73	44	53

Key:
WG = Western Germany, EG = Eastern Germany, USA = United States, J = Japan, UK = United Kingdom, F = France, NL = The Netherlands, B = Belgium

Source: After Tüsselmann (1999). His calculations based on data from: Institut der deutschen Wirtschaft, IW Trends – Quartalshefte zur Empirischen; Wirtschaftsforschung, no. 2, 1997 and no. 3, 1997; Bundesministerium für Wirtschaft, Wirtschaft in Zahmen, September 1997

the 1990s. Outflows increased by 120 per cent from 1983–89 to 1990–96, with inflows amounting to just 20 per cent of outflows in the latter period (Tüsselmann 1999). However, it is too narrow a perspective to attribute increases in outflows solely to cost factors. In addition to labour costs and corporate taxation, qualitative factors such as the skills level of the workforce, density and tightness of regulatory frameworks, market demand, geo-political location and national culture all play a role in multinational location and investment decisions (Buckley and Mucchielli 1997). Indeed, 80 per cent of German FDI has gone to western industrialised countries, not low-wage locations. Only a small proportion of total FDI has been driven by wage and related rewards/benefits factors, despite the popular press attention.

Rewards are notoriously difficult to compare across countries for many reasons. Flexibility deals that surround pay conditions can mask inflated or deflated pay levels and simple comparisons of unit labour costs and hourly manufacturing wage rates hide many complexities. For example, in Germany, wage rates averaged DM48 an hour in manufacturing in 1996, higher than any of the other fifty-two countries surveyed by the World Economic Forum. However, the number of hours actually worked also varies markedly. Data from the International Institute for Management Development (*Economist* 1999a) show that the annual hours worked by full-time employees in the United States is 1,920 compared to 1,840 in the UK, 1,830 in Sweden, 1,810 in Japan, 1,750 in France, but only 1,700 in Germany. Moves to a shorter working week and early retirement increase the proportion of gross wages that must be used to cover social costs. Given the ageing workforce, the Federation of German Industry estimates that social security costs will amount to 55 per cent of gross wages by 2040. Today's 20-year-olds can expect zero returns on half of their lifetime contributions, whereas today's 60-year-olds receive three times what they have paid in. This said, the younger generation benefits from and can expect about three times as much inherited wealth in terms of savings and property than their grandparents had. The *Kostenkrise* will lead to some rewards system reform, but the business rhetoric often ignores the subtle ways in which national systems can balance out rewards and benefits across societal groups.

The risutora *process in Japan*

Japan has also changed from being a role model for HRM policies and practices, to becoming a major target for those who argue for the break-up of national business systems (Wood 1994). The restructuring process associated with the revitalisation of its post-bubble economy is called *risutora* (Dirks 1997). Within the HRM arena, attention has focused on:

- the introduction of performance-based career and compensation standards
- open feedback systems regarding performance evaluation
- even more differentiated employment tracks between core, specialist and flexible employment groups

- externalisation of much corporate welfare; and non-discriminatory hiring practices.

In order swiftly to lower or alleviate labour costs, in the short term Japanese firms have reduced the level of overtime payments, and transferred employees between companies. The social contract, based on lifetime employment and seniority-based pay, is slowly breaking down as forces of internationalisation, global competition, demography, slowed economic growth and the collapse of investment banks begin to bite. In practice, the substantial bonus proportion of annual wages and the introduction of job ability-based grading schemes (*shokunōkaku seido*) have simply been added on to existing seniority-dominated practices, in that most firms linked bonus pay and ability-related remuneration largely to the age of employees and the length of employment with the firm (Sasajima 1997; Rōdōsho 1997, cited by Dirks 1998).

Some of the rewards problems facing Japanese organisations reflect structural issues, such as demographic pressures. Salaries and earnings in Japan peak at age 50–54 (compared to 45–49 in the UK), but by the year 2000 a quarter of the Japanese workforce will be aged 55 or older, creating high fixed cost. The chairman of the Japan Federation of Employers Association (Nikkeiren) urged pay restraint in wage and bonus demands, stating that Japanese companies employ 1.2 million excess workers (Sparrow 1998). Deregulation is expected to lead to 10 per cent job losses in the finance, public administration and construction sectors. Despite apparent collectivist preferences, employees in Japan have regularly been found to be dissatisfied with the opaqueness of work and performance evaluation systems and the highly centralised nature of decision-making (Fujimura 1997). Flexibility in rewards is an issue in Japan, but although wage increases are flexible, the annual wage bargaining ritual known as 'shunto' (or spring labour offensive) in practice means that wages increase uniformly across sectors, as awards have been made irrespective of productivity. There was some divergence from the uniform agreements in 1997, when profitable firms like Toyota offered well above the average, whilst Nissan and Honda fell behind. The seniority-based wage system has also come under threat within organisations. Honda and Sony introduced pay systems placing greater emphasis on performance; Mitsubishi Corporation allowed the pay of managers of the same age to vary by plus or minus 10 per cent; and many firms are introducing what on the surface resembles western-style, performance-related pay schemes. Matsushita introduced the first tiered wage system in Japan, which differentiates between those following a lifetime employment 'contract', newcomers who want to bring forward and forgo the substantial retirement benefits, and those with specialist skills in demand, who wish to contract-out of most age- and service-related benefits.

Several commentators now argue that more dramatic changes are needed if '*risutora*' is to prove viable in the long run (Nikkeiren 1995; Yoshida 1997), such as regrouping and reclassifying employees into different employment tracks (core groups, specialists and flexible labour reserves) in order to make the introduction of standardised norms and performance criteria, customised training pro-

grammes, incentive schemes, and strategically motivated cost externalisation programmes more manageable (Dirks 1998). Basic wages in Japan make up about 70
per cent of total compensation. Although nominal wage rises in Japan have been
relatively low, bonuses and overtime can still offset wage moderation. The move to
a 40-hour working week in 1997 was accompanied by a 10.5 per cent increase in
overtime work (Robinson 1997). Although employees are not taxed in Japan until
earnings amount to $38,000 (compared to $28,000 in Germany, $20,000 in the
US, and $8,000 in the UK), 70 per cent of all tax revenue still comes from direct
taxes on earnings in Japan, so the incentive impact of salaries is diminished, and
the top individual tax rate at 65 per cent (53 per cent in Germany) is one of the
highest in advanced economies (*Economist* 1999b).

However, a loss of loyalty to the employer is being observed (Morita 1996) as
Japanese employees realise that they have limited opportunity to express grievances over unfair evaluations, and feel that neither the evaluation criteria nor the
results are being communicated to them (Japan Productivity Centre for Socio-
Economic Development 1997). There are concerns that these restructuring
strategies, in aiming at the introduction of standardised evaluation schemes and
individualised remuneration systems, are potentially counter-productive:

> [T]hese two trends are fraught with considerable misunderstandings and
> even contradictions . . . many Japanese firms are thus embarking on a perilous
> road leading to two clearly undesirable effects simultaneously: the unravelling
> of a corporate culture based on team work orientation and labour organisa-
> tion flexibility on the one hand, the systematic destruction of individual
> motivation and personal loyalty on the other.
>
> (Dirks 1998: 91)

The new glorious rich in China

Nowhere is wide-scale transition more apparent than in China. Until recently
Chinese employment arrangements centred around 'the administrative allocation
of life-time jobs by the state, the virtual non-existence of unemployment, redundancy or retrenchment, and a strict separation maintained between urban and
rural labour' (O'Leary 1992: 373).

In addition to divisions between 'the new glorious rich' and those working in
the state sector, sharp divisions also exist in the state-owned sector between
labourers (*gongren*) and cadres (*ganbu*) based upon the level of completed education
and job assignment. The two groups represent different labour markets and are
administered by different organisations or bureaux: the Ministry of Labour and
Ministry of Personnel. Historically, employment planning was fairly basic, politic-
ally influenced and constrained by a shortage of trained personnel. The labour–
management relation system was unsophisticated, although a number of practices
had been institutionalised. Morale and material rewards were subjugated to
ideology. Selection and appraisal were based on group norms, and human
resource development was conducted within a narrow framework (Warner 1993).

This system showed the fallacy of viewing rewards simply in western terms, i.e. focusing attention on direct financial benefits and areas of organisational autonomy, since in the People's Republic of China (PRC) factories had to

> strive to establish and maintain a health-care system, schools, meal services, entertainment facilities, a guest house, and a car pool and also try to find employment for the offspring of employees and fund the pensions of retired workers. It organises sports teams and cultural events.
>
> (Stewart and DeLisle 1994: 107)

The labour market has been portrayed as the 'iron rice-bowl', a system with built-in rigidities, but one that offered cheap housing, free health and welfare benefits and jobs-for-life for those (albeit a minority) in the state-owned enterprises (SOEs) (Warner 1994). Such traditions still resonate today. None the less, a long process of reform has attempted to create floating wage systems that link individual wages to enterprise or individual performance. The range of wage fluctuation is usually half or less of total income (Jackson 1988; Takahara 1992). Wage-fixing powers for more of the structural elements of the wage system – such as basic pay, job-related pay, seniority pay (based on the length of service) and bonuses – were handed down to enterprises in 1987. Four major working factors were emphasised in 1992 – the knowledge and skills required, responsibility assumed, work intensity (load) and working conditions (Hu and He 1992) in order to make it easier to quantify a worker's performance and link it to pay (Zhao and Nichols 1996). A survey of 440 Chinese organisations (104 state-owned enterprises; forty-five collectively owned enterprises; sixteen privately owned enterprises; and fifty-three foreign-invested enterprises) found that pay has become more linked to individual performance and an important incentive to Chinese employees (Zhu *et al.* 1998).

As in Japan, demographic factors are playing an important role, and there is an increasing drain on resources from an ageing population. Many enterprises are now imposing an early retirement age of 45 for women and 50 for men, five years before the retirement age set by the state. This situation is only expected to get worse as dramatic changes continue to take place within the Chinese business structure, and it continues to move towards a labour contract system whereby employers assume total responsibility for all welfare programmes, subsidies and pensions during one to five year contracts. In 1997 President Jiang Zemin announced an acceleration in this transition, consolidating the previous pattern of reform. Such transitions are altering the social contract.

Factors that create distinctive national rewards systems

The scope for national differences in rewards systems is broad and the presence of any specific attitude towards rewards or compensation practices reflects a range of determinants. Simple recourse to 'culture' as an explanation of the behaviour or presence of the practice is very often misleading.

To what extent do the changes discussed above in Germany, Japan and China signal deep shifts that determine the future frame of reference for rewards behaviour within organisations? Questions are being raised about the assumptions that underlie much reward behaviour, and the implications of perceived changes in trust, motivation and commitment. It is important to understand what pay means to people in different cultures. Psychological analysis of rewards behaviour suggests that there is a generic cross-cultural process of pay satisfaction and the subsequent influence that this has on work behaviour. Pay tends to have four meanings (Thierry 1998). It carries motivational properties. People differ in the extent to which they see pay as a good means of achieving important objectives. Pay signals relative position, both in terms of achievement of tasks or goals, and in relation to performance in comparison with others. Pay carries meaning in relation to the relative level of control an individual has, through the different composition of the pay package and perceived ability to influence others and create autonomy over reward. Finally, pay carries meaning in terms of the utility it creates, the ease or difficulty with which it can be spent. The structure of a pay system (elements of pay, form of payment, and climate factors such as level of secrecy or participation) can determine the meaning that individuals derive from it and, as we have seen, the structure of pay systems varies markedly across societies. So too does the extent to which a pay policy is integrated into the strategic context of the firm, and is tailored to the goals of other HRM policies such as selection, evaluation and management development. Of these four meanings, 'relative position' seems to be the most powerful influence on motivation (Thierry 1998). Relative deprivation models of pay satisfaction suggest that pay satisfaction falls when there is:

- a discrepancy between desired and received pay
- a discrepancy between received pay and other comparable referents
- a discrepancy between received pay and historical parity (in terms of inflationary factors and grading systems)
- a low future expectation of more pay.

The pay motivation *process* has been assumed to be generic across societies, even though the *content* (i.e. what motivates people) has long been known to differ across countries. Should we assume that even the pay motivation process is generic? National culture should influence many of the causal dynamics between perceived meaning of pay and actual satisfaction.

National culture and rewards-related preferences

National culture influences the efficiency of various pay formulae and techniques (Gomez-Mejia and Welbourne 1991). Unravelling the complex set of influences that culture can have on rewards behaviour has become a focus of recent research. When the individual behaviour of a broad set of people is considered (behaviour of non-managerial workforces, and the external labour pool from which and to which pay policies are applied), then evidence of convergence in rewards behaviour is not as marked. A number of important mechanisms must be considered. White *et al.* (1998) note that international comparisons of pay systems focus on four aspects. If we overlay our knowledge of national culture on to these, we can see that each of these factors can have a cultural cause:

1   the locus of decision-taking (reflecting the emphasis on centralisation and hierarchical authority, attitudes to worker participation)
2   management criteria for pay determination decisions (reflecting the different mindsets, perceived causal factors, and cognitive schemata that managers use to interpret differentially what might be a common idea)
3   the effect of particular reward strategies on employees' behaviour (reflecting the role of values and the attitudes and actual behaviour that these values will generate)
4   the content and practice of the actual rewards packages in various countries (acting as an amalgam of the above three factors).

The role of cultural value orientations

The analysis of values has formed the basis of much comparative work on rewards. Why? Principally because they have been found to be less malleable and more stable than attitudes about pay. They also influence an employee's activity indirectly by shaping their attitudes and goals (Roe and Ester 1999). The theoretical process through which cultural factors, including values, account for differences in the effectiveness of many management interventions and tools has been examined by Erez and Earley (1993). In this process, values become important because they reflect:

• enduring beliefs that a specific mode of conduct is personally or socially preferable (Rokeach 1973)
• an objective state of mind, relationship or material condition that people seek to attain (Super 1980)
• normative standards that are used to judge and choose among alternative modes of behaviour (Schwartz 1992)
• conceptions of the desirable that guide the way that leaders, policy-makers and individuals select actions, evaluate events and explain their actions (Schwartz 1999).

Unlike attitudes to pay (which may be negative or positive), values have to reflect a positive position – a conscious judgement in favour of something. They clearly mediate the four meanings of pay outlined above. Values might also enable better prediction of employee response to new pay policies. If the objection to a particular pay policy tool or technique is due to the cultural values held by individual employees, then international HRM managers have a real problem. Values are more predictive of behaviour than specific attitudes, and if the policy is counter-cultural, it will either simply be rejected locally, or will be modified in a way that the organisation did not intend, or even worse will apparently be adopted but will actually be operated on a totally different set of behavioural and decision rules (Sparrow 1998). The international HRM manager needs to know which HRM policies are values-free and which are values-linked.

A recent analysis by Schuler and Rogovsky (1998) has begun to address this question. They examined data from three international HRM surveys: the IBM/ Towers Perrin world-wide study of HR practices; the International Social Survey Programme (ISSP); and the Price Waterhouse/Cranfield project. Under the ISSP programme, data have been gathered for eleven countries covering the US and Europe. Standardised stratified survey data for over 6,600 employees have allowed for sophisticated statistical analysis of work value and orientation data covering such components as high income, job security and interesting work. By controlling for the effects of occupational grouping and demographic variables of age and sex, it was found that both line of country, and the cultural value orientation prescribed by Hofstede (1980) for that country, were the most significant predictors of work values. Those compensation practices that were based on status were linked to national culture. Countries with a high level of 'uncertainty avoidance' (such as Greece, Portugal, Italy and Japan) were more in favour of compensation being based on either seniority or level of competence and skill; they were less inclined to favour a focus on individual performance or on employee ownership plans, but favoured benefits such as provision of workplace childcare and career break schemes. Countries with a strong individualistic culture (such as the United States, Britain, Australia, and The Netherlands) understandably preferred pay for performance, a focus on individual performance, employee stock options and commission paid to clerical and manual staff. Countries with feminine cultures that do not respect aggressive goal-orientated behaviour (such as Norway and Sweden) favoured flexible benefits, workplace childcare schemes, and career break and maternity break schemes for all levels of staff. Countries with high-power distance (such as France, Greece, Brazil, India or Far Eastern countries) were set against employee share options or share ownership for manual, clerical or technical employees.

Given the comments made about the role of German non-wage costs, it is important also to consider the impact that national culture has on employee benefits plans. The need to understand and to co-ordinate global benefits plans is evidenced by the alliances and mergers that occurred between US benefits consulting firms and overseas consulting firms throughout the 1990s. National culture helps determine how easy it is to meld workers into the desired corporate culture (Hempel 1999) – an important point given that a significant motive behind many benefits programmes is a desire to facilitate or reflect changes in corporate culture. Benefits lie at the heart of the employment relationship. Indeed, the lifetime employment system that Japan once held was seen as a cornerstone benefit within their employment relationship. As with the Schuler and Rogovsky analysis, Hempel (1999) relates various Hofstede cultural dimensions to rewards and benefits policies, such as levels of pension income, and job and income protection schemes. For example, power distance scores for Belgium (65), Japan (54) and Norway (31) are negatively linked to the level of redistribution of income achieved through social pension income replacement ratios. In high-power distance societies, retirees below or above national average earnings levels all receive a smaller level of income replacement. In low-power distance societies those below average earnings receive a far higher level of income replacement than those with above-average earnings. Similarly, high-uncertainty avoidance scores are associated with greater levels of job protection and income protection. More feminine societies, where quality of life considerations are typically important, tend to prefer income protection rather than job protection benefits programmes. In designing culturally acceptable pension schemes, Hempel argues that multi-national organisations should provide separate plans for different employee groups in high-power distance countries, and provide defined benefits plans and highly formalised low-risk pension systems in high-uncertainty avoidance societies.

These two analyses link national data on cultural values post hoc to national rewards policies or attitude data. Some studies have examined the operation of specific processes that can be involved in decisions that influence reward. For example, will employees from different cultures apply upwards appraisal assessments in the same way? If not, multinational organisations have to think carefully about applying many advanced performance management systems. Adsit *et al.* (1997) examined attitude survey data from 6,400 employees making upwards appraisal ratings of 751 managers in a multinational electronics and consumer products firm headquartered in Europe. Data were analysed for employees from France, Germany, Poland, the US, Mexico, Brazil, Singapore, Malaysia, Hong Kong and Thailand. Items were linked to those that formed part of Hofstede's four cultural scales. Countries differed in the extent to which their employees rated managers across various items, so that in Germany employees had high expectations for managerial performance, especially compared to Poland, Mexico and Brazil. In France managers were rated particularly highly on understanding customer responsiveness. Managers from Thailand and Poland were perceived by their subordinates as placing more emphasis on clarifying goals and giving feedback about performance. Brazilian managers were perceived as being poor at this. What is impossible to tease out from such data is whether the managers from the respective countries were better truly at the noted characteristics, or whether national culture values tempt employees towards more leniency or strictness in making upwards assessments. Similar patterns might be expected in downwards assessments. For multinationals, it is important to know what the answer is before converging international rewards around performance-related pay or competency-based pay systems that will rely on such assessment processes.

These types of analysis move us towards a better understanding of the relative importance of national culture. But just how important a variable is national culture? In the Schuler and Rogovsky (1998) analysis, aggregated data on Hofstede's values accounted for about 7 per cent of the cross-national variance in the importance accorded to the work value for high income. However, do such culture–rewards attitude relationships hold at the individual level?

Sparrow and Wu (1998) examined the relationship between individual orientations across four of Kluckhohn and Strodtbeck's (1961) value orientations: human nature (good–bad, changeable–immutable); human position towards nature (subjugation–mastery–harmony); activity (being–doing–thinking); and relational (collective–individual–hierarchical). They similarly found that national value orientations accounted for around 10 per cent of HRM preference when examined at the individual level, but also found that many HRM choices appear to be values-free, i.e. bear no relationship to the underlying national value orientations held by the individual. Starting from the most values-free HRM functions, they found that 50 per cent of compensation choices, 44 per cent of staffing choices, 44 per cent of performance appraisal choices, 36 per cent of planning choices, but only 29 per cent of training and development choices fall into this category. In relation to compensation, individual preferences for market-based (as opposed to internal-equity based) pay rates, linkage of compensation to functional flexibility, separation of fringe benefits from wages, rewards of a financial rather than non-monetary nature, and rewards based on individual needs and individual choice were all values-free. As an international HRM manager operating in Taiwan, the message was that whilst many HRM policies were clearly not seen as appropriate, dependent on the individual's national value orientations, at least the above list of rewards policies would not offend the basic value orientations of local employees.

Distributional justice

Another cultural factor that the design of comparative rewards systems has to account for is distributional justice. Studies of distributional justice concern themselves with the rules and standards by which decisions about the allocation of resources (financial or non-financial) are both made and perceived to be fair (Meindl *et al.* 1990). Exploring the nature of these decisions and the motives that surround them is seen as one way in which researchers can gain insight into the social systems that surround rewards behaviour. Allocation problems are resolved by resorting to a series of decision rules that determine the entitlement of recipients. In practice, these rules reflect the familiar, normative rules of a society that concern issues of social and industrial justice. They are also seen to embody decision logics and the value position of individuals and their motives. These logics and value positions are linked to national culture: 'the particular cognitive and behavioural manifestations of justice, as they take place in the resolution of allocation problems, may be conditioned by the culture at large within which the organisation is embedded' (Meindl *et al.* 1990: 224).

When there is a pot of 'reward' to be shared out, what is the fairest way to do it? Several rule-sets have been identified. The two most potent rule-sets distinguish between principles of meritocracy and egalitarianism. They are based on principles of:

- 'equity' – whereby entitlements are based on relative contributions and differential reward is legitimate as long as it is based on an equitable way of differentiating performance. These are felt to be dominant in the US and related national cultures such as the UK, Australia and Canada
- 'parity' or 'equality' – in which allocation solutions are insensitive to input differences and call for resources to be distributed equally to all, regardless of relative productivity. These are felt to be applicable in collectivist cultures such as China and Japan (Leung and Bond 1984; Leung and Park 1986). The decision rule is clearly bounded, in that collectivists make a clear distinction between in-group and out-group members and do not apply equality rules to out-group members (Triandis 1995). Where teams operate as in-groups, incentives and bonuses should only be given to the group, not to individuals (Wasti 1998).

There is evidence however, especially in the special economic zones of China, that a radically altered institutional and social environment can change previously deep-seated psychological determinants of rewards behaviour, such as distributive justice. The 'new glorious rich' in China's free market challenge the underlying value of equality-based rather than equity-based justice held by the many. Meindl, Cheng and Jun (1990) analysed justice rules amongst a small sample of eighty-six Chinese managers and ninety-six US managers. The analysis showed that the Chinese managers were more equity-driven than might be expected. They were also more unsophisticated in their allocation rules. US managers were prepared to override equity rules in situations where there was high work interdependence and where values of solidarity (low conflict) were present. The Chinese managers pushed equity-based solutions in all contexts. This might reflect low levels of experience of actually making these decisions and so a lack of sophistication. It might also reflect a process of 'going native' in that, knowing that foreign systems are being vaunted as worthy of emulation, respondents conform to the new rhetoric somewhat unthinkingly. A similar picture emerged in another cross-cultural study into distributive justice, which compared 277 employees in three state-owned enterprises and 205 employees in two US companies (Chen 1995). In-basket role plays were used to establish preferences for reward type, allocation rules and goal priorities. Chinese employees emphasised economic organisational goals over the US humanistic goals and a differential logic for the allocation of both material and socio-emotional rewards. The study revealed a complex pattern of continuity and change. Confucian values were still evidenced in the continued emphasis on the social hierarchy, with a higher ranking for differential rewards according to rank and seniority in the Chinese sample. However, performance and job needs outranked seniority and rank as a differential allocation rule. This new emphasis of Chinese employees towards an economic logic and rejection of equality-based rules was felt to be more a product of recent environmental pressure and institutional practice than any shift in underlying cultural values. Such research suggests that some individuals can make a transition in deep-seated drivers of rewards behaviour, whilst others may not, and some can do it intelligently, whilst others may apply new rule-sets rather uncritically.

Socially healthy pay versus increasing pay differentials

A final concept, related to the justice rules above, is that of 'socially healthy pay'. Within societies there are boundaries placed around the range of pay differentials or multiples deemed to be legitimate. These are generally measured by metrics such as the ratio between the highest and average, or highest and lowest paid. In the US high multiples are both legitimate and expected. In continental Europe much narrower multiples are felt to be appropriate. If differentials move beyond accepted limits, then social reaction can be marked. Research on pay differentials has shown that the gap between the remuneration of workers and the most senior managers in organisations has increased markedly in recent years across the world. For example, the pay differential ratio between the average worker and the CEO in the US has increased from 41 in 1960, to 79 in 1970, 157 in 1992, 152 in 1993, 209 in 1996 and 326 in 1997. When the pay differential between the average worker and the highest paid executive is considered, by 1997 the differential was a ratio of 8,130 (Tang *et al.* 1998). In the United States there has, however, been a groundswell against salary imbalances between those at the top and the average employee. Research by the United Auto Workers Union suggests that in 1965 US CEOs were paid forty-five times the average wage, rising to 187 times average wage by 1995 (Griffith 1997). O'Reilly and Pollock (cited in Griffith 1997) tracked 120 large public companies over five years and found that employee turnover levels were higher than average in the firms that paid CEOs above the industry norm.

The power of market competition to overcome norms about socially healthy pay and to alter rules of distributional justice should not be ignored. Research that has examined employee preferences and motivational factors across countries shows that financial factors have high motivational value amongst Chinese employees these days (Silverthorne 1992; Fisher and Yuan 1998). Survey data from 785 employees of a western-owned hotel group in Shanghai showed that good wages rated as the highest motivational factor. Comparing this to other national data produced by Silverthorne (1992), it is clear that good wages in China are ranked much higher as a source of pay motivation than in the US (ranked fifth most important out of ten) or Russia (ranked tenth). In Taiwan good wages are similarly rated as highly motivating (second most important factor).

This issue of increased attention to financial matters in an apparently egalitarian society is also seen in the debate around 'executive pay with Chinese characteristics'. Official guidelines, applied to 70 per cent of the workforce in state-owned enterprises, recommend that directors' pay be tied to company assets and in principle should be no more than three times that of the average worker. However, consultancy market reports from the region and the financial press indicate that grey income (in the form of benefits, hidden compensation, directorships on subsidiaries and graft) is significant. It is estimated by Chinese government economists to be such that real compensation is at least three times the stated figure. There is no separation between personal and private income at senior levels of the hierarchy in Chinese SOEs. General managers can ensure that the education of their children, holidays, cars and carpets, are all paid for, and receive free chauffeur-driven sedans, luxurious housing, domestic staff, comprehensive travel expenses at home and abroad, free banquets and unlimited expenses for wining and dining, especially as they near retirement. If the Chinese tax authorities cannot estimate the true extent of hidden compensations, then academic research into international pay comparability certainly will not. To combat grey income and staunch pay differentials between the state and private sector, the Shanghai authorities introduced a bonus scheme that allowed managers in some SOEs (such as Baoshan Iron and Steel) to earn bonuses worth up to three times official pay. Therefore research on grey income is likely to counter many apparent cross-cultural differences in rewards behaviour.

Continued pressure for change is also anticipated in Europe. As US multinationals expand in Europe and pursue strategies built around pan-European structures and teams, the level of competition for talent is forcing change in rewards behaviour. So too will the Euro, which is anticipated to unleash powerful market forces that will transform work practices through the creation of mergers and acquisitions, changes to corporate tax rates, a shift towards an equity culture as shareholders gain more influence over corporate governance, and harmonisation of rewards levels. To close the competitive gap with other peripheral countries in the Euro zone, German wages would have to fall by 2 per cent a year for several years to come (Hirsch 1999). Many European managers now have from 10 per cent to 50 per cent of their pay tied to the financial performance of the firm, and the trend is for increased compensation at senior levels, though not to US levels. Bonus plans, merit raises and stock options are becoming more commonplace. Daimler-Benz was one of the first German firms to offer a stock option plan – a move challenged in the courts by a German shareholder.

Conclusions

Research on cultural value orientations, distributional justice and pay differentials suggests that MNCs attempting to harmonise rewards systems will face predictable patterns of resistance across different countries. These aspects of national culture are amenable to change, but only amongst highly selected groups. Whilst there may be convergence in pay philosophies across national HR systems, the need to engage the local institutional context means that there should be considerable local autonomy of practice allowed within MNCs, and distinctive practices will remain within domestic organisations. Institutional differences – legal and economic constraints such as employment law, tax law, and minimum wage legislation – will continue to play a vital role in pay systems because they limit the freedom of action of employers (White *et al.* 1998). When considering a converging policy objective such as individual performance-related pay, it is the how of organisational implementation that reveals just how bounded the convergence actually is. Whilst most managers around the world would now subscribe, for example, to the policy objective of a pay–performance linkage, the cultural inter-pretation of it differs: 'the difficulty is that they all mean different things by pay and different things by performance' (Trompenaars 1993: 176).

The first level at which these different meanings become evident is when we consider the 'drivers' of the policy objective. These differential drivers reflect the fact that whilst managers might have signed up to the same HR policy objective, the local institutional context is different, as are the local labour market concerns. Managers might therefore come to the conclusion that individual performance-related pay is an important and necessary HR policy objective through a very different logic. More importantly, as far as rewards practitioners are concerned, this different logic means that the 'political' messages that must be communicated in order to 'sell' the convergent policy objective soon become immersed in national culture. A good deal of 'spin doctoring' becomes necessary in the 'selling strategies' adopted by HR managers. They have to find 'engagement points' with the national culture on which they can play to make the audience more receptive to the policy objective.

Consider the following interpretation of White *et al.*'s (1998) analysis of rewards systems in British and Hong Kong banks. Both the British and Hong Kong banks stressed the importance of individual performance-related pay. In the British context, however, the message that was sold stressed the following logic: 'A job for life is no longer possible, nor is much vertical grade movement, so if you want pay progression, linking it to individual contribution makes sense'. By championing the right of the individual to equitable reward, the point at which local managers engaged with the message was through a set of 'individualistic' values – if I work hard in this uncertain world but my colleague shirks, then I deserve additional reward. In Hong Kong, however, where deferred gratification and a more collective perspective might be expected to work against a performance-related pay objective, the point of engagement was actually another cultural dimension – the 'money ethic' or 'cash mentality'. Given the desire for financial well-being after high levels of migration from China, considerable importance is given to the role of immediate cash. The point of engagement with the local audience was through the money ethic, not individualism.

From the perspective of an international HRM manager, the future agenda for comparative rewards system research must surely concentrate on understanding how facets of national culture mediate the operation of new pay systems, includ-ing initiatives such as broad-banding and competency-based. It must also identify the appropriate 'engagement points' through which policy objectives can be deemed to be in line with underlying values.

References

Adsit, D.J., London, M., Crom, S. and Jones, D. (1997) 'Cross-cultural differences in upward ratings in a multinational company', *International Journal of HRM*, 8 (4): 386–401.

Buckley, P. and Muccielli, J. (1997) *Multinational Firms and International Relocation*, Cheltenham: Edward Elgar.

Chen, C.C. (1995) 'New trends in rewards allocation preferences: a Sino-U.S. comparison', *Academy of Management Journal*, 38 (2): 408–28.

Dirks, D. (1997) 'Out of recession and beyond: indications for a new type of Japanese management?', *Euro Asia Journal of Management*, 12 January 1997: 5–23.

Dirks, D. (1998) 'Experimenting with standardisation and individualisation: human resource management and restructuring in Japan', *Management International Review*, 38 (2): 89–103.

The Economist (1999a) 'A survey of Germany: the Berlin Republic', *The Economist*, 350 (8105): 10.

The Economist (1999b) 'Japan: in search of friends', *The Economist*, 350 (8105), 6 February: 76.

Erez, M. and Earley, P.C. (1993) *Culture, Self-identity and Work*, Oxford: Oxford University Press.

Fisher, C.D. and Yuan, A.X.Y. (1998) 'What motivates employees? A comparison of US and Chinese responses', *International Journal of HRM*, 9 (3): 516–28.

Fujimura, H. (1997) *Are Middle-aged Employees of No Value for the Firm?*, Tokyo: Seisansei Shuppan.

Gomez-Mejia, I. and Welbourne, T. (1991) 'Compensation strategies in a global context', *Human Resource Planning*, 14 (1): 29–42.

Griffith, V. (1997) 'Fat cats dog morale', *Financial Times*, 16 April: 23.

Hempel, P.S. (1999) 'Designing multinational benefits programs: the role of national culture', *Journal of World Business*, 33 (3): 277–94.

Hirsch, M. (1999) 'New Europe, new world', *Newsweek*, special issue on the Euro, 5–8.

Hofstede, G. (1980) *Culture's Consequences: International Differences in Work-related Values*, Beverly Hills, Ca: Sage.

Hu, X.Y. and He, P. (1992) (eds) *The Implementation of Post-plus Skills Wage System*, Beijing: Wage Research Institute of the Ministry of Labour of China.

Jackson, S. (1988) 'Management and labour in Chinese industry: a review of the literature', *Labour and Industry*, 1 (2): 335–63.

Japan Productivity Centre for Socio-Economic Development (1997) *Best Practice Cases of Personnel Appraisal Systems*, Tokyo: Shakai Keizai Seisansei Honbu.

Kluckhohn, F.R. and Strodtbeck, F.L. (1961) *Variations in Value Orientations*. New York: Harper & Row.

Leung, K. and Bond, M.H. (1984) 'The impact of cultural collectivism on reward allocation', *Journal of Personality and Social Psychology*, 4: 793–804.

Leung, K. and Park, H.J. (1986) 'Effects of interactional goal on choice of allocation rules: a cross-national study', *Organizational Behaviour and Human Decision Processes*, 37: 111–20.

Meindl, J.R. (1989) 'Managing to be fair: an exploration of values, motives and leadership', *Administrative Science Quarterly*, 34: 252–76.

Meindl, J.R., Cheng, Y.K. and Jun, L. (1990) 'Distributive justice in the workplace: preliminary data on managerial preferences in the PRC'. In *Research in Personnel and Human Resource Management, Supplement* 2, New York: JAI Press.

Morita, M. (1996) 'New personnel management systems and the actual situation under the discretionary work system', *Kansai Daigaku Shakai Gakubu Kiyo*, 28 (1): 143–69.

Naisbitt, J. and Aburdene, P. (1990) *Megatrends 2000*, London: Sidgwick & Jackson.

Nikkeiren (1995) *Japanese Management in a New Age*, Tokyo: Nikkeiren.

O'Leary, G. (1992) 'Chinese trade unions and economic reform'. In K.Y. Chen,

R. Lansbury, N. Sek-Hong and S. Stewart (eds) *Labour–Management Relations in the Asia-Pacific Region*, Hong Kong: Centre of Asian Studies, 364–83.

Rôdôsho (1997) *Whitebook on Labour*, Tokyo: Nihon Rôdô Kenkyû Kiko.

Robinson, G. (1997) 'Japan gets round 40 hour week: corporate culture means salarymen are clocking in more overtime', *Financial Times*, 2 May.

Roe, R.A. and Ester, P. (1999) 'Values and work: empirical findings and theoretical perspectives', *Applied Psychology: An International Review*, 48 (1): 1–22.

Rokeach, M. (1973) *The Nature of Human Values*, New York: Free Press.

Samuelson, R.J. (1999) 'A foolish gamble', *Newsweek*, special issue on the Euro, 20–1.

Sasajima, Y. (1997) 'Prospects regarding the reform of wages and personnel management'. In Y. Sasajima (ed.) *Personnel and Wages under the Performance Principle: Case Studies of Eight Leading Companies*, Tokyo: Seisansei Rôdô Jôhô Sent.

Schuler, R.S. and Rogovsky, N. (1998) 'Understanding compensation practice variations across firms: the impact of national culture', *Journal of International Business Studies*, 29 (1): 159–78.

Schwartz, S.H. (1992) 'Universals in the content and structure of values: theoretical advances and empirical tests in 20 countries'. In M. Zanna (ed.) *Advances in Experimental Social Psychology*, New York: Academic Press.

Schwartz, S.H. (1999) 'A theory of cultural values and some implications for work', *Applied Psychology: An International Review*, 48 (1): 23–48.

Silverthorne, C.P. (1992) 'Work motivation in the United States, Russia and the Republic of China (Taiwan): a comparison', *Journal of Applied Social Psychology*, 22: 564–76.

Sparrow, P.R. (1998) 'International rewards systems: to converge or not converge'. In C. Brewster and H. Harris (eds) *International HRM: Contemporary Issues in Europe*, London: Routledge.

Sparrow, P.R. and Hiltrop, J.M. (1997) 'Redefining the field of European human resource management: a battle between national mindsets and forces of business transition', *Human Resource Management*, 36 (2): 201–19.

Sparrow, P.R. and Marchington, M. (eds) (1998) *Human Resource Management: the New Agenda*, London: Pitman.

Sparrow, P.R. and Wu, P.C. (1998) 'Does national culture really matter? Predicting HRM preferences of Taiwanese employees', *Employee Relations*, 20 (1): 26–56.

Sparrow, P.R., Schuler, R.S. and Jackson, S. (1994) 'Convergence or divergence: human resource practices and policies for competitive advantage worldwide', *International Journal of Human Resource Management*, 5 (2): 267–99.

Stewart, S. and DeLisle, P. (1994) 'Hong Kong expatriates in the People's Republic of China', *International Studies of Management and Organisation*, 24 (3): 105–18.

Super, D.E. (1980) 'A life-span approach to career development', *Journal of Occupational Psychology*, 52: 129–48.

Takahara, A. (1992) *The Politics of Wage Policy in Post-revolutionary China*, London: Macmillan Press.

Tang, T.L.P., Tang, D.S.H., Tang, C.S.Y. and Dozier, T.S. (1998) 'CEO pay, pay differentials and pay–performance linkage', *Journal of Compensation and Benefits*, 14 (3): 41–6.

Thierry, H. (1998) 'Compensating work'. In P.J.D. Drenth, H.Thierry and C.J. de Wolff (eds) *Handbook of Work and Organisational Psychology. Volume 4: Organisational Psychology*, Brighton: Psychology Press.

Triandis, H.C. (1995) *Individualism and Collectivism*, Boulder, Co.: Westview Press.

Trompenaars, F. (1993) *Riding the Waves of Culture*, London: Economist Books.

Tüsselmann, H.-J. (1999) 'Standort Deutschland: German direct foreign investment –

exodus of German industry and export of jobs', *Journal of World Business*, 33 (3): 295–313.

Warner, M. (1993) 'Human resource management "with Chinese characteristics"', *International Journal of Human Resource Management*, 4 (1): 45–65.

Warner, M. (1994) 'Review symposium: recent contributions on international human resource management', *International Journal of Human Resource Management*, 5 (2): 491–4.

Wasti, S.A. (1998) 'Cultural barriers in the transferability of Japanese and American human resources practices to developing countries: the Turkish case', *International Journal of Human Resource Management*, 9 (4): 608–31.

White, G., Luk, V., Druker, J. and Chiu, R. (1998) 'Paying their way: a comparison of managerial reward systems in the London and Hong Kong banking industries', *Asia Pacific Journal of Human Resources*, 36 (1): 54–71.

Wood, C. (1994) *The End of Japan Inc.*, New York: Simon & Schuster.

Yoshida, H. (1997) *A Personnel System for the Future*, Tokyo: Doyukan.

Zhao, M.H. and Nichols, T. (1996) 'Management control of labour in state-owned enterprises: cases from the textile industry', *The China Journal*, 36, July: 1–21.

Zhu, C.J., De Cieri, H. and Dowling, P. (1998) 'The reform of employee compensation in China's industrial enterprises', *Management International Review*, 38 (2): 65–88.

10 Coda

Reward management into the twenty-first century

Janet Druker and Geoff White

This book has highlighted the uneven and often contradictory tendencies that are apparent in the evolution of pay practices. There are marked contrasts in attitudes between different cultures and societies as to what is socially acceptable in terms of income distribution and pay differentials, as Paul Sparrow shows in Chapter 9. Attitudes and values are of fundamental importance in determining the approach that employers may take in establishing pay regimes – and there is no necessary requirement in the UK that an employer should adopt one coherent and consistent approach to pay within the organisation. Reward practices may serve to create or to minimise divisions within the workforce, for example, between white-collar and blue-collar workers – or between occupations or grades dominated by men and those filled for the most part by women. The choice that is made and the approach that is taken are not simply technical matters. Pay is the subject of conflict; moreover influence over the form and the level of wages has, historically, provided trade unions with a lever to enhance workplace influence. Wider issues, conceptions of skill and social status for example, are important but philosophical and ethical issues – questions of equity and equality – must also be addressed.

When job evaluation and formalised grading structures were being established in the post-war years, they were justified by a notion of fairness within internal labour markets. Fairness in this context meant that there was a systematic analysis or ranking of work processes, with coherent grading and pay structures based on the criteria determined and the information gathered about the jobs that people did within an organisation. Pay levels may have been benchmarked against the external labour market, but the overall approach was intended to provide an internal coherence in the treatment of one group of workers relative to another, or between one class of job and another. This concept of 'fairness' has to be located in its social context, which assumed differential treatment for men and for women; or for managerial, professional and administrative employees on the one hand as against craft, process workers and other manual workers on the other. As Sue Hastings has demonstrated in Chapter 4, the notion of 'fairness' could not be separated from the social values embodied in the notion of 'skill'. As these values mutated, so the 'fair' standards of early job evaluation processes were perceived to be distorted in favour of the skills that were traditionally exercised by men.

Before the 1980s there was, in some measure, a collective notion of what was 'fair'. It was based around the tasks and the responsibilities that were undertaken and the individual was positioned as part of a grade or rank within a larger structure. Such arrangements provided for a centralised control of pay costs which, within the unionised workplace, accommodated trade union influence at workplace level. The traditional scientific management approach to pay and grading went hand in hand with the concept of a rate for the job, which in turn provided a focus for union activity (Mahoney 1992). On one hand trade unions served to reinforce sectional interests – for example, by supporting higher pay and differentials for skilled and unionised workers, who most frequently were men. Paradoxically though, they also campaigned for fair treatment and bargained for general principles – for example, to improve the lot of the lowest paid (often women) within the workforce – as Ed Heery shows in Chapter 3.

The 'New Pay' theorists challenge job evaluation and associated notions of pay equity on the grounds that the focus for pay determination should be on people, their skills and their performance relative to business needs, rather than on the specified duties of particular jobs (Lawler 1990). According to this approach, it is performance and skill that are significant and so if one individual works harder than another, it seems only fair that that person should be paid more (Lawler 1990; Schuster and Zingheim 1992). Such an approach seems to preclude legitimate differences of view about the appropriate value, status or reward for a particular job. The reference point is locked into business strategy and needs, and there is little attempt to accommodate employee priorities or conflicts of interest concerned with equity of treatment. The 'New Pay' represents an increased risk for employees whose earnings are contingent upon performance. This risk is in effect downloaded from the employer. In this respect the New Pay represents 'a fairly hard edged set of proposals for transferring the risks inherent in economic activity from those who are powerful to those who are less able to bear them' (Heery 1999).

Our contributors demonstrate that, whilst the rhetoric of the New Pay has in some ways been influential within the UK, New Pay theories have not been translated fully or easily into pay practice. In seeking to identify change in reward practice, a number of different issues have been identified. The first is the erosion of traditional distinctions between 'blue-collar' and 'white-collar' workers. There are fewer manual workers now than there were twenty-five years ago and they are less likely than in the past to receive incentive payments. This could be regarded as a standardisation of reward practice and, indeed, one important report has stressed the extent to which variability in conditions of work are being reduced (Brown *et al.* 1998). This is confirmed in Chapter 7, where Ian Smith points to the absence of innovation in the management of benefits. Whilst single-status working has not been uniformly adopted, however, some of the conventional demarcation between key groups within the firm has been blurred as skills have been redefined and grading boundaries have been redrawn. Yet there are many waged workers who have not experienced such changes. Some traditional areas of waged employment (e.g. in retail and distribution) have grown, whilst new types of routinised work (e.g. in call centres) have emerged. Moreover harmonisation of the terms and conditions of blue- and white-collar workers may be concerned with limited innovation rather than with more costly processes of full implementation of single-status working.

The most convincing support for the influence of 'New Pay' ideas rests in the growing use of flexible pay – particularly the more widespread use of performance-related pay for professional, administrative and managerial workers. The constraints on internal career progression have been accompanied by tighter controls and more individualised reward arrangements for many salaried employees. Marc Thompson in Chapter 6 demonstrates both the importance but also the limitations of payment for the person, suggesting that the momentum to introduce performance-related pay in its various forms has declined or may even have been reversed. In discussing the difficulties associated with the assessment of performance of salaried employees, he points to the absence of consistency in managerial assessment, a problem that has also been highlighted by Dickens (1998). Organisational characteristics shape managerial assessment and may further undermine the equity of performance-based pay – for example, through the imposition of quotas on high ratings and a consensus within the organisation that salary costs need to be contained. In other cases where there has been a growth in variable or flexible pay – for example, through schemes of financial participation – it may not serve the purposes originally anticipated. As Jeff Hyman shows in Chapter 8, financial participation schemes in the form of employee share ownership or profit-sharing do not necessarily or automatically impact positively on employee attitudes, behaviour or performance, nor on organisational performance overall.

The current interest in more flexible pay systems is international in scope – partly because multinational corporations themselves operate across national frontiers, but also because ideas about management are transmitted globally. In Chapter 9 Paul Sparrow points to international convergence around the interest in pay flexibility – illustrating his theme with reference to the implications of high labour costs in Germany, the restructuring of business in Japan, and the marketisation of the Chinese economy. He also highlights the diversity of international experience, with particular attention to national cultural variations in attitude and values. Sparrow distinguishes between the principles of the meritocratic society (such as the US and the UK), which accepts differential contribution and reward, and more egalitarian societies (such as Japan and China) in which there is a more equitable distribution of resources. He also points to the ways in which cultural values may change in the context of particularly rapid economic development, as in the special economic zones in China.

These developments must be understood in the context of prevailing fiscal standards, social values and national laws. Within the European Union the law is founded on the equality of status of citizens of the European Union. This in turn governs the notion of what is acceptable in terms of pay practice and equal pay. Whilst the 1970 Equal Pay Act preceded United Kingdom membership of the European Community, European legislation was subsequently important in strengthening claims for equal pay in British law. In Chapter 4 Sue Hastings tracks employer responses to the requirement that work of equal value should be rewarded by equal pay. The legal connection between 'equal value' and job evaluation is an important one, given that a fair and non-discriminatory analytical job evaluation scheme offers employers a defence against claims for equal pay/ equal value. At a time when American 'New Pay' influences were underlining the individualisation of pay relations, European legislation concerned with equal pay was reinforcing the important principles of pay equity and comparability within the organisation.

Similarly, European directives on working time, on parental leave and on part-time workers are eroding what remains of the traditional voluntarist approach to determining pay and conditions in the UK. In the future there will be a floor of minimum pay, terms and conditions laid down by statute. The 1998 Working Time Regulations, which gave effect to the 1993 Working Time Directive, laid down not only maximum working periods but, more importantly perhaps for many employers and workers, minimum paid holiday entitlement of four weeks per year. Figures from the *Labour Force Survey* show that, prior to the Directive becoming law, around 640,000 full-time employees and 1.7 million part-time workers had no paid holiday (White 1999). Forthcoming regulations on part-time employment will finally end the possibility of lawful discrimination against part-timers in terms of pay and conditions, although case law has already led to substantial changes in employer practice.

The election of a Labour government in May 1997 led to a change in political direction at national level – to one that was more amenable to European social legislation. While retaining many features of Conservative economic policy, the new employee relations rhetoric is one of 'fairness at work' and 'social partnership'. The full significance of this terminology has yet to be made evident, but the creation of the Low Pay Commission in 1997 and the passing of the National Minimum Wage Act in 1998 were first steps in establishing minimum standards in terms of the level of pay. The *New Earnings Survey* for April 1999 showed that at its inception the minimum wage provided modest gains for low-paid workers, especially women. In the year to April 1999, women's pay increased by 5.2 per cent, compared to 2.1 per cent for men, while the percentage increase for women part-timers was 6.3 per cent. The pay of manual women increased by 5.4 per cent. While the full impact of minimum wage legislation depends on the scale and regularity of uprating, the prime beneficiaries so far have been the lowest-paid women workers.

Following the passage of the 1998 National Minimum Wage Act and the 1999 Employment Relations Act, it is clear that there is greater congruence between national and European level initiatives than there was before 1997. The emphasis is on minimum legislative standards – whether this is to address questions of trade union recognition or to implement European initiatives concerned with parental leave. It follows therefore that over and above these minimum standards, the question of pay determination will remain very largely one to be determined at organisational level.

The management of reward is a complex and often perplexing task. It is one that is bound up with meeting strategic business objectives, but reward decisions are concerned essentially with the motivation of workers in a range of different roles. New Pay ideas sit uneasily alongside current preoccupations with employee involvement and commitment. One thing then is clear. It is a matter both of what is decided and also how decisions are reached. Without transparency in the decision-taking processes and a forum through which employees can make their voice heard, the task will be much harder.

References

Brown, W., Deakin, S., Hudson, M., Pratten, C. and Ryan, P. (1998) 'The individualisation of employment contracts in Britain'. Department of Trade and Industry, research paper. London, DTI.

Dickens, L. (1998) 'What HRM means for gender equality'. *Human Resource Management Journal* 8 (1): 23–40.

Heery, E. (1999) 'The new pay: risk and representation at work'. In Winstanley, D. and Woodall, J. (eds) *Ethical Issues in Contemporary Human Resource Management*. London, Macmillan.

Lawler, E. (1990) *Strategic Pay: Aligning Organizational Strategies and Pay Systems*. San Francisco, Jossey Bass.

Mahoney, T.A. (1992) 'Multiple pay contingencies: strategic design of compensation'. In Salaman, G. (ed.) *Human Resource Strategies*. London, Sage.

Schuster, J.R. and Zingheim, P. (1992) *The New Pay: Linking Employee and Organisational Performance*. New York, Lexington Books.

White, G. (1999) *Pay Structures and the Minimum Wage*. Low Pay Commission Occasional Paper 3. September. London, Low Pay Commission.

Index

Note: Page numbers in bold type refer to figures; those in italic type refer to tables; those followed by 'n' refer to notes.